D1221945

TOP GUNS

Impiger et Acer
Energetic and Keen

The motto of 29 (Fighter) Squadron

TOP GUNS

Hugh McManners

Photographs by John Cassidy

NETWORK BOOKS

This book is published to accompany the television series entitled *Top Guns*. The series was made by Folio Productions and produced and directed by Charles Thompson.

Network Books is an imprint of BBC Books,
a division of BBC Worldwide Publishing.
BBC Worldwide Limited, Woodlands,
80 Wood Lane, London W12 0TT

First published 1996
© Hugh McManners 1996
The moral right of the author has been asserted
ISBN 0 563 38707 6

Designed by Keith Watson Art Direction
Map by Keith Watson Art Direction
Photographs by John Cassidy

Text set in Bembo; headings set in Franklin Gothic Bold
Printed in Great Britain by Cambus Litho Ltd, East Kilbride
Bound in Great Britain by Hunter and Foulis Ltd, Edinburgh
Colour separations by Radstock Reproductions Ltd, Midsomer Norton
Jacket printed by Lawrence Allen Ltd, Weston-super-Mare

References to horizontal and vertical measurements in the air coincide with the official practice of aviators to calculate distance in feet or nautical miles.

For Deborah, William and Joseph,
with all my love

ACKNOWLEDGEMENTS

There are a great many people to thank for their help in the creation of this book. The most important by far are its subjects, the men (and women) of 29 (F) Squadron, and the individual officers of the Royal Air Force whose support and work enabled both this book and the television series *Top Guns* to be made. The Director of RAF Public Relations, Air Commodore Gordon McRobbie, was first and foremost in this.

The quality and accuracy of any project of this type depends upon harmonious interaction with its subjects. Air Commodore McRobbie deserves special thanks for appointing a superb liaison officer, Tornado navigator Squadron Leader Peter Budd. Without Peter Budd's astute and unstinting efforts, the television series would simply never have happened, and this book would not have been published. While he is certainly not to blame for any errors in this book (for which I alone am responsible), Peter Budd's hard work has given book and film the vital hard edge of realism, for which very many thanks. I am grateful also to RAF Strike Command's Chief Press Officer, Chris Shepherd.

I would have to list everybody in 29 (F) Squadron if I were to acknowledge their efforts fully. I hope they will understand if I restrict myself to the hierarchy and their Boss, Wing Commander Martin Routledge; his friendly professionalism set the tone from which everything else followed. I am very grateful to them all, particularly to those who waded through and corrected the manuscript of the book.

On the television side, many thanks to Folio Productions and the film crew. Particular thanks to West Country Television and Anglia Television, and to The Discovery Channel's in-house aviation expert Chris Hawe (also its senior Commissioning Editor), who commissioned the television series.

As always, Network Books have worked flat-out producing this book. Editor Tessa Clark has worked wonders pulling together text and pictures, turning impenetrable fighter pilot jargon (with which I became a touch infected) into plain English. Designer Keith Watson has enhanced the splendour of John Cassidy's photography. Joint Editorial Director Suzanne Webber played a blinder in commissioning this book, and provided timely authorial support and inspiration, very ably abetted by her deputy Nicky Copeland.

Final, but particular, thanks to photographer John Cassidy, who took all the photographs in this book. John's aviation expertise was invaluable, not only in getting pictures to support the story, but in latching on to the story in the first place. I look forward to working with him again.

Contents

Introduction

The image of a fighter pilot has been hopelessly romanticized ever since men first flew to war in aircraft. Today, exacting and highly selective training courses encourage the idea that they are a god-like élite, with physical and mental capabilities well beyond the range of ordinary people. Although today's fighter pilots are a technocracy – an élite within the armed forces by virtue of their ability to master mental and physical skills beyond the abilities of others – it was not always so. The first Royal Flying Corps pilots could barely fly their aircraft and learnt the skills once they had arrived in front-line squadrons, in the air over the trenches with German aviators their ruthless instructors. You learned – or you died. The fighter pilot image came not from the men themselves, but from others who looked at them and drew the wrong conclusions.

The devil-may-care part of the fighter pilot ethos was created out of fear as, during wartime, men desperately socialized between missions, living life to the full in the knowledge that tomorrow they could quite easily die. Unlike soldiers in front-line trenches, or sailors at sea in battleships, they lived normal lives most of the time, on air bases, in pubs, with girlfriends and wives providing a familiar background to the actual war fighting – a bizarre contrast that made unwilling gods of ordinary, frightened men, and one that today's fighter pilots experienced for themselves during the Gulf War. Flying dangerous missions deep into Iraq, many returned at dawn to five-star hotels, and a peculiarly cosmopolitan social scene. Churchill's 'Few' would have understood the problems all too well.

The cautionary legend of Icarus is too near the knuckle for the men who fight each other in the sky. Their war is one of lonely battles against gravity, fear and flame, high in the clear blue of an indistinct, radar-delineated environment in which speed, altitude and mental acuity decide who lives, and who dies. Normal concepts of time, space or distance do not apply. One minute in the air is time enough to traverse huge slabs of airspace, and win or lose a complete battle with a lethal but unseen enemy. In the unimaginable alternative life these people live, a few seconds of thought followed by decisive action determines everything thereafter, an entire day is taken up planning and flying one astonishingly high pressure, ninety-minute mission.

A remarkable continuity of experience and attitude links the first combat pilots with the technocrats who fly today's jet fighters, many of whom are science graduates, and all of whom have had science training at the highest level in order to be able to operate aircraft that represent the most radical and advanced of interfaces between man and machine. In the early days the machine was basic and suicidally flimsy, made of wood and thin, glue-brushed canvas held together by wire and string. Its military purpose was equally basic: to drop hand-grenade-type bombs into enemy trench positions and attack other aircraft with revolvers and machine guns mounted on simple pivots. At heart all fighter aircrew, regardless of the technology they are flying, are trying to do exactly what their pioneering forefathers did: kill the enemy.

Britain started its Royal Flying Corps as part of the army – a gallant new replacement for cavalry made obsolete by the machine gun (they were to make their last horse-borne attack during the Palestine campaign). The Royal Flying Corps became the Royal Air Force and developed different specializations: bombers, fighters and the communications and command control facilities needed to co-ordinate these assets. As technology extended the scope of this new combat arm, the air became a theatre of war in its own right and air forces provided the vital umbrella under which land and sea operations could take place.

As today, the ground has always been the true enemy of all flyers. Defying gravity depends upon having power and lift in a flyable aircraft. The ground can be either a saviour or a threat to combat pilots, who dive towards it for shelter from enemy radars, land on it at the end of dangerous missions – or are killed by it when their luck eventually runs out. In those early days, open cockpits and oily, unreliable engines made the reality of this new form of warfare very much harsher than it appeared to be to the rest of the army, who were living and dying far below in the violent misery of the trenches. There were no parachutes, so if an aircraft was hit its crew had no choice but to keep it flying and try to land. Engines often caught fire, offering incineration as an alternative to bailing out into cool clean air – a longer, agonizing death, or the chance to die a few seconds later as the ground rushed up to hit them.

Air combat between biplanes was the result of their initial role: to thwart enemy artillery observers who adjusted their guns on to ground targets from airborne observation positions. Fighter aircraft tried to prevent their observers being shot down, and so the air-to-air fighter – the air defender – came into being. Although these early dogfights offered welcome entertainment to troops in the trenches, aviators were not popular. The presence of a biplane from either side over any part of the front led to increased activity – either because it indicated that enemy artillery observers were doing aerial spotting prior to a bombardment, or as a reaction to friendly forces' aerial spotting. Although it is possible that ground troops found it difficult to tell one type of aeroplane from another, they did in fact fire on their own aircraft as well as those of the enemy in order to make these troublesome machines go away to some other part of the front – and leave them in peace.

The aviators themselves had problems getting senior officers to understand their type of warfare. Freezing in open cockpits, they were totally at the mercy of the weather – and suffered the additional cold of being at higher altitudes. It was, for example, difficult to persuade army supply officers to authorize a regular supply of silk scarves. Although these appeared to be a totally unnecessary luxury they were essential: pilots constantly swivelled their heads to spot enemy aircraft and without the scarves their necks rapidly became chafed to the point where they simply could not fly. The oil thrown backwards by the forward-mounted engines rotted clothing and affected exposed skin – requiring a constant supply of protective clothing that seemed to some to be extravagant. It was not until the fledgling air force achieved pilots in more senior appointments that such irritating problems could be solved by people who understood what the new type of warfare was all about.

Flying biplanes was simple enough, but air combat was another matter – and many died before learning the basics. A combat-experienced pilot is radically more effective than his un-blooded equivalent. Aircrew are therefore afforded a great measure of esteem in the RAF and enormous efforts are made to give them as much experience as possible against the day when they have to do it for real.

In this context Maple Flag, the exercise described in this book, is vital front-line training with the specific aim of giving younger aircrew the experience that will help them adjust faster to the harsh realities of real combat – if ever they have to do it. If there is one enormous difference amid all the many similarities between today's fighter pilots and those of the past, it is that their Second and First World War forebears did the business for real. And in doing so the less able

– and the unlucky – were killed. Although modern military training tries to differentiate between the two so that the ones most likely to survive are actually flying the aeroplanes, nobody gets shot down. And although there are deaths in fast-jet training, certainly nobody is killed deliberately. So while there is tremendous camaraderie between fighter aircrew of different vintages this one, tremendous, difference – of which every modern fighter jock is acutely aware – remains.

All modern fighter crew regard the various piston-engine Second World War fighters with affection, particularly the Mustang and Thunderbolt. The most affection, however, is reserved for the Spitfire. Fast-jet bar room banter is at its most interesting when flyers talk about the performance of these aircraft in comparison with modern jets. Most agree that if a Spitfire was in combat with any of today's fighters, and both were equipped only with cannon, the Spitfire with its superior turning capabilities would turn inside the jet and kill it every time. Sheer nostalgia, but very interesting nevertheless.

It is, however, important to realize that air warfare requires much more of aircrew today than it ever did in the past. A Spitfire pilot could do too much and tear the wings off his aircraft, whereas modern jets (especially those such as the Eurofighter that are under development now) use new, very light, load-bearing materials and are much more manoeuvrable, faster and able to climb better. Electronics monitor everything the pilot does so he or she cannot inadvertently damage the aircraft. However, the physical pressures of such hard flying are extreme, especially when coupled with the lethality, complexity and speed of modern air combat which demand constant and brain-numbing mental effort. The sheer workload of flying and fighting turns a ninety-minute sortie into an exhausting, mentally demanding roller-coaster of furious concentration, mental flexibility, and determination. These basic character traits are the same for fighter pilots of all eras, and it never was an easy thing to do.

The 'top guns' of the 1990s have to be just as tough-minded as any of their battle-hardened forebears.

This book concentrates on the aircrew of the Tornado F3s of the RAF's 29 Fighter Squadron as they undergo the rigorous training cycle of Exercise Maple Flag held at the Canadian Air Force base of Cold Lake in the heart of the Alberta prairie. Fighter squadrons from NATO allies take part in these exercises flying their aircraft and ground crews over to Canada for the duration.

Maple Flag is one of the American-organized 'Flag' series of air combat exercises in which two fully configured air forces fly real-life missions against each other over a series of two-week periods. Twice every day, between ninety and a hundred aircraft take part in these exercises, a concentration of combat aircraft that would only be seen in the largest air war, between very well equipped air forces. One hopes that it is therefore an unlikely scenario. As training, however, it is invaluable.

At the end of their two-week exercise period, 29 (F) Squadron fly back to England in the bowels of an RAF Tristar tanker aircraft. After all the hard work, they leave their Tornados in Canada, for another RAF F3 squadron (111 Squadron) to use in the second two-week exercise period. After a few days at RAF Coningsby, their home base, the squadron will set off for Spain and another multi-national exercise, before starting training for a NATO United Nations tour patrolling the no-fly zone over Bosnia-Herzegovina.

This book is a snapshot of their incredibly busy lives; an intimate, detailed examination of what it takes to be one of today's flying élite, the very best pilots and navigators in the world – that incredibly tiny percentage of aircrew judged good enough to be trusted with millions of pounds' worth of lethal technology – the real 'top guns'.

CHAPTER ONE

29 (F) Squadron

Eight Tornados from the RAF's 29 Fighter Squadron are flying across the Atlantic from the United Kingdom to Canada. Their destination is Cold Lake in Alberta for an 'air war' with other NATO allies: Exercise Maple Flag. The aircrew have been training for weeks for this detachment – a 'det.' in RAF parlance – and it has been much looked forward to: because it is abroad it should offer social as well as professional challenges.

Maple Flag is part of a series of 'Flag' exercises organized by the Americans as a result of research into aircrew casualties. Data compiled from the First and Second World Wars, and from Vietnam, showed that most combat losses took place in a flyer's first ten missions. It also showed that anyone who made it through them greatly increased his chances of survival. When the Vietnam War ended, the Americans decided to provide an exercise that would give their young pilots those first life-saving combat missions. The first one, Red Flag, was held over the Nevada desert in 1975, but by the late 1970s the United States Air Force was looking for somewhere more like central Europe – and they looked to Canada. Maple Flag One, in 1978, assumed a Soviet threat in central Europe. Today the series has progressed to simulate United Nations coalition efforts. The aim is the same: to give the junior, newly combat-ready pilot who has just arrived on squadron, and who has not seen any action, his first ten missions – in a realistic scenario that increases his chances of surviving when he does go to war.

Exercise Maple Flag lasts for six weeks, and comprises three identical two-week packages, in which contingents from the US Air Force, the US Navy, Canada, the German Luftwaffe and the Italian and Spanish air forces will participate. With everything from bombers, fighter escorts, jamming aircraft, radar-destroying jets known as 'HARM shooters', and airborne tankers, these exercises are the nearest thing to real war that it is possible to get without people actually being shot down. During 29 (F) Squadron's two-week detachment they, with six Canadian Air Force CF–18s and the American Aggressor Squadron, who fly specially painted F–16s and use Soviet combat tactics to give their adversaries more realistic training experience, are Red Air: the enemy. These aircraft will form a fighter air-to-air defence screen through which Blue Air bombers and escorts must fight in order to drop their bombs on target. Blue Air are two Canadian squadrons – 410 Cougar flying CF–18 Hornet fighter-bombers, and 441 (the Silver Foxes) who will fly the CF–18s as air defenders – and the Luftwaffe's Richthofen Squadron with its Phantom F–4s. The exercise will get harder as the two weeks progress with more threats being put in the way of the flyers to evaluate their reactions. The fighters are supported by the full range of other aircraft, from airborne tankers to American and British AWACS sentry aircraft.

The 29 (Fighter) Squadron badge depicts an eagle spreading its wings in triumph while delivering a 'Bruce Lee' kick at a cross-looking buzzard that is reeling earthwards in disarray. Its motto is *Impiger et Acer* (energetic and keen). The squadron's semi-official marking is three Xs – thirty in Roman numerals and not twenty-nine – a 'mistake' that dates back to the end of the First World War. Aircrew blame numerically illiterate ground crew – perhaps a sign-writer interrupted by a scramble – or perhaps it was the instructions given: 'Two Xs, one X'. Whatever the reason, 29 (F) Squadron decided that three Xs emblazoned on the sides of their biplanes looked good. Today their jets still wear that mark – and nobody gives a 'XXX' how many Xs make twenty-nine.

Based at RAF Coningsby in the heart of Lincolnshire, the squadron comprises nearly 200 people, whose sole aim in life is the maintenance and operation of their eleven Tornado F3 fighters – two-seater, twin-engined jets, configured for the air defence role. There are seven other Tornado F3 squadrons in the RAF: 5 Squadron, 56 Squadron and the Operational Conversion Unit (OCU), also based at Coningsby, with two squadrons (11 and 25) at Leeming and two (43 and 111) at Leuchars in Scotland.

Since its formation in November 1915, the squadron has flown, maintained and repaired thirty-one different aircraft including, in the First World War, the Avro, Caudron G111, Nieuport 17c, Sopwith Pup, Sopwith Camel and Bristol Fighter; in the Second World War, de Havilland Mosquitos and various versions of Bristol Beaufighters; then post-war, Gloster Meteors and Javelins, the English Electric Lightning F3 and the McDonnell-Douglas Phantom FGR–2. It has been flying the

Tornado F–3 since 1987. During the First World War, the squadron's pilots had to retrain on eleven different aeroplanes; in the Second World War only six – but they had also to develop tactics and techniques for the revolutionary new radar system.

29 (F)'s present 'boss' is Wing Commander Martin Routledge, a relaxed, brown-haired navigator of slender build, with an easy-going sense of humour who, before converting to Tornados, had flown in Phantoms. Before becoming its commanding officer, Routledge had never been a member of 29 (F) Squadron, although he had served in rival air defence squadrons (111, 56 and 74).

'I'd known 29 Squadron while I was flying the F–4s. They had a very good reputation, and still have I hasten to add – but reputations can fluctuate. I was very pleased to be given the job, as squadrons are hard to get hold of these days.'

Cut-backs have reduced the number of squadrons to the extent that only the very best officers are likely to get command – and even then an element of good fortune is involved. Commanding a squadron is perhaps the most professionally satisfying time in the life of a career officer, particularly as it is likely to be the last time he flies as part of an operational unit. Routledge:

'Coningsby is not my favourite place, but I'd prefer to be a squadron commander here, rather than not a squadron commander somewhere else. My wife, however, might not see it in such black-and-white terms.'

Most aircrew officers prefer to remain operational for as long as possible; 'flying a desk' is a fate to be avoided. Nevertheless, it is a vital imperative for any air force that aircrew, particularly pilots, achieve high rank and RAF career planners must therefore ensure that their better people do jobs outside flying. Thus Martin Routledge's curriculum vitae is typical of a career officer destined for promotion into the realms of headquarters, staff work and higher command. Like most officers he has a degree (in engineering). He started flying, in Chipmunks and Bulldogs, with Southampton University Air Squadron. In the summer of 1977, after professional training at Cranwell and Finningly (as a navigator), he started on the Phantom F–4 operational conversion unit learning the air defence role. After four flying tours and a critical change to desk-style work at the RAF Staff College at Bracknell, he worked at NATO headquarters for the Deputy Commander-in-Chief Central Europe. The air marshal clearly approved of him, he gained the appropriate ticks in the right boxes and after only a year he was promoted to wing commander and moved to HQ Strike Command at High Wycombe in Buckinghamshire where he worked in the plans department.

Routledge is bright, sharp and dedicated, clearly able to handle himself in the cockpit, aircrew briefing room, or among the top brass at the RAF's operational

Wing Commander Martin Routledge; as 29 (F) Squadron's 'boss' he has almost 200 aircrew and ground crew under his command and is responsible for their operational efficiency.

headquarters in High Wycombe. He found the work at Strike Command very different:

'There "plans" doesn't mean aircrew tactics, or even operational plans, but very large-scale, force structure planning – build-ups, draw-downs and so on. As we were in the middle of the "Options for Change" review, it was a very busy time, re-structuring and re-organizing the entire Royal Air Force.'

After two and a half years he moved into the Operations Division, a new structure created by Options for Change to run out-of-area operations at bases like Insulik for northern Iraq and Italy for Operation 'Deny Flight' in Bosnia. At this stage he had been 'grounded' for over five years, and the Phantom (his aeroplane) was no longer in service:

'… in fact one of the things I'd done in Plans was the draw-downs and disposals that actually got rid of it!'

He was appointed Officer Commanding (OC) 29 (F) Squadron, which required re-training in the Operational Conversion Unit on a completely new aircraft – the Tornado F3 – and found that much had changed:

'There is more out-of-area work like policing and escorting. And the Tornado is a lot more capable than the Phantom. Its radar can track considerably more targets, builds a much bigger picture of what's going on, and is manipulated very differently to the way the F–4 radar was used.'

Starting again, in a totally unfamiliar jet, was far from easy:

'For example, handling the F3 radar is not an automatic, natural thing – it has a predominantly digital read-out, and you have to read the various lines to see what the target is doing … There are some pictures of where things are going, but generally it's a very manually intensive job, tagging targets and getting things sorted out.'

Routledge's experience is typical of air force life. Throughout the RAF's seventy-six years, technological change has been very much part of the job.

Technology apart, his most important responsibility is for people. Even without the hurdle of the operational conversion unit, taking command of an operational, front-line fighter squadron packed with aggressive, determined fighter crew is a daunting prospect:

'Coming back after five years on the ground, re-learning the flying, plus taking command of a squadron is hard – but quite common in the air force, although in many ways not ideal.'

Performance in the air is very important for the boss of a fighter squadron, particularly for his own self-esteem:

'Until I'm actually happy flying the aeroplane, I don't quite feel I can go in there and lay down the law as much as if I'd come from another F3 squadron.'

However, although ground tours have placed Martin Routledge at a temporary disadvantage, he is in a very different position to the other aircrew on his squadron. He has already succeeded in the jobs that they are doing now – albeit using a different aeroplane. Commanding the squadron demands of him a very much greater spectrum of abilities, experience and knowledge than their jobs require of them:

'I'm no longer employed just as a navigator. My ability to lead and work with people, plus handle the staffwork side, hasn't changed just because the aircraft is different. I'm up to speed with the administrative side, so my learning curve is very much in flying the aeroplane.'

The pressure to do well in the air is nevertheless always there – a constant itch to be scratched whenever possible:

'Since starting flying again seven months ago, I've got in around a hundred and twenty hours, which is not actually much – particularly as there are so many different things you need to be able to do with the Tornado, and different styles of operating it. There's a lot to learn.'

As squadron boss Routledge is responsible for almost 200 highly (and variously) qualified people doing a wide range of different tasks. The operational efficiency of 29 (F) Squadron is the sum total of their efforts – for which he is held responsible by his superiors, and by which he is judged. It is a sudden responsibility:

'There is very little training to show you how to handle the next level – apart from having watched your own superiors do it. Personal experience isn't much use – being a squadron commander is not like being a sort of super flight commander. You have the ground crew, the administrative element and the long-term demands for which the squadron has to be correctly configured. Delegation becomes vital. You have to organize things so that the flight commanders and engineers can do their jobs.

'Becoming the squadron commander is not difficult – You Are It! But the problems start coming your way very rapidly! Until recently I was lucky to have a very experienced F3 man, Buzz Turner, as my executive officer. He'd done two and a half years on 29 Squadron, and kept most of the administrative crap off my back while I got on with the flying. I got a lot of flying done in those first few months ...

'Commanding a squadron really grows on you. It all boils down to personalities. Some people go in and start banging on the table, saying "I'm in charge, you buggers do this, this and this; you're all useless and weak" ... I'm not that sort of person. I like to sit back a bit, consider things, listen to both sides of the story – with perhaps a more gently-gently approach. At least I like to think I do ... letting my flight commanders handle the detailed, short-term planning so that I can concentrate on planning ahead.

'But at the same time, I won't put up with any crap from the guys. If I don't like what's going on, I tell them. What I tend not to do, however, is interfere – unless what they're doing is actually bad. It's counter-productive to change something that would work. I don't subscribe to the democratic style of leadership – but at the same time I'm not up there with Attila the Hun!'

The squadron's hectic pace of life requires its personnel to work flat out on what they are doing now, while planning a year or so ahead for other exercise and operational tours. To do the job properly, fighter squadrons can't just deploy – particularly into a war zone. Although they are combat-ready for all roles, each theatre has subtle differences and they need to train for specific conditions. In May of 1995 Routledge was already looking at 29 (F)'s 'Deny Flight' Bosnia deployment in November:

'Once I've thought about it, I'll get one of the flight commanders to do more detailed planning. As soon as we return to the United Kingdom after our next exercise – in Spain – we'll have to start actually training for it.'

The aircrew of a fighter squadron is divided into two flights – A Flight and B Flight – each commanded by a squadron leader who is responsible to the squadron's commanding officer. The current officer commanding (OC) A Flight is Squadron Leader Ian Gale. Fair-haired and well over 1.9 metres (six foot four inches), unusually tall for a fighter pilot, he is known as 'Stilts'. The division of responsibility between the Squadron OC and his two flight commanders is clearly understood. Gale:

'The boss manages the whole squadron, while between us we run it.'

Gale is responsible for all operational aspects: devising flying programmes and ensuring that the squadron fulfils its training requirements. Squadron Leader Dave Hartill, officer commanding B Flight, is responsible for transition to war operations, tactical evaluation exercises (TACEVAL) and deployments like Operation Deny Flight in Bosnia. Squadron Leader Graham Bond is the executive officer (XO) – the deputy boss, who administers the squadron, and apportions jobs to others

Overleaf: A Tornado F3 prepares to taxi; eight of these aircraft will take part in Exercise Maple Flag.

guided by Routledge. Flight Lieutenants Tim 'Beavis' Taylor and Harry McBryde are the qualified weapons instructors, and Squadron Leader Andy Crawford is the qualified flying instructor responsible for all flying standards.

Gale believes that his most important responsibility is the welfare and careers of the sixteen pilots and navigators under his command. That takes a lot of work and he has to use his experience to evaluate and grade his officers:

'They get a confidential report every year, so they're well aware of what I think of them. I'm supposed to assess the guys first as officers, and as aviators second. However, I make no distinction between these abilities because in war their officer qualities are not going to be what saves my life. The best fighting men are not necessarily officer material. There are other vital factors too: military life requires specific qualities that many civilians couldn't tolerate – particularly the discipline, and accepting that you might have to go to war at short notice – which puts very heavy demands on your family life … especially these days.'

Before starting this job, with the exception of two years as a staff officer, Gale had concentrated upon flying (like the boss, in Phantoms). As with Martin Routledge, command was a significant change:

'There's very little preparation for commanding a flight. Even if you get to be a deputy flight commander, it's really doing admin. without the responsibility.'

Ambition is not something the services are frightened of; indeed, people without ambition are unlikely even to survive in an operational environment – let alone do well. It is only natural that as leaders, officers should be ambitious enough to want to lead others. One senior officer has been quoted as saying that all he wanted to be as a junior officer was a flight commander; but that once he became a flight commander, the only thing he wanted to be was a boss; and then when he was a boss, the only thing he wanted to be was a station commander.

Service life thrives on change, on getting people through careers in which their abilities are stretched, their capabilities evaluated. Ian Gale believes he could not have done another tour as a junior officer and got any sort of job satisfaction:

'You get stale. I'll have to make the most of it here, do well, and if I remain long enough in the air force and am lucky enough, I'll get the added responsibility of being a squadron commander one day.'

He joined the RAF in February 1979 when he was nineteen. He had been an air cadet and already had a private pilot's licence and glider pilot's wings, so his objective to be a military pilot had been well established by the time he was fifteen. He endured what he describes as 'the rigours of officer training at Cranwell' (the drill square, 'bulling' boots, physical training and the enforced fresh air of outward-bound) then passed flying training, 'with one stumble', at RAF Valley in Wales – in the Hawk. Tactical weapon training at Chivenor was hard flying, hard work and extremely demanding:

'We came out very sharp. I wasn't the least bit interested in being an air-to-ground pilot, so when I got the posting I wanted – to Phantoms – I really was delighted.'

He finished OCU and went to 111 Squadron at Leuchars, then to 74 Squadron where Routledge was his flight commander for a while. Gale considers this to be undoubtedly his best Phantom tour:

'We were flying the F–4J, bought to replace those used in the Falklands – the best Phantoms the air force ever operated.'

After seven years and 1300 hours in various aircraft, Gale was grounded for being too tall:

'It was a bit of a surprise! However, after almost two years as a staff officer at 11 Group, I was posted to Australia, to fly F–18 Hornets.'

After eighteen months on the ground, and having flown nothing but fairly early generation, two-seater, air-to-air fighters, converting to the Hornet was a big step. It is a very modern, single-seater, multi-role aircraft with a much higher workload than a two-seater plane and, in addition, Gale had never done any air-to-ground:

'I had a whole new job to learn – very quickly, burning the candle to get through. Exchange tours are a fighter pilot's dream anyway – to go and fly somebody else's aircraft, especially one as good as the F–18. It was a dream posting: great aeroplane, lovely place – near Newcastle in New South Wales – great people. Then the dream came to an end, as they generally tend to, and I was posted back to Coningsby!'

Again, another aircraft to learn to fly. A very short course on the F3, then into 29 (F) Squadron to make a mark all over again:

'Only as a flight commander, so much more is expected of you.'

Like every fighter squadron, 29 (F) is split very distinctly down the middle into ground crew and aircrew – and back in the United Kingdom they are in geographically separate sites on Coningsby air base (dispersed in concrete shelters to limit bomb damage). Often the only time aircrew and ground crew meet is at the aeroplane, before and after flights. Also, all air crew are officers – living and working in an almost exclusively 'officer' world. Although bridging the divide between such different jobs and ranks is not easy without the common aim of wartime, Routledge believes that rank is less important in the air force than it might be in the other two services:

'The divide between ground crew and aircrew is functional. Culturally, however, the officers are closer to their men in terms of educational standards and so on, than either of the other two services.

'Also the men are not under the direct command of officers, most of whom are aircrew. Because of this, you don't get the sort of tension that develops when men feel they must leap to attention and do what they're told all the time. The flight commanders command the aircrew flights, but not the ground crew shifts, which are under the senior engineering officer's command – and mine. People generally get on very well, although this does vary from squadron to squadron.'

29 (F) Squadron's ground crew are commanded by Squadron Leader Chris Gould, the senior engineering officer (SENGO), who is responsible to Wing Commander Routledge for everything to do with engineering. He looks at long-term planning, while Flight Lieutenants Dave Mudd and John King, the two junior engineering officers (JENGOs), are responsible for the two shifts that deal with day-to-day matters. Each of these shifts has a flight sergeant as senior NCO, and trade managers, who also have jobs on one of the shifts, on permanent day shift. All the trade managers work with the various specialists in the rectification ('rect') teams who provide the hit team which sorts out any crewing snags reported by aircrew on the flight line before taxiing, and is responsible for the immediate repair of faults. The rect team also provides crash cover.

Line control keep the aircraft going, handling the see-offs and see-ins, site maintenance, replenishments and all the checks of the aircraft. The line teams, usually six teams of three men, are under the line controller – a sergeant. If an aircraft declares an emergency, the JENGO goes in with one of the line teams to make an initial assessment, then an emergency rectification team with a manager from each trade sorts it out.

Whereas aircrew (and other officers) are posted every two or three years, ground crew can remain on the same squadron indefinitely. Squadron Leader Chris Gould:

'Guys have been here for seven years – which in service terms is a long time – and they enjoy the stability. However when eventually they are posted somewhere else, it's possibly worse. People are posted out on promotion – which obviously they accept.'

There are no 'dead man's shoes' promotions within the squadron. All promotions are made by the RAF personnel branches, invariably to job vacancies in other units. The decision for a member of the ground crew is often whether to accept promotion – or stay with 29 (F):

'A few guys have been promoted, gone away, then returned after tours elsewhere. Others are still here in the same rank.'

29 (F) Squadron has one female officer: Flying Officer Vania Pearson, the intelligence officer, a job that normally calls for the nickname 'Squinto' (short for Squadron Intelligence Officer). Out of deference to her sex, however, the squadron's politically incorrect lobby would appear metaphorically to have had its way with her, and she wears the name patch 'Squintess'. Like most members of the squadron, she had always wanted to join the air force:

'I wanted to fly, but at that time they weren't taking female aircrew. They suggested I should become a fighter controller so I could fly in the E3 – which I did; two years at Buchan in north-east Scotland, then a posting to this squadron.'

Fighter squadrons did not have intelligence officers of their own until the Gulf War started in 1991, when it became apparent that the vast amount of intelligence and target information involved was too much for aircrew to assimilate unaided before missions.

In war the intelligence officer is responsible for collecting information about threats, aircraft, weapons and electronic counter measures (protection measures against hostile radar, and procedures to cope with jamming, known as ECM), then correlating what is important and putting it on to the computer system to be passed via Station Intelligence to the people who need to know about it. This process is carried out on exercises but the scenarios are never as important as when they relate to the real world.

Vania Pearson does not have an intelligence role on Maple Flag; this is being handled by the Canadians and Americans. Instead, she has been looking ahead:

'Our next detachment is Exercise Link Seas – an exercise similar to this in Spain – which starts the week after we get back from here. I'm off with the advance party a few days after our return. I'm not married – thankfully as I'd need a very understanding husband. It would be great strain – a woman going off with forty men for weeks at a time!'

CHAPTER TWO

Cyclone Trail

Getting a fighter squadron from its United Kingdom base to a remote military air base abroad requires first-class administration and logistics. In an operation known as 'trailing', fighter squadrons travel *en masse*, aircraft and personnel together, down the same route, accompanied by tankers so that they can refuel in the air as they go.

These operations take up large amounts of airspace into which other aircraft are not allowed to stray. In war, interlopers would risk being shot down. Without trailing and air-to-air refuelling it would not be possible to project air power beyond the fuel ranges of individual bombers and fighters. These are vital skills for all air forces with responsibilities beyond their own national borders. The much-vaunted geopolitical theory of 'power projection' is turned into reality, air power reaching across the world to help keep the peace, prosecute a war or act as a deterrent. Power projection is the basis of all military operations in the post-Cold-War world.

29 (F) Squadron is well used to trailing, having toured the world with brand-new Tornados when the aircraft first came into service, and has taken part in countless international exercises. The operation was also essential to their role in the Gulf War in 1991 – and, more recently, when they travelled to Gioia del Colle in Italy for United Nation duties over Bosnia-Herzegovina.

The planning of trail operations takes an enormous amount of work. To ensure safety, each tanker and its 'chicks' – the aircraft it refuels – must rendezvous together and travel in the same block of airspace. This block of air moves along the route at a predetermined speed, like an enormous, rectangular fish tank. Within the fish tank, RAF aircraft may manoeuvre as they wish; for planning purposes they are regarded by International Air Traffic Control as one aircraft.

Flight Lieutenant Steve Sansford and the Tanker Planning Cell at 38 Group

HQ planned this particular trail. Tornado trails are codenamed 'Cyclone', and this one is designated the 'A03 Cyclone Trail'. First the fighter squadron submits a route and fuel usage request, from which the various fuel burns are calculated, and a route determined, with decision points that allow aircraft to refuel or, if something goes wrong, divert to airfields in safety. Each tanker has three hoses, but only two are planned for. Fuel consumption is calculated using '85 per cent statistical met' from RAF Bracknell, rare and precious weather forecasts guaranteed to be 85 per cent better than predicted.

Today there is a tail wind, but the whole operation is planned on the basis of a 30 knot head wind that would have slowed the aircraft down. The squadron therefore expects to be twenty minutes early at its destination, Goose Bay on the east coast of Canada. Safety margins are built in to ensure that each aircraft reaches its destination in safety, with fuel in hand. Sansford has presented all his calculations in the form of a graph, to which every navigator refers throughout the operation.

The four tankers are starting from Brize Norton in Oxfordshire, and the graph shows that there would be insufficient fuel for the transit to Goose Bay. Sansford has therefore arranged for two VC10 tankers to pre-position from Prestwick in Scotland (a few hundred miles into the planned route), one of which (called 'the whirler') will refuel the other tankers then turn back to go home empty. A third VC10, a C3 with greater fuel-carrying capacity, would fly from Brize Norton.

HQ 38 Group is in operational control of the deployment and has arranged for a Nimrod Early Warning aircraft from Kinloss to follow the squadron down the route doing search and rescue, ready to find, mark and throw dinghies and survival packs to any crew forced to ditch into the sea, and then co-ordinate their rescue. For further safety, the plan is calculated on the F3s having only minimum start fuel. The tankers' route runs from Brize Norton to Prestwick, then north-west of point QN9 near Cape Wrath. The F3s come up from their base at Coningsby in Lincolnshire, via Leuchars, then to a rendezvous at QN9 under the control of Scottish Military Air Traffic Control. Between Stornoway and point 59N 10W, they refuel for the first time, leaving United Kingdom Domestic Airspace for the Oceanic Airspace Control – where the VC10s will refuel from the whirler. The trail will then route to point 60N 20W, then 60N 30W where the F3s refuel again, just south of Iceland. After point 59N 40W, the third and final refuelling takes place south of Greenland, after which the trail passes over Point Loach and into Goose Bay.

The refuelling plan gives brackets within which everyone must refuel, and an abort point just after the bracket, by which anybody who has not refuelled must abort and divert from the route to an allocated airfield. This point is carefully calculated to leave enough fuel for the aircraft to be able to divert safely to specified airfields. The decision is very much the preserve of navigators, who in this instance tell the pilots what to do. It nevertheless remains the responsibility of pilots (who are personally responsible for their aircraft) to decide what they actually do if they miss a rendezvous or, in the event of a tank malfunction or mechanical failure, whether they divert to a closer airfield.

Once the refuelling plan is worked out, HQ 38 Group produce an altitude reservation request for a 2000-foot block of airspace (from 22 000 to 24 000 feet), in which they ask the controller of Oceanic Air Space (UK Prestwick–Shanwick Ltd), and Gander Air Space for exclusive use at specific times. The idea is that a rectangle of air moving along the route should belong to the trail, based upon the Tornados' take-off times. EUCARF (the European Central Air Space Facility in Ramstein near Frankfurt) co-ordinates this request. A one-hour delay facility is built into the plan; any longer, and Flight Lieutenant Sansford will have to re-negotiate the whole operation.

For the second day's flight – across Canada to Cold Lake – another altitude reservation request·is submitted to Canadian airspace controllers in Ottawa, which includes booking accommodation, the aircraft categories in case they crash, and a plethora of other details. Diplomatic clearances have also to be obtained – which are straightforward in Canada, but can be complicated to achieve in other parts of the world. Finally, all RAF departments and units receive an air-to-air refuelling operations order (AROP) which tells everybody what is happening and gives complete details of airframes, personnel, routes, fuel, etc. This information also goes out on the civilian terminal to every airline, port and landing agent, as well as into the RAF message system. Flight Lieutenant Sansford travels with the trail. If anything goes wrong, it will take him all night to re-plan for the next day.

Hardly surprisingly, it is not necessary for civilian airlines to go through all this paperwork. There is, however, little comparison between what they do and military operations in which lethal weapons are likely to be carried, by fully armed aircraft. A host of other considerations include military crew flying hours: fast-jet aircrew wearing 'g' suits have shorter peacetime duty limits than tanker crew, who are allowed to work for up to fourteen hours – starting two hours before take-off.

Prestwick Airport: 0800 hours Zulu, Tuesday 25 April 1995

On a raw Scottish morning, passengers on board, the crew of VC10 frame number ZA141 – more usually known by its tail letter 'Bravo' – settle back in their seats while Air Loadmaster Flight Sergeant Annie Dobson makes sure that everything from the coffee machine to cargo is correct as per the manifest.

The Royal Air Force is the only organization in the world still operating VC10s, long-serving passenger jets several generations the ancestors of today's commercial aircraft. Keeping them going involves a four-year cycle of maintenance, with serious stripping down every two years, and a four-yearly total rebuild. Because of the sheer age of the aircraft, although fitted with much of the latest technology, it suffers avionics snags, and hydraulic problems due to the movement of the airframe. On out-of-base missions, four ground crew technicians fly with the aircraft: Senior Aircraftsmen Marcus Collett, the airframes expert, Eric Dunlop, the propulsion engineer, Scott Keen, the avionics expert and Phil Byran, the electrician. This team is able to do anything from changing a tyre to fitting new engines. Because this is an overseas detachment, the squadron crew chief, Flight Sergeant Tony King, a very experienced aviation engineer with sixteen years' experience on VC10s, is also on board.

After a short delay, the VC10 taxis and takes off into a damp, grey sky, on a cold, dank day. The aircraft has 143 000 kilograms of fuel on board, some 9000 kilograms short of its total capacity because of the weight of passengers and equipment also being carried. The main body of 29 (F) Squadron is travelling in a Tristar from 216 Squadron, which combines a large passenger and cargo capacity with being a fuel tanker. As well as carrying 160 non-flying squadron personnel, the Tristar, call sign 9412, will also refuel two of the F3s.

A second VC10 tanker, call sign 9213, will follow down the route forty minutes later, having taken off from RAF Brize Norton in Oxfordshire. VC10 ZA150J will 'whirl' from Prestwick and go home to Brize Norton totally empty except for pre-calculated 'get back home fuel'. (In the Gulf War tankers often went back with next to nothing by way of fuel, so that the fighters could be absolutely full before their missions. Safety, however, is paramount, particularly over water.) The trail route diverts north over Iceland, to the south of Greenland, then back to Labrador, so that in an emergency the F3s could divert to the United States military base at Keflavik in Iceland, to Sonderstrom Fjord in Greenland or to Goose Bay.

Once airborne, the technicians – with nothing to do until they land at Goose Bay – are recharging their physiological batteries after a night in the glittering nightspots of Ayr. Crammed into the VC10's tiny passenger cabin, 24 000 feet above the Atlantic, they are drinking coffee from Styrofoam cups and eating sandwiches from white, service-issue cardboard lunch-boxes. The aircraft was built in October 1963 and is older than its ground crew. The three rows of passenger seats face backwards – a safety measure most civilian airlines would like to adopt, except that customer research has indicated that their paying passengers would object. The seats face a blank, grey bulkhead with a single door – which opens suddenly letting in a blast of chilled, dry air, and the sudden surge of engine noise. Air Loadmaster Annie Dobson returns from checking the cargo bay, rubs her hands together and grins, before stowing a large inspection lamp in one of the luggage lockers.

ZA141B no longer earns her living carrying passengers. Beyond the bulkhead her fuselage is filled with a long, stainless steel cylinder containing 150 000 kilograms of highly inflammable aviation fuel called 'Avtur' – aviation turbine fuel – a form of kerosene. The insulated pipework that leads off from the tank turns the gangways on either side into an obstacle course. The gleaming stainless steel feels icy and is dangerous to touch – without gloves, hands could stick to it. The air is very cold and gets colder further aft, making gloves and flying jacket essential for Annie Dobson's regular rounds of inspection. The lack of sound insulation requires ear protection – and makes communication impossible, other than by shouting directly into the ears of others.

Through the circular windows – the only reminder of the aircraft's former passenger role – the sun shines relentlessly, hard, white light reflecting up from a puffy floor of altostratus and cumulus clouds, in an otherwize empty sky. On the flight deck, aircraft captain Dave Mutty, co-pilot Mark Robson, navigator Neil Bishop and flight engineer Hugh Pender – all flight lieutenants – are preparing for their first customers of the trip. Neil Bishop is head down in the corner, at the rear-facing navigator's desk behind the captain on the port side, poring over the route chart and trail graph, checking his calculations and timings. Hugh Pender sits on the other side of the entrance door behind the co-pilot, the myriad dials of his banks of consoles occupying the entire bulkhead around him and curving over his head. Tanking is a critical operation for him, as he is responsible for all aspects of the fuel – its safety, delivery and distribution. In the front seats, Mark Robson is scanning the route plot, double-checking the times at which they are to enter the refuel boxes; while the aircraft's captain, dark-haired and wearing sunglasses, savours a last cup of coffee before the Tornados arrive.

Tornado aircrew describe air-to-air refuelling (AAR) as like 'taking a running fuck at a rolling doughnut'. The rendezvous position is pre-planned but, as the sky is a very large place, the F3's dual inertial navigation system (a gyroscopic system that measures movement from known points and is accurate to within half a mile) requires a little additional assistance. Radar is used – both on-board radar, ground radar (if within range), and the aircraft's air-to-air tactical air navigation (TACAN) system to help tanker and chicks find each other. Tankers usually fly on their own, with a fighter escort if tactically necessary. If several refuellings are needed (three will be required today) F3s and tanker will stay together after the rendezvous, separating once the fighters have enough fuel to accelerate ahead to land … to get the best rooms in the hotel, shower and generally relax. All this, however, is hours away.

In the Tornados, long transit flights are one of the few occasions when auto-pilot is used – making the journey rather uneventful and potentially boring. People resort to various diversions like playing a particularly imaginative version of 'I-spy', for five hours in an empty sky. With little leg room, strapped in tightly, wearing close-fitting g suits, it is far from comfortable for long periods of time. Care has to be taken with liquid consumption, as unstrapping and unzipping to use the pee bag is less than amusing.

Flight Lieutenant Mark 'Britvic' Gorringe, a former fighter controller, is aged thirty, and flies in the back seat as Flight Lieutenant Mark Boyes' navigator:

'It's a pain undoing five or six layers of immersion suit, and unstrapping. You can't move around much, and although the footrests go all the way out, they're not that comfortable, so you tend to get a sore bum – especially if you're big.

'The transit was pretty boring for us. We navigators just put the route up on to the plan display, then follow the little sperm, or the tanker – which has a bit better idea of where we are. Our navigation system is generally only a couple of miles out, which we can fix on the way in anyway.

'So we can take it easy – while keeping an eye on things. When we're close to other aircraft, it isn't so relaxed … !'

ZA141B is cruising towards the first refuelling box, between Stornoway and point 59N 10W. Three Tornado F3s crewed by flight lieutenants Tim Taylor and his navigator Paul 'Vicars' Vicary, Graham 'Stumpy' Stobart and Mark 'Giz' Harding, and Mike Jones with Graham Bond will be taking on fuel. As the slot time approaches, Air Loadmaster Annie Dobson puts her flying jacket back on,

Overleaf: Tornados over the Atlantic, in transit from Prestwick, Scotland, to Goose Bay, Labrador, Canada, on AO3 Cyclone Trail; the long range fuel tanks under their wings would be dumped immediately before air combat.

ready to take up an icy station on the intercom at the rear of the tanker fuel bay. Flight engineer Hugh Pender swivels the rear-facing video camera, and prepares to let out two of the three fuel hoses – one from each wing, so the F3s can refuel in pairs. (The centre fuselage hose is used only for larger aircraft like the AWACS, Tristar or a single fighter.) Neil Bishop has already picked up the F3s on his radar. They are approaching steadily from the east in close formation, at a speed timed to arrive exactly as the tanker enters the refuelling box.

The three F3s are a 'three-ship' flying formation on their leader, Tim Taylor:

'It's important never go to a tanker without enough fuel to divert or get home. You could damage your probe when approaching, or something could go wrong with the fuel feed system … so tanking must never be your only option.'

Once radio communications have been established between tanker and receivers – the chicks – Vicary, Taylor's navigator, closes in using much the same intercept techniques he would use when stalking an enemy bomber. As always the approach is from astern. The receivers stay at a safety margin of 1000 feet below the tanker, which flies straight and level and only marginally faster. Taylor sees the tanker, an occasionally glinting speck above the clouds, at about eight miles. As they close, he pulls his three-ship over to the left, gradually climbing to the same altitude as the VC10 to join it on its port wing.

Both tanker and chicks start running through their refuelling check lists. The tanker loads its signal pistol – an emergency measure to order the fighters off if something serious or dangerous is about to happen – de-selects its HF (high frequency) radio, which is too powerful to transmit so close to other aircraft, turns off its lights, and puts the cabin seat belt signs to 'On' so the travelling ground crew will not be hurt if the tanker has to manoeuvre suddenly during the F3s' close approach.

Flight Lieutenant Dave Mutty slips the autopilot into manual mode. Once refuelling starts he becomes responsible for all four aircraft, determining where they are going, and their altitude and flight safety, which he can only do by flying the aircraft himself – by hand. Optimum limiting speeds for the type of aircraft being refuelled have been calculated, so he knows what airspeed to maintain.

The radios go on to single side band split mode – a short-range, low power option – and the air-to-air refuelling lights are set. Like small traffic lights beside the hose drum units (HDUs pronounced 'hoodoos'), these red, amber and green lights give basic instructions to the receivers. They are backed up by radio – but in war refuelling is done in radio silence: the fighters arriving silently, working to the hoodoo lights. Pender runs out the two wing hoses and their thick, black pipes quiver in the slipstream, dragged backwards by the baskets at their ends.

Once the hoses are out, Mutty clears the first two F3s astern. Followed by Stobart's F3, Taylor drops back, then pulls in behind, matching speed to fly formation on the tanker. Taylor and Stobart alter their positions to line up exactly behind the hoses. Their navigators have already read out the F3 pre-AAR check list from the pile of reminder cards they keep in the back. As they approach, they check off the last few items: 'HF radio off, probe out, own fuel switching …' The Tornados move in towards the baskets, their navigators giving a running commentary. The idea is to come in steadily and make the final connection with carefully calculated firmness. The hoodoo lights show red and amber, inviting the F3s to come in close behind the basket, then the red goes out. The single amber means 'Make contact and plug in'. The hose has a thick orange marker halfway along which has to be pushed back into the hoodoo. A good push, and the amber is replaced by a green light indicating that fuel is flowing.

On the VC10 flight deck, Hugh Pender has been following the action on his television screens, altering the hoodoo lights, noting the leap of his fuel delivery gauges from zero to 500 kilograms per minute – the usual pumping speed – as the probes engage and fuel flows. Each suck takes around seven minutes, the F3s getting an average of 3500 kilograms weight of fuel. When Stobart finishes, Jones moves on to the other wing hose – his blocking presence in the slipstream creating a slight increase in turbulence for the tanker. Hugh Pender monitors the flow, adjusting fuel levels in the VC10's various tanks as it loses weight.

In the Tornados, buffeted by the slipstream, the pilots are concentrating on keeping the huge picture of the VC10 nice and stable in exactly the same position above them. To keep the probe inserted, they must match the tanker's every move, using their throttles and sticks to hold position in the heaving air stream. As they take on fuel, their weight increases, requiring more throttle. The pilots watch the fuel flow, checking that the automatic routing system is balancing the fuel across the fuselage and wing tanks. Fuel can also be stored in the Tornado's large tail fin although for reasons of stability these F3s are not doing this. The aircraft's fuel groups must be monitored; each comprises a number of smaller tanks, which are divided into cells to prevent unstable sloshing around, and minimize fire and leak risks if punctured. On long transits like today's, or in war, under-wing fuel tanks – each containing 2250 litres – are added, which can

Overleaf: A three-ship of Tornados flies formation on its tanker VC10; two of the aircraft are taking in fuel while the third 'chick' flies alongside.

be ditched in the event of emergency or enemy action. The navigator monitors the fuel totalizer, which tells him how much fuel he has in all his tanks.

Pender has a fuel gauge for each hose on the top panel of his console. The exact amount of fuel required by each aircraft at each refuelling has been pre-calculated, and they refuel according to this plan. In war, where fuel requirements are impossible to predetermine, aircraft fill to their total capacity. When each aircraft is full Pender gets a back-pressure reading (like that at a filling station), the fuel flow is blocked automatically and the green light starts to flash.

Taylor has finished first. In war, when aircraft need the maximum amount of fuel, they refuel in pairs. Taylor would have stayed plugged in while Mike Jones finished off, dribbling fuel in at the same rate as he burnt it, in effect using the tanker's fuel to fly. Once everybody is full, and the tanker's green flashing hoodoo lights have given them clearance to break contact, all three aircraft drop back and pull over to starboard to fly in the same airspace as the VC10.

ZA141B's scheduled refuellings take place without incident, including a very bumpy forty-five minutes as Dave Mutty takes on fuel from the whirler VC10:

'We're taking on around 90 tons of fuel, but I don't actually feel any changing of our centre of gravity, because the aircraft trims itself automatically. It's very heavy, like a huge ship which takes ages to stop or turn. You have to anticipate things well in advance and fly very accurately. Being thirty years old, it has a limited performance. At maximum weight, it's hard to alter speed, and the gap between top speed and slowest speed narrows greatly. The buffet speeds come right down, with 290 knots as the minimum – which makes it difficult to slow down enough, for example, to tank a C–130 whose maximum speed is around 230 knots.'

Buffet speeds are determined in brackets that are based upon the amount of g or gravitational force being generated. Turns generate g, which increases according to speed and the tightness of the turn. Any slight amount of turn requires additional speed above minimum stall speed, or the aircraft will stall – go unstable and fall out of the sky. In a fully loaded VC10, a modest turn pulling 1.35 g causes buffeting which can turn rapidly into a stall. It is easy to enter the 135 buffet bracket (1.35 g) when manoeuvring. Higher altitude also narrows down the buffets so the maximum height is around 43 000 feet.

As planned, after the VC10 has refuelled from the whirler and the F3s have had their third suck, Taylor and his three-ship ease their throttles forward a touch and vanish off ahead.

CHAPTER THREE

Goose Bay

It is the afternoon of 25 April 1995 at Goose Bay, Labrador. It is snowing and the F3s arrive without warning, screaming war birds dropping suddenly from a lead-grey sky like migrating geese. Squadron Leader Ian Gale, the commander of A Flight, with Flight Lieutenant Paddy Dickson sweating it out in the back seat, comes in completely blind, enshrouded in snow. Just as he is about to have to pull up and come round for a second approach, Gale catches sight of the sequentially flashing 'running rabbit' landing lights that run towards the beginning of the runway and touches down almost immediately.

It is not essential for the aircrew to see anything on landing. They can take a precision approach radar (PAR) from the air traffic controller who talks them down from his two-screened radar – one screen for height and the other for azimuth (giving the jet's horizontal position). The controller guides the aircraft down a line keeping it on the glide path and azimuth. At 200 feet the crew look out and try to see the airfield. If it is not visible they keep going round until they run low on fuel and have to divert. The other method of assisted landing is by ILS (instrument landing system), where an electronic beam indicates the correct glide path and azimuth. The pilot flies according to his azimuth and glide path indicator to stay on the beam. Again, if nothing is visible at 200 feet the aircraft goes on round again.

Before aircraft are even allowed to take off, the weather at both their diversion and 'crash' diversion airfields, as well at their home base, must be suitable for an emergency landing. Coningsby has only one runway, so if the weather is good there but bad everywhere else no one takes off: if an aircraft crashed, the others would have nowhere to land. Goose Bay has two runways, so if one goes out of service it is always possible to run back round and land on the other.

The RAF hangar complex at Goose Bay is a hub of activity with crew buses arriving every fifteen minutes to drop off ground crew and flyers exhausted from the long flight across the Atlantic. On arrival in their C–130, the advance ground crew has gone straight into action, getting the line kits into position, marking slots for the aircraft and laying out the chocks in the snow, ready to see the jets in. Once the planes are on the ground they service them and change all the ejector seat personal survival packs (PSPs) from normal United Kingdom ones to the special Arctic versions. (They have to change these back again, after reports that spring has arrived at Cold Lake, and the snow is melting.) They will then leave the jets to the sweeper ground crew, who followed everybody down the route and who will fix any problems that might develop. The advance team then take off for Cold Lake in their Hercules.

The sweeper party is the last to arrive at Goose Bay, its C–130 Hercules landing into driving sleet long after the VC10 and Tristar tankers. Its members stumble down the rear ramp, still wearing ear-defenders, heads ringing from over eight hours of mind-numbing noise in the hold of the transport aircraft. Like the rest of the squadron's ground crew, they had been working solidly for the past seven days getting the F3s ready for this trip.

The Tornados had taken some five hours (pushed along by tail winds – an unusual weather phenomenon when travelling west) to cross from Lincolnshire to Goose Bay to land using instruments. On a bitterly cold, wet evening, the

Squadron Leader Ian Gale, commander of A Flight, in the cockpit of his F3; he devises the squadron's flying programmes and makes sure it fulfils its training requirements.

Tornado and tanker crews gather in the operations centre at the RAF's new hangar (part of a £3million rebuild that prompts several cynics to comment that withdrawal from Canada is imminent). The F3 aircrew look weather-beaten, their faces marked by tight-fitting flying helmets and oxygen masks.

Once everyone has arrived, the briefing for the next day's flight to Cold Lake is held. The briefers are brisk and to the point, knowing that the tired crew need to unwind and sleep, before another exacting day of tanking. The Goose Bay detachment's British air traffic controller is the first to speak:

'We've got less than ideal weather for the trip to Cold Lake so I've changed the RVs to make joining a little easier. At the first bracket, you fill to full, then on the second, to the amount shown. The Tristar will take four chicks to Edmonton, so if one F3 goes u/s [unserviceable] it can be escorted back to Goose Bay by the other one, the Tristar continuing. If any chicks with the VC10 go u/s, that whole wave will return for yet another night at Goose Bay ...'

A slight groan goes through the audience. Goose Bay is clearly not the preferred night-out. Second-in-command Squadron Leader Ian Gale, runs quickly through timings for the next morning:

'We should have no problems with body clocks for tomorrow's start time – outside ready to go at 7 a.m. local, 11 a.m. GMT.'

He looks around the briefing room, knowing that in order to sleep most people would be drinking the odd beer.

'So you can stand outside in the cold for half an hour to wake up if necessary.'

The Goose Bay base commander offers advice:

'Don't go down town and annoy the local people. We're not very popular here at the moment due to the low flying around Goose Bay.'

In any case, nobody intends leaving the base. Wing Commander Martin Routledge urges everybody to have a few drinks –'But don't go mad' – and a good sleep before announcing the mandatory watching of a flight safety video about the problems of flying low level, which has a special relevance to the forthcoming exercise.

Made by the United States Air Force, the film is a compilation of low-level flying accidents and brings out the findings of the post-accident investigations. In each one, experienced fast-jet pilots inexplicably flew into the ground, trees or hillsides – and as they were killed, were not able to explain why. The investigations are as much psychological as technical and physical, explaining how particular and unusual circumstances fooled aircrew into making fatal mistakes. Fast-jet aircrew are selected for their rationality and determination – and do not easily make mistakes, especially fatal ones. It is therefore vital to discover what fooled them, and to pass on the information so that these mistakes are not repeated.

Canada is very different from the RAF's usual low-level flying areas. It is flat, endless and covered with trees, often with few marks of human habitation to indicate location. Aircrew call it the 'GCFA' – the Great Canadian Fuck-All. Judging altitude at low level depends upon knowing the usual height of standard objects on the ground like telephone wires, buildings and trees. Several accidents have resulted from pilots mistaking bushes or young pines for full-size trees and flying into the ground. At 600 knots low level, the ground becomes an indistinct green blur flashing underneath the aircraft. Particularly in hilly or mountainous terrain, pilots are easily lured into canyons or valleys which appear to be longer than in fact they are, or which have less than obvious hills shadowed by the mountains behind. At speed, it takes a lot of air (and distance along the ground) to turn or climb a jet, and once an aircraft is closer to a hill than its maximum climb capability a crash is unavoidable. To compound the scope for error, deceptive terrain causes optical illusions: 'A goldfish bowl effect like you've never seen before.'

The film is long-winded, and everybody groans at the repeated use of the phrase 'the crew were fatally injured in this incident'. ('Does that mean killed?' asks somebody.) Flying low level is dangerous, leaving little time to react to the unexpected. The sky reflected in still water gives no indication of where the water surface might be. And water is lethal even at low speeds – and as hard as concrete at 500 miles an hour. False horizons lure people towards hills, forcing impossibly steep climbs followed by apparently inexplicable crashes into hillsides. Hills blend in with bigger hills behind, vanishing in light and shadow, particularly early and late in the day.

Flight safety investigators have also noted what they call the 'chain link fence' illusion, in which pilots look through trees in the foreground of their vision (as if they were the links of a fence seen close up) and concentrate on the vegetation and terrain beyond. They end up flying into the trees – and crashing.

Goose Bay, Labrador: Wednesday 26 April 1995

Goose Bay is the staging post for many of the NATO military aircraft *en route* to Maple Flag. Only the best aircrew may attend the exercise – those with the flying hours in various types of mission. Even the most experienced squadrons have spent several weeks working up to the standard required. For the European nations, who cannot do as much low-level training because of environmental restrictions, this is not always possible. The Italians and Germans therefore descended upon Goose Bay *en masse* several weeks previously for an additional work-up period before flying further west, on to Cold Lake.

As a usually quiet military base, Goose Bay is emerging from the grip of winter with scenes of great activity, particularly this morning as Cyclone Trail A03, somewhat time-lagged, but well refreshed from the odd can of Labatts the previous evening, prepares to taxi. Fighter and other military aircraft from Canada, Italy and Germany, plus the eight F3s, two VC10s and the Tristar from the trail, are waiting in line to taxi in what is called the 'cascade' – prepared to take off early if the aircraft in front goes unserviceable at any stage of the process.

The Tristar is due to take off before ZA141B which will be preceded by its four chicks. In the VC10's cockpit everybody is peering out, trying to work out how the complicated and endless procession of jets from different nationalities is going to get airborne. The first two 29 (F) Squadron F3s emerge from the pan around one side of the hangar at the same time as a second pair emerge from the other side. They end up moving towards each other on a slow collision course as a dark green Luftwaffe C–130 waits its turn to join the queue, and a long line of Luftwaffe F–4F Phantoms looks on. The F3s circle each other like Indians round a campfire before moving off in the correct direction.

'Torville and Dean would have been proud of them,' says Dave Mutty.

Air traffic control is pressurizing ZA141B to take off or wait for one hour. Confusingly, but for obvious military reasons, all timings are in Greenwich Mean Time – Zulu. The Tristar has started its engines, which are sucking up small tornadoes of water from the pan which swirl into the engines and then out as water vapour. It looks very heavy and is about to turn to face its engines towards the VC10.

'Tell Annie to make sure everything is secure – we're about to be buffeted by the jet wash as they start moving,' Mutty warns.

The 'follow me' vehicle is gesticulating furiously at the Tristar, trying to get it moving forwards on to the flight line. Something appears to be wrong. In the meantime two German Phantoms jump the queue, followed by the C–130. The VC10's co-pilot Mark Robson makes a comment about German beach towels and sun loungers. The Tristar says that for some reason he cannot move. ZA141B's crew can see that his rear chocks are still in place, but no reason why he should not move forward. Mutty asks one of the on-board ground crew to leap out and have a look. The VC10's door is opened and two senior aircraftsmen

Overleaf: A Luftwaffe Phantom F-4F, one of the aircraft that will participate in Maple Flag; only the best aircrew from the participating NATO nations may take part in the exercise.

nip down the steps on to the pan. Mutty is concerned that the Tristar's back blast might injure them, so Hugh Pender also leaps out and runs across the apron to speak with them. The Tristar gets moving and joins the queue for the runway.

The Germans' formation call sign is 'Starship', the RAF's transit call sign the much less evocative 'Ascot' (a hangover from the old days of Air Support Command's operational air traffic call sign) or the even less imaginative 'RAF Air'. The F3s will be 'Triplex', 'Magpie' or 'Buzzard' followed by their numerical call signs, and the tankers have alpha–numerical call signs, plus their numbers. So in radio-speak, Tristar Ascot 9412 will refuel Ascot 9621, 9622 and 9623 and 9624; VC10 Bravo Ascot 9211 (ZA141B) will be responsible for 9625 and 9626; and VC10 Juliet Ascot 9213 will refuel 9627 and 96288.

Any F3s that fail to take off lose their call sign and the aircraft that takes their place ('cascades') gets it.

Today's trail will be simple, with only two refuelling brackets. The first will be of 3.5 tons and the second 3 tons, with an abort point after the bracket depending on where the abort airfields are. The whole operation takes place over thousands of square miles of GCFA, the scale of which is breathtaking. Goose Bay and Labrador are the size of Britain and Denmark put together, with only 500 000 inhabitants.

Confusion continues in the cascade; one F3 has failed to start properly and has been replaced. If it cannot be fixed its accompanying aircraft – its wingman – and the other VC10 may also have to stay behind for another night at Goose Bay.

Dave Mutty starts his take-off checks:

'Fuel sixty-nine tons.'

'They promised me that they'd put in seventy, so it'll probably come up ...' Hugh Pender starts the first engine.

Another F3 goes unserviceable and taxis back to the aircraft servicing platform (ASP) – the pan, otherwise known in American air parlance as 'the ramp'. Pender starts engine four:

'Best hope that nothing goes wrong with us now ...'

Confusion is setting in. The unserviceable F3 rejoins the queue:

'Why can't they rejoin at the end – and use a squadron call sign?' asks Mutty. 'Something like Buggalugs One ...'

'No,' says Pender, 'more like Eject Two.'

As the VC10 is about to go forward, three German Phantoms move into the taxi queue. The four F3s taxi off and ZA141B continues with checks. All four engines are now running as they should. The doors are locked and 'follow me' truck 'Pulldog 405' starts flashing its green 'follow me' sign and moves slowly forwards. The VC10 is cleared to taxi to runway 08, and the steps are removed. Brakes off, Mutty decides to get ahead of the remaining F3s. He steers by turning the nose wheel – using a hand wheel by his left-hand knee. There are several aircraft around, so Pender stands up to scan rearwards out of the starboard windscreen. Bravo Hotel, the unserviceable F3, comes back in towards the ramp area moving fast, so the VC10 has to stop and let him past. Navigator Neil Bishop, squinting over his left shoulder, suggests that they 'Taxi it straight to the skip'. The tanker moves forward again, turning sharply right into the taxiway.

'I can't turn the bloody thing,' grunts Mutty, straining to turn the hand wheel round the tight corner. 'Give me a hand.'

'It's OK, you've got enough room.'

The VC10 turns on to the taxiway, following one of its two F3s. The Tristar's F3s are making one last attempt to take off before they must submit to air traffic control and wait for one hour to let everybody else get off. A German Phantom cuts in front of ZA141B so it slows down yet again.

'This is turning out to be really hard work,' comments Mutty.

The tanker follows 365 metres (400 yards) behind the Phantom. Mutty tells Robson to speed up. He has seen another German C–130 lurking, propellers turning, in one of the side taxiways and fears (rightly) that it too will queue-barge. As the VC10 hits the long straight tarmac of the main taxiway, a line of Phantoms and F3s, spaced evenly until the holding area at the end, becomes visible. The aircraft passes the German C–130 that jumped in front of it earlier:

'Don't mention the war,' comments one wag.

'We could always wave,' says another – so they do.

One of the F3s takes off with a distant roar. Air traffic control tells of a fresh problem regarding the VC10's take-off time. Mutty queries this and is told to check with Channel 11. His aircraft needs to leave at its designated time because it has specific altitude clearances for its trail route. It appears that because the Tristar is flying with four chicks and was late taking off, air traffic control has to allow at least thirty minutes along the route between them and ZA141B. Mutty argues the score, but remains philosophical:

'If we have to sit here and hold for thirty minutes, I don't suppose it's going to cut that much into the fuel plan.'

The aircraft pulls over into the holding area, close to the tails of its two F3s – Charlie Bravo and Charlie Victor. Air traffic control announce a new take-off time, and everybody waits – all three aircraft are treated as if they were one.

The F3s move forward on to the runway, side by side. Charlie Victor goes to full throttle and accelerates away, flame powering out of both engines. He rotates, nose pulling suddenly upward, rear wheels leaving the ground a moment later. Charlie Bravo's engine roars into max dry — maximum power without using burners. The VC10 turns smoothly on to the runway, nose wheel on the centre line, and Dave pushes the four throttles forward. Pender, who has a duplicate set of throttle levers to the left of his engineer's desk, checks the power. Robson calls out the ground speed — 'Eighty-three knots … V1 … Rotate' — and the nose pulls sharply upwards. Galloping tarmac is replaced by the grey of the sky.

Aircraft are safer, and their crews happier, once airborne. Take-off, when the engines are put under greatest strain, is the most potentially dangerous part of any normal flight. If anything goes wrong, particularly with engines, instant decisions must be taken with no space or time for error. A series of calculations is therefore made before take-off, to determine the exact point at which it would have to be abandoned.

V1 is the speed at which the aircraft can get airborne even if it loses one engine. It is calculated taking into account air temperature, the all-up weight of the aircraft and the length of the runway, plus other factors like wind speed and the runway's gradient. If an engine malfunctions before reaching V1 the take-off is aborted. If it malfunctions after V1, the aircraft keeps going. VR is the velocity at which the aircraft's nose is pulled up (rotated) when the stick is pulled back, and V2 is the speed at which it will climb with three engines. Runway length is important. Civilian Aviation Authority rules require civilian aircraft to have gained enough altitude by the end of a runway to be able to clear a 10.5 metre (35 foot) fence — a rule that doesn't apply to the RAF. For this take-off, V1 was calculated as 133 knots (153 m.p.h.), VR was 154 knots (177 m.p.h.) and V2 was 163 knots (187 m.p.h.). These are indicated airspeeds; if an aircraft was taking off into a 30 knot head wind, the ground speed would be 30 knots less but indicated speed would be the same.

The VC10 climbs steeply and levels off at 10 000 feet. The F3s are not visible but the tactical air navigation (TACAN) system indicates that they are at twenty miles range. Their radar homing warning receiver (RHWR), the Elettronica ARI 23284 radar-warning radar, enables aircraft type to be determined; for some reason it thinks the F3s are Sea Harriers — the wrong sort of bird for this terrain. The TACAN distance closes, indicating that the Tornados have turned to port and circled round behind the VC10, which settles down to an airspeed of 290 knots. Its F3 'Sea Harrier' chicks cruise unseen four miles behind it.

Although Neil Bishop could use his inertial navigation system (INS) he will follow radio beacons along the route, which runs obliquely to the usual air transit routes. He updates the flight deck: the VC10 was airborne at 13.57, and will land at Edmonton at 18.49. As with all RAF operations worldwide, timings are in Greenwich Mean Time – Zulu time – which requires a quick conversion to local time: take-off was at 09.57, expected landing time is 14.59 hours. He glances through the refuelling plan: the tanker will enter the first refuelling bracket at 14.53 Zulu, in just under an hour's time. Seated behind the co-pilot, Hugh Pender monitors the engines, controlling the four throttles:

'On this aircraft, it's easy to overpower the engines, so I monitor them very closely, over-riding the pilots if that looks like happening. They only actually use the throttles themselves when taking off or doing formation flying – and even then I'll take over if we have problems.'

The AAR and flight go smoothly, according to plan. There is heavy cloud over Edmonton and the city can only be glimpsed as the VC10 descends from cruising altitude. Edmonton air traffic control upsets its orientation by altering the runway because of a changing wind direction, forcing it to turn on to a different heading. As it turns Dave Mutty asks Air Loadmaster Annie Dobson to warn the passengers to belt in and brace for a rough ride. The aircraft descends into the tops of some cumulus clouds, Mutty calling out 'Going dirty' as it enters. Neil Bishop starts calling out the distances:

'Thirteen miles from Golf now; eighteen miles to touchdown.'

The VC10 emerges from the cloud:

'The lakes round here are not frozen,' notes Mutty, '250 knots please.'

Pender controls the throttles. Neil Bishop is straining over his right shoulder, looking out of the port windscreen:

'Flock of birds at nine o'clock.'

Mutty swivels left, then relaxes; they are well clear of this potentially lethal hazard. Edmonton and the surrounding countryside are visible now, and Bishop and Mutty identify the various landmarks:

'What's the airfield look like?' Mutty asks.

There is a slight pause, then:

'Like an airfield,' replies Bishop.

'210 knots Hugh. I thought the airfield was to the north of the town.'

'No, to the south.'

'I must have my map upside-down.'

'Nine miles to touchdown.'

'Turning to port, flaps down, speed's good ...'

'And you get eighty per cent,' adds Pender, commenting on the power level of the engine.

'Airfield then to port.'

'Undercarriage down.'

'Eight miles to touchdown.'

Mark Robson: 'You're high but it's all right.'

'Going down, landing checks …'

'Speed brake, touch flap …'

Air Traffic Control Edmonton offer them a second circuit as the change of runway has put them off the desired track. Mutty turns on to the correct heading:

'We'll take it now,' he replies.

'Cabin OK, checks are complete.'

'Four miles to run.'

Ahead, to the side of the runway, a bank of lights gives last-minute glide path instructions to the pilot.

'We have three greens to land.'

'Eighty-two per cent,' says Pender, monitoring engine revolutions per minute.

'At six hundred feet.'

'Two reds, two whites.'

'Eighty-three per cent … eighty-two per cent.'

The aircraft has turned and lost height rapidly to make the new heading and approach, levelling out as it closes with the beginning of the runway. The centre line moves up to meet it, wavering slightly as the VC10 floats towards it. The plane touches down.

'Full reverse.'

Hugh uses all four engines to slow the aircraft down.

'Idle reverse' and he shuts off the power. The VC10 coasts along the tarmac, while co-pilot and captain contact both air traffic control and 'company' to find out where it should taxi, and which 'finger' in the terminal it will occupy. Although there are only some half a dozen aircraft on the apron, air traffic control and company manage to give contradictory instructions, until finally a marshaller waves ZA141B into Finger 14 with its connecting walkway arm. Unfortunately, as tanker VC10s have their (normal) port-side doors welded shut, the Edmonton ground crew's attempts to open this door (despite explanations from the cockpit) fail, and steps are brought to the starboard side.

'It happens everywhere,' comments Mutty sadly. 'I'd really love to walk off down one of those tunnels, but it hasn't happened yet …'

CHAPTER FOUR

Strapping In

One experienced Maple Flag pilot commented that, 'You don't take Junior on this exercise.' All aircrew taking part in Maple Flag have had to qualify by having flown a minimum number of operational hours, of particular sorts of mission, up to a specified standard. However, even 'Junior' is extraordinarily well qualified.

Fast-jet navigators and pilots have survived one of the most rigorous selection processes in the world. Many have science degrees and every single one is very highly motivated. In the RAF, the Officer and Aircrew Selection Centre at Cranwell is the great watershed, selecting for both officer potential (as aircrew are officers first) and aircrew potential. (The famous Biggin Hill selection centre closed down about four years ago.) Selectors are looking for 'the controlled extrovert', and employ flying-based manual dexterity and hand-eye co-ordination tests, problem-solving exercises and 'Crystal Maze' type leadership tests that also measure team member potential. After three days of intensive assessment, candidates are told whether they are potential fast-jet pilots or navigators – or not – and are offered a job, depending upon vacancies. If fast-jet aircrew are not being recruited at that time, something else would be offered.

Having accepted the job offer, all officers go to Cranwell for basic officer induction and training; twenty-six weeks of square bashing, turn-out, skill-at-arms, leadership and basic military skills, with camps at places like Sennybridge Ranges and Otterburn, plus lots of physical activity. Those pilots who pass go to elementary flying training on the Slingsby Firefly; then basic flying training on the Tucano at Linton-on-Ouse, and are streamed into rotary wing, multi-engined or fast jets, depending upon how well they've done in the training.

After basic fast-jet training, both pilots and navigators go to the Operational

Conversion Unit to 'convert' to the jets they will fly operationally: Tornado F3s or GR1s, Harriers or Jaguars. After learning to fly these new and very much more powerful aircraft, they start to operate them as weapons systems. From pure flying, they are now getting into fighting and the training harnesses the aggression that has kept them going all the way through the previous weeks.

OCU starts with aviation medicine training – hypoxia and pressure-breathing drills – survival, sea survival and a four-week ground school. Navigators deal with weapon selection, looking out for other aircraft and monitoring systems, so their actual navigation has to be automatic. (They still have the map and stopwatch, in case the systems fail.) The pilots must think tactically, not just about their own aircraft but about others in their formation – and about the enemy. On completion, both pilots and navigators are ready to be posted to a fast-jet squadron, in a state called 'limited combat ready'.

Flight Lieutenant Marc 'Fizz' Physic, RAF exchange officer with the Canadian 410 Cougar Squadron, had to convert from the Phantom to the CF–18 Hornet:

'It's not easy to convert to different aircraft. The older the dog you are, the harder it is to learn new tricks. Three weeks of ground school, six months of flying in all the various situations – none of it easy or gradual. The fourth trip was solo – so it's like drinking from a fire hose. Big-time hard work, up to midnight swotting most nights. Also, I had come to an air traffic control system which is very different to the UK's and it took a lot of hard work to understand it.'

Flight Lieutenant Mike Jones believes that nobody should join the military, especially for flying training, unless they're really sure they want to do it.

'You can waste three years – it's a long haul. There's horrendous waste, and you've got to be committed to your long-term aim or you'll blow it off.

'I'd gone to Liverpool to do mechanical engineering so I'd got another string to my bow. I was what the Americans call pretty focused to my goal, so I didn't think about failing.'

Flight Lieutenant Richard 'Ritchie' Bedford of B Flight took a B.Sc. in business and computing at Hatfield Polytechnic, and was accepted as a pilot by British Airways as well as the RAF. But he really wanted to fly fast jets and said he was not interested in doing anything else. His aptitude results were good so the RAF offered him pilot training.

'The most difficult part of the training was the initial course at Swinderby. I went solo after nine trips which was daunting – and the process of actually being taught to fly, never having even been in a civvie aircraft before, was a shock. They had to find out if I'd be able to cope – so I was pushed hard. You really

Flight Lieutenant Marc Physic, pilot; as an exchange officer with Canada's 410 Cougar Squadron he spent six months learning to convert from Phantoms to the Cougar's CF–18s.

do need confidence to get through. There are so many stages and aspects of flying training – and I had doubts throughout the course.'

Flying training is very structured with a steep learning curve. Low-level flying, night flying, instrument flying, formation flying, general handling and tactical skills like multi-plane formations are relatively small building blocks, but every stage has to be mastered. A trainee who cannot cope with one stage will not cope at all.

There is time to take in information but not to become proficient. Pilots have to learn what their instructors are trying to teach them and put it into practice so that they can cope with a lot more later in the course.

The whole job is about working on overload, and coping – and there is no respite.

Those who cope are pushed even harder. Bedford:

'On low-level sorties, they'll make you go off track for bad weather; or simulate an in-flight emergency like bird strike or engine failure – real possibilities – to load you up and see how far they can push you. Military pilots have to be as flexible as possible, as anything can happen on an operational sortie.'

Fast-jet flying is at the heart of the air force image, ethos and aspiration. All aircrew, especially those who fail to be streamed fast jet, or are 'chopped', have fast-jet values instilled into them. RAF multi-engine pilots have to be able to fly in close formation, maybe in a Tristar – with other Tristars, VC10s and fast jets, flying in ways that would give their civilian counterparts recurring nightmares. Aggression, versatility and hard-minded professional skill exists across the board in the RAF. The dividing line between the potential of fast-jet aircrew and other aircrew is actually quite thin, based only upon performance and maturity during training – and the speed with which individuals manage to assimilate the training. Flight Lieutenant Tim Taylor did not want to fly fast jets:

'Throughout flying training, I found I was waking every morning with a sickly feeling in the pit of my stomach, and realized that I didn't like fast jets … I actually wanted to be a helicopter pilot. The training is very repetitive. You'd be taken up, shown something, then ten minutes later you'd have to demonstrate it, and ten minutes after that, do it on your own. Very "monkey see, monkey do". Anybody can fly an aeroplane. It's not difficult to do what you've been shown.'

Flying training lasts a very intense eighteen months, of which mainly the social side seems to stick in people's minds. The pressure and work load can make people introspective, often fearful of failure, and constant assessment is a serious limiting factor. Taylor:

'There's no reward for thinking for yourself. It's only quite late into the course that they ask you to extrapolate from what you've learned and prove what you can do – which came too late for me.'

Taylor felt strait-jacketed. He found the flying was hard, but unfulfilling.

'Everything was learned by rote. Every five minutes, even if you haven't moved an inch, you will check the fuel … You will do set things at set speeds and set heights … It's all vital – and sticks in your brain. But at the time you think, "I wish he'd stop badgering me, bugger off and leave me for a minute or two." Before the OCU, where you learn to drop bombs and kill people, at the end of the fast-jet pilot stage, I came up for my last test, the final handling test – and failed.'

Pilots have one hour or so to demonstrate everything they have learned over eight months. The trainee takes off in close formation and does high-level formation and aerobatics. The instructor gives him or her an emergency, some low-level flying, then after another emergency he diverts to another airfield, overshoots, comes back, then demonstrates academic flying – instruments only in different forms, including aerobatics. Taylor says that he failed through being generally scrappy:

'Everything was below par. I thought, "Oh well, nobody told me about that," and took two or three practice rides, coasted along until the next test, and failed again – which was unheard of. Nobody fails twice.

'So it was into the boss man for a chat – "Pull your socks up …" – and then I flew with a couple of people I'd not flown with before, who boxed me around the ears. I was under-confident in some bits, over-confident in others, lazy or hyperactive in other bits. They smoothed off edges, and pushed me in different directions, until I took the test a third time. Thankfully I passed – which was just as well as I was due to get my wings the following day. It would have been embarrassing for my parents to come up for the parade – and then for me not to get them!

'But having passed for fast jet, when I applied to fly helicopters, they called me in and said you can't do that … Having spent all this money on me, I had to be a fast-jet pilot.

'I'd got it into my mind that I didn't want to go rushing around fast at low level. I wanted something more sedate – to cut straight from being twenty years old to being thirty-odd with pipe and slippers. Which is where I am now! I wanted to miss out on all the dangerous stuff. I thought that if I felt like this flying training jets, extrapolating upwards to Tornados the feeling would be worse. So I was pretty miserable … I never thought I was cut out for fast jets.

'The trouble is that in training, only ten per cent of the instructors were fast-jet pilots, so the only things you get to know about fast-jet flying is what you read in magazines, which can be quite nebulous. OCU was the big change. Getting your wings means you've made it – at least that's what you think. You finally shrug off the training environment, and you're on your own. Being given £20 million worth of aeroplane, and after a very short time being told to have a go on your own, is a big boost.

'That whole summer was a formative period – halcyon days, sitting in the sun with a black Labrador sort of stuff! Some of my friends had difficulties, which at that stage colours the rest of your time in the air force as you spend the next few years trying to shake off the bad memories.'

OCU is very different to those first flying lessons, where the instructor does most of the actual flying.

Pilots are told what to do and where to find out how to do it. They practise in the air, with a trainee navigator, then demonstrate that they can master the technique – without having been shown exactly how to do it. Like earlier training, it is the building block system. There is lots of free time to work everything out in simulators as it is too expensive and politically sensitive for a pilot to go out flying all the time.

But, as with all the training, it is necessary to learn at the required rate. Taylor did not find this particularly difficult. It took him seven months to become operationally ready – what is known as the 'convex' period. Once he arrived at 25 Squadron at RAF Leeming, it was very different:

'Flying with a real aeroplane, on an operational, front-line squadron, was completely different from what I'd thought – a real buzz – great, a constant high, working with very single-minded people. You learn by osmosis half the time, passing on everything you learn. It's work hard, play hard – a bit of the old Biggles, rushing around with your hair on fire …'

For quite a while, the air force has only ever recruited people with enough flying potential to become fast-jet aircrew, relying on fall-out from the fast-jet programme to crew the multi-engine and rotary wing branches. Flight Lieutenant Graham Stobart:

'To an extent the RAF is crewed by frustrated fast-jet people, some of whom feel that they were unjustly chopped – that given the chance they could have made it – and are jealous of others who were given those extra chances whereas they weren't …

'Some of the people chopped as pilot, end up as navigators on fast-jet squadrons – which they prefer to being a pilot elsewhere. Personally I'd rather be a pilot of anything than be a navigator! You don't get chopped as a navigator and then go on to pilot training!'

Although it is possible to reapply to fly fast jets after being chopped, not many people bother because it means starting again at the bottom. But with the benefit of more experience and maturity, those who do generally succeed.

Stobart got all the way through on fast jet, but could not come up to speed flying the Lightning during OCU:

'I was unsafe so, not surprisingly, I didn't continue. The Lightning used a lot of fuel, so flights lasted around thirty minutes – half the time of other aircraft. I couldn't pick things up fast enough and ran out of time. Maybe given more fuel, time and instruction, I could have made the grade – but would I have learned fast enough on the squadron? Flying is very expensive. You've got to make a certain grade in time or you're out. And as enough people make the grade within the time to fill the squadrons, that's the way they work.

'I went into multi-engines flying Nimrods, but always fancied coming back to fast jets.

'The Tornado was supposed to be like a big Hawk, which is a very easy aircraft to fly. I thought I could probably crack that, so I kept asking for a cross-over back to fast jets – and in the end I got it. I did a bit of training to bring me back up to fast-jet standard, went through the F3 OCU, and here I am.

'Once you make it into fast jets, you've passed everything in the RAF system. Only a few loonies get through to fast jet, then apply to be transport pilots!'

Once a flyer reaches a squadron he has proved that he can learn quickly and improve. But there is no time to relax. The standards officers constantly check people out. It is up to the flyer as an individual – and up to the squadron to try and help him out. Stobart:

'If he wants to be the best fighter pilot or navigator in the world and know everything about his jet, it is up to him. Equally, if he wants to be idle that is also up to him.'

The secret of being a good flyer is hard work – planning, preparation, thinking about sorties, learning from one's own and other people's mistakes. A lot of studying is also involved as everything that needs to be known in the air can be learned on the ground. Experience is essential, with a handful of natural ability thrown in. Taylor:

Flight Lieutenant Graham Stobart, pilot; he was originally streamed into flying multi-engined Nimrods but kept on asking for a cross-over to fast jets – and got it.

'When you're fresh from OCU, almost all your brain power is used up simply flying the plane. It gradually becomes second nature, until you can afford to look out of the window and enjoy the view – or devote that spare capacity to helping the navigator or improving the job. As you continue, both pilot and navigator use less and less brain power simply flying, and more improving this mysterious situational awareness – dealing in the third dimension – that we all talk about. Some people are a lot better at it than others, and some (comparatively) haven't got a clue. Like everything else, there's people of a higher ability, and people of a lower ability. I'm not higher I should add.'

Natural pilots do exist. They fly the aeroplane perfectly, never drop out of formation, excel in air combat and never let anybody beat them. But there are not too many of them around. Stobart:

'On this squadron there aren't any naturals – although others might disagree. There are a few good pilots, but "good" in flying the aeroplane is in reality secondary to operating it. A Tornado's not an able fighter in dogfights. No matter how well it is flown it will not compare with the American fighters. The best Tornado pilot in the entire world will lose against F–15s, 16s and 18s in close visual combat – they are such superb aeroplanes. It's being a good operator of the weapon platform that counts, knowing how to use your aeroplane and formation to the best of its ability, leading them effectively around the sky.'

Being good is more a question of how you react than how you fly. Taylor:

'It's working out what might be happening, then reacting and using the information early rather than later so that you can make it do what you want to do. If you give two people the same information, they'll do different things. One will be completely reactive, while the other will think ahead giving the impression that he's driving events – which he isn't – but he gives off the aura that he is. People have got it or they haven't. You can go on being reactive and be good at it. But there's a limit to the effectiveness of people who are reactive.'

Looking ahead, coupled with speed of thought and action, is a fundamental quality. A minority of RAF aircrew are in fighters. Within that very rarefied group of very talented people, they categorize themselves as the 'god-like', the average, and the 'awful'. A squadron is a very competitive place. Taylor:

'Among our sixteen pilots, we have some junior pilots who are very good, some very experienced pilots who are very good; and some junior pilots who are not very good. Only three are QWI pilots – who are gradeable into the best, middle and worst. You place people in the squadron – the best navigator, the worst pilot … you can't help it. It's not always a conscious thing, and you don't use the information. But it's always there in the back of your mind. It's competitive too, as everybody wants to be better than anyone else and be recognized by the system. On the other hand, if you get some good information, you have to share it because it's expected that others will do the same for you, and for the overall improvement of the squadron. We're very caring, sharing people!'

Flying a fast jet is essentially an introverted job – sitting in isolation, peering into screens, concentrating furiously on making the right decisions. Yet aircrew are clearly extroverted people, selected by psychological testing and subsequent group moulding for team spirit and outgoing qualities.

Fighter aircrew do not become fully operational until they can prove their combat readiness, after which they are awarded their operational badge. Before they get this all 29 (F) Squadron's new navigators have to fly their operational 'op check' ride with Tim Taylor who, as the squadron's qualified weapons instructor, is responsible for testing new crews. New pilots have to fly with Flight

Lieutenant Harry McBryde, the QWI navigator. Taylor says that there is nothing more demoralizing than a really low quality check ride – fighting with the aircraft, working too hard and losing out:

'I then have to go into great detail and point out a whole load of negative things, which makes them miserable. It can go horribly wrong, so we don't put anybody in until they've got enough experience to decide on their own way of doing things. And everybody gets a check ride every year.'

Both pilots and navigators also undergo a tactical evaluation check ('tac check') which involves planning, briefing and then flying a mission with a senior flight commander or weapons instructor, who declares them combat ready. They need to have gained enough experience to be able to put on a well-balanced sortie, which is well briefed, well led and de-briefed to a good standard. Everything must be second nature, so that they have the capacity to cope with complications during the mission.

People then progress, at their own pace.

The formalized steps through the squadron start with leading a two-ship, then a four-ship, then, in recognition of experience and supervisory capability, the better people become authorizing officers who decide who is capable of doing missions. People progress by being given more responsibility and work load, rather than by any sort of 'ace-of-the-base' competition. Somebody who is doing well and coping well will be given additional tasks – and assessed again. There is a pecking order of flying ability determined by the squadron's commander. Some people will get made up to lead a formation of four jets before others, while some may get their fours lead taken away from them.

Most of the leading is done during planning and briefing on the ground. Leaders have to be able to set realistic game plans, aims and objectives for their sorties, then specify what they want from wingmen and the leaders of elements like two-ships, four-ships or formations. The more experienced leaders are able to make what they want crystal clear to everybody.

Navigator training starts at Cranwell, then at Linton and RAF Valley in Wales. Trainees start with ground training, learning the basics and the systems of the particular aircraft they are using. Everybody aims to get 100 per cent in ground school examinations, nobody willing to admit there might be gaps in their

Overleaf: Flight Lieutenant Paul Vicary, Flight Lieutenant Tim Taylor's navigator, in his cockpit; he is the lead navigator in A flight.

knowledge. Flying starts on the Bulldog: something new is demonstrated, the trainee gets time to practise it, then he is tested.

Training is also progressive, to the faster Tucano, learning to fly lower and with the additional pressure of flying on time over a target — on the principle that there is no point in a military aeroplane taking off unless its crew hits the target. Trainees develop mental dead reckoning without instruments, working out wind speed from smoke on the ground or the weather, calculating ground speed and drift in their heads. No mental techniques are totally accurate but it is necessary to be quick and as exact as possible. In the Tucano, it's visual navigation, with nothing at night.

Techniques to cope with being lost are also taught; as any navigator knows, there is a lot to be learned through losing your way. The greatest pressure on him, however, is fear of failure, particularly in the eyes of his peer group — six or so fellow pupils.

Squadron Leader Peter Budd is a Tornado navigator, and former instructor:

'Our aim as instructors was to pass everybody. Unfortunately some guys do not have the ability and get suspended. Most realize that they are failing and suspension when it comes is a relief. Very rarely is the person close to failure unaware of it. If suspended, they are still valuable officers, and re-muster to other trades.'

The next stage is to the Domine business jet where they navigate using radar at medium altitudes. Two pupils share the navigating, overseen by an instructor. Once they are used to this, they come down to 500 feet low level, the windows are blanked out and they fly completely blind to hit targets on time. This is extremely demanding.

Using a weather radar as an attack radar is the most difficult — trying to recognize patterns. It is a display that looks like a bowl of lumpy goo, and it is known as 'orange porridge'. To complicate matters further, navigators have to sit backwards and are unable to see out. Pupils have to actually fly over the target — a dam, power station or something else that will show up on the radar. Initially they are given a set of predictions of what the radar picture should look like which they try to match to what they are seeing on the screen. Then, as training proceeds, they have to work it our for themselves, selecting what they hope will be radar-significant features from the map to use as reference points (off-sets) for the run-ins. It is a lot easier if there is a coastline to follow, but over land it is very difficult. Time on targets (ToTs) of plus or minus five seconds have to be achieved. As the course develops, the instructors throw in emergencies, diversions and other tasks.

The trainees learn by orientating the radar to the route, and feeding in accurate fixes of where they are to update the avionic system. They also have to monitor all other aspects of the mission: ToT, fuel, routing and simulated emergencies. It is a busy and testing process but it takes place at slow speeds of around 210 knots.

Halfway through the Domine stage navigators, like pilots, are streamed into rotary wing, multi-engine or fast-jet aircraft. Budd:

'They really grow in confidence and stature during this phase. It's hard and demanding, and they feel they have really achieved something by the end of it.'

The next stage is the Hawk, still with staff pilots, but the learning process speeds up significantly with low-level flying and visual navigation at speeds of up to 420 knots, with ToT and some air-to-air combat. Trainees are then streamed into either air defence or ground attack fast jets. Ground attack navigators require good, low-level navigation, whereas air defenders require better situational awareness (SA). Some people are good at both, so they can be given a choice. Once streamed, they do specific training: air-to-air navigators do more combat and intercepts; air-to-ground people more targeting, both as singletons and pairs. After this phase they graduate, after some 130 hours and fifteen months.

Even though they are no longer trainees, there is little relief until they get their 'op patch' – the heraldic flying badge which they can wear once they are judged combat ready. Once they have achieved this status they can fly on bigger exercises and more complicated sorties, and work up from being two-ship to a four-ship leader, then to a six.

CHAPTER FIVE

In the Air

The huge ranges and high speeds of modern air combat are very different to the deadly, close-in aerobatics of Second World War dogfighting. Modern jet fighters do still 'merge' and slog it out with each other, but over enormous chunks of sky, with longer range missile systems. The accuracy and speed of medium and short range missiles are likely to further increase the ranges at which dogfighting takes place. On Exercise Maple Flag, 29 (F) Squadron do not have the American AMRAAM missile which, because of its long range, speed and accuracy, will dictate their tactics – making them underdogs from the outset.

Close range air combat in air war today is about twenty miles, and fighters are basically defensive against the 'big stick' (29 (F) Squadron's name for AMRAAM). They try to destroy the enemy's situational awareness and defeat the missile basically by running away.

Situational awareness is an intangible, three-dimensional sense of exactly where everything is and what it is doing. Acquiring and retaining it takes enormous mental effort, but without it a fighter crew is helpless – and an easy target. In computer terms, SA can be thought of as being the interface between the human super-computers in each aircrew member's head and the aircraft's on-board computers and sensors. To stay alive, all the aircraft's weapons systems – and especially the crew – must be on line and working. Losing SA is worse than being blinded by electronic jamming or spoofing because good SA can be used to overcome electronic warfare (EW).

When fighters are running away they perform massive height changes as well as splitting to the four winds. If their manoeuvres were to be only two-dimensional, the enemy could keep track of them much more easily. In the face of a missile that is utterly lethal once it has been launched correctly at its target, the aim of these tactics is to enable some of the fighters to re-commit – turn back towards the enemy and kill him. Flight Lieutenant Justin 'Reuts' Reuter is a navigator in 29 (F) Squadron:

'If you stay in the same piece of sky all the time, then eventually the enemy will find you. But if you keep changing altitude and position all the time, it's much harder for him to keep track of you – and very labour intensive. We're trying to max the guy out, saturate him so he can no longer do his job properly.

'Obviously, to an extent all these manoeuvres defeat your own SA, but you try to hold on to enough of it to do your job while completely screwing his air picture so that he doesn't know what's happening. Although he's got automated equipment to help him, he's still got a lot to do manually. He's trying to keep track of lots of different people, all at different heights, all changing rapidly.'

Not every fighter will be able to re-commit, and whoever does so must be untargeted. If a plane turns back only to get hit by a missile, there is no point in getting airborne. With the high speed, heavy g forces and enormous mental effort required to both fly and keep track of what is going on, air combat is physically exhausting. The battle, however, is one of wits, brain power and intelligence, to achieve enough of a psychological advantage to slip through the enemy's fighter escort. Reuter:

'The idea is to get a group of our fighters past the enemy and into the bomber package. As soon as he loses SA, you're in.'

Flight Lieutenant Paddy Dickson:

'The problem with air defence is that unlike the bombers, who can plan everything in detail, we can plan the initial presentation in great depth but thereafter we don't know what's going to happen. We can only plan "what ifs". What if he does this or that? Or I'm radar down …

'The difficult bit is keeping situational awareness, and retaining the capacity to be flexible enough to take the situation as you see it. It all comes down to the crew in the cockpit. If they think they're untargeted they have to be able to schneagle in, the best way they can, and get some killing done.'

It is very much a team game, with the wide range of other air defence assets on whom air battles depend – like the AWACS 'eye in the sky' sentry aircraft, electronic jamming aircraft and ground-based radar, jammers and fighter controllers – and also with the other fighters. Reuter:

'We try to keep together in our pairs whenever possible, so we can cover each other in a defensive formation. It's the one you didn't see that kills you. You always fly with a height split, sharing the search responsibility between you, covering half the sky more thoroughly.

'However, because the weapon we're up against is so good we have to do even more, and bigger and better, things to defeat people's SA. Often we have to operate alone – which you just don't do ordinarily. It's risky and difficult, but gives you more chance. Six aircraft operating in six separate tracks are more difficult for the enemy to track than three groups of pairs.'

The Tornado's defensive manoeuvres rely upon violent height changes, from 250 to 35 000 feet. If it goes any higher it uses too much fuel. In war, the jets go down to fifty feet – as low and as fast as is necessary to defeat the enemy's weapons, hiding behind hills or other features. Their defensive airspace is a rectangle around thirty miles across as the enemy looks at it, with as much depth as possible. Reuter:

'The visual fight is a lot larger than you'd think. You can see an awfully long way – up to ten miles. You can see Phantoms twenty miles away with their smoky old engines. Also, if aircraft are really high, they start to contrail, like airliners. These days if you can see somebody, you can kill him. Missiles are as accurate as your eyes.'

Because it is a two-seater, the Tornado has one big advantage over the single-seat American-made F–16s and F–18s – even though these are armed with the dreaded AMRAAM. A pilot on his own has to fly the aeroplane as well as keeping track of what the enemy is doing, while fighting in a Tornado is done by two people: the pilot and the navigator. And two brains are able to retain SA and work out intercept solutions – and evade – much better than one.

Although pilots say things like 'No stick, no vote,' and although the pilot and his navigator both have set jobs, in reality their responsibilities overlap to such an extent that it is difficult to separate them. Reuter:

'We're both needed to keep each other alive and do the job which, in basic terms, is getting in there and killing people before they drop bombs on your grandparents.'

Dickson: 'I'm not too fussed about the grandparents, but the wife would piss me off.'

Reuter: 'Yeah, it would … and actually … I mean my wife and not necessarily your wife, or possibly wives in general …'

Dickson: 'As air defenders, we have to get through the enemy's fighter escorts first, so we can get at their bombers …'

Reuter: 'I don't mind as much if they bomb your wife rather than mine …'

'Vice versa,' agrees Dickson.

'We want that on the record.'

Fast-jet flying is incredibly absorbing and very physical, but enormously and unimaginably demanding. Former instructor Squadron Leader Peter Budd:

'When people have problems with fast-jet flying, it can almost always be put down to a lack of mental capacity, which doesn't mean intelligence but the ability to cope with changes and a vast amount of information. Some people are fine when things are going well, but go to pieces when changes occur, unable to deal with situations as they deteriorate. It's very difficult to define what this might be – the ability to absorb, assimilate and act upon a lot of information while listening to several radios and the intercom, looking out to spot other aeroplanes ... Then things start getting worse, and you've got to deal with problems as well.

'All the way though flying training the guys I saw suspended were suspended because of a lack of the mental capacity to deal with the unexpected. On operations nothing runs on rails exactly to plan. You have to be able to deal with the unexpected as it happens.'

As soon as an aircraft gets airborne, the navigator starts to build up a picture. He sets up a combat air patrol (CAP) in an area to cover an enemy approach, then commits from advance warning information – either from a JTIDS picture (the RAF's new data link system) passed from another radar or his own radar, or by a voice radio order.

The navigator starts off looking into his screen. All the radar controls (except some dogfighting modes that the pilot controls) are in the back. He looks at the enemy and does the geometrical calculations that make the tactics work, building a picture so that if the pilot enters a 'visual merge' – sees the enemy – he'll know how many aircraft there are, their formation, roughly how high they are and where he can expect to see them.

A merge is where two sets of forces come together and have a fight. There are 'pre-merge' and 'post-merge' tactics: pre-merge the aircraft manoeuvre and radar lock over longer distances with different ranges; whereas post-merge they are too close to do this. When the jets are in pairs searching the airspace for targets they use strong search disciplines, scanning different sectors to make sure they cover the whole sky. When they discover a target, both navigators roll down their radars so that they are both looking at it – which is known as 'merging the radar'. However, they do not do this immediately as it is necessary to keep scanning the whole sky to ensure nobody else creeps in.

The navigator's contract is to give maximum useful information to his pilot and the others in his formation, in order to achieve targeting (which group to attack), then sorting (assigning radar responsibility within the formation) so that each of

Flight Lieutenant Paddy Dickson, navigator; fast-jet flying requires the ability to cope with a vast amount of information while listening to radios and the intercom, and watching out for other aircraft. Navigators give pilots that invaluable 'second brain' in the cockpit.

the enemy's aircraft is threatened and can be shot at. All the navigators pass the information from the radar to their colleagues in the formation as well as to their pilots. With the high pressure of working and assimilating all the information, some of them talk more than others. The element leaders have primary control over how their formation scans the sky, building up their air picture and SA, but otherwise it's very flexible. If a navigator sees something that is different from what the leader is calling, he calls it and starts building his picture up.

Meanwhile the pilots fly the aircraft in a good defensive formation, giving each other mutual support, doing a lot of look-out and getting as much situational awareness as they can from their navigator and others. All the time, both pilot and navigator monitor the radar homing warning receiver (RHWR) which will give first indication that somebody else's weapon system is looking at them. Reuter:

'You can tell by his aspect on the radar, whether an enemy aircraft is pointing at you. You start to work out whether he's trying to run away or whether he's a bomber or transporter, who doesn't want to fight. These are the guys you want to kill, who are going to be dropping bombs on to your wife and kids, or paratroopers over your home town to storm your local pub.

'If he's pointing at you all the time, you've got information on your radar warning receiver that he's looking at you or locking you up with his radar. With certain types of aircraft, you'll know he's fired at you and you start to think he might be a fighter. Our radar warning receiver is superb, one of the best around, and provides extremely accurate information about what's looking at you.

'So he's being aggressive, he's high, he's fast. Who am I up against? If he's a bomber who doesn't have much opportunity to fire back at me, then great, I want to press him, shoot at him, force him away from his track, make him lose time, make him miss his time-on-target, screw him up as much as possible so he can't get a bomb on target.

'In the meantime you're also thinking, well if he keeps looking at me, he's got to be a fighter, so he could shoot at me. What sort of missile could he shoot at me? Who's got the best weapon? What can I do to defeat him? Or how can I avoid him, so I can get at the guys I bet he's protecting? 'Cos if there's fighters coming across into your home territory, you know the guys carrying the nukes are behind them – the guys you're really interested in.'

The navigator works the radar, building up the picture of what the Tornados are up against and what the enemy is doing, monitoring the threat and passing on information. As the F3 gets closer in he manages the radar to achieve a sort –

making sure each fighter is locked up to the correct aircraft in order to shoot it. With some systems like AMRAAM and certain radars, multiple groups can be targeted without locking up, which means that the systems can look at other aircraft while they are targeting yet others. Tornados, however, have to go 'single target track' – lock up one enemy and then shoot him. The sort therefore ensures that all the formation's missiles have a different target and that no enemy aircraft slips through the net. When one target is locked up all the information on the others is effectively dumped, so it is important to know what the enemy's other aircraft are doing.

Once a sort has been achieved the aim is to get a rocket off as quickly as possible. A long range missile like Skyflash, the Tornado's primary weapon, is shot in the head sector (straight ahead). The fighters like to be travelling high and fast in order to throw it for maximum reach. Skyflash is used beyond visual range (BVR) if an aircraft can be positively identified as the enemy – which AWACS is able to do.

If there is no positive identification the fighters have to close with it visually, which is extremely dangerous. Whoever recognizes the other first and gets a missile away, wins. The other will die – especially against AMRAAM. The first indication that another aircraft is not a friend is when a missile comes off his rail.

At the same time, the Tornado will do defensive manoeuvres so that the enemy has the least possible opportunity to shoot back. If totally outgunned, Tornado crew have to confuse their opponent's air picture so much that they can get in untargeted – either to the enemy aircraft or past it to whatever is coming behind.

All the time the pilot is building up his situational awareness so that using his eyes (and his navigator's eyes) he knows where the enemy is. If the radar missile is unsuccessful, he will quickly shoot a visual missile into him – or, as a last resort, use the gun, a 27 mm cannon. Reuter:

'If the pilot doesn't see all the players, then somebody will get unsighted and shoot him down – and it's your little pink body too.

'You decide early to blow straight through – going as fast as possible – with minimal risk, out the other side to separate, then build up your own air picture before turning back to re-engage. The pilot is eyes-out the whole time, plus he can switch the radar and the navs' plan display through from the rear and is monitoring the warning receiver all the way in …

'Each of us covers the other's job. When you start training, the instructors make you tell the pilot to do everything – like come up, come left, turn right, roll out, go up, go down, shoot now … but when you get to fly with a guy on an operational squadron he's already thinking the same things as you, so as soon as you start thinking about the geometry of your intercept he's looked at it and has thought the same – and is beginning to do things for you. You don't actually need to ask him to climb or descend, and equally he doesn't need to ask you to lock, 'cos at the same time as he's thinking "Why haven't we locked this guy up?" you're doing it. You're always looking at each other's jobs but doing your own as well. And the pilot is flying the plane in formation, to protect the other aircraft.

'The visual arena is where the pilot gets to do the Biggles stuff – pull the wings off, and shoot other guys down. You are then his second set of eyes, his extra brain, to optimize his performance. He's looking out all the time – 'cos that's what's going to save his life and end everybody else's life. You can look out, keep track of everybody else in the fight, tell him things he should really know about, like "Break right now otherwise we're going to die". Also you can both be putting out chaff and flares to defeat other people's missiles. You keep glancing in, to watch things like altitude and fuel. If you hit the ground or run out of fuel, you'll die just the same.'

Tremendous concentration is required and aircrew find that they go into 'automatic mode'. Many of the things they have practised and trained for become basic functions that they don't have to think about. Reuter:

'Monitoring all your sensors and fighting heavy radar and communications jamming, which sap your brain, plus managing your tactics, calls for an incredibly high level of concentration. After an hour or so you are physically whacked – and have sweated a lot – simply because of the concentration. And ten minutes or so of dogfighting – pulling a lot of g and thinking at the same time – is physically demanding.

'In training, when the g comes on you start consciously to strain against it, greying out, eventually blacking out as the blood rushes from your head. I only consciously strain once a week or so – as usually I'm already straining and ready.'

Dickson: 'You learn a special straining manoeuvre to keep the blood in your upper body, which involves clenching your stomach muscles as if somebody was going to hit you. You do the same thing with your leg muscles – instantaneously for about three seconds. You also do a big breath in, which you let out in little puffs, then another big breath and let it out. You make a loud grunting sound as

Overleaf: A pilot leaves his aircraft after a long flight; a one-hour mission can involve an exhausting eight-hour day that starts with a 6 a.m. briefing.

you do it. If you do it correctly on the ground you'll see stars and feel dizzy because you've pumped too much oxygen to your brain. Up there, it's all being forced away.

'There's no time for the pilot to warn the nav. about g coming on, but you generally know when to expect it. Sometimes it can catch you – if you're looking in on the radar, not expecting it. Ordinarily you talk as you do things – a constant flow of information, or talking on the radio, which helps you strain.

'The pilot will routinely tell you as he pulls up at the end of a very heavy dive, say 80 degrees nose down – which is amazing as you lose so much height so quickly, and all you see is the earth screaming at you. Pulling out of a dive is when the g is heaviest. You know exactly from the aircraft fit – the weapon load that determines its flying limitations – when you must start pulling out. The pilot will routinely then say "g's coming on" so that I know he's about to pull up and we're not about to dig our own graves ... And also so that I don't start blacking out, and the last thing that I knew was the ground screaming up towards me – so as navigator in the back, what am I going to do? I'm going to save my arse.'

'Toosh!'

'Yeah, I'm going to bang out – eject, and you've just thrown away a perfectly serviceable aeroplane.'

Fighter aircrew are so well conditioned that all their decisions are automatic, even though they are based upon circumstances and complex calculations that would defeat most normal people – even if they were sitting in an armchair in front of the fire.

They have a general awareness of where their jet is at all times – their air picture. And they know their attitude – how the aircraft is placed – even at night. They make so many checks of the altimeter while in cloud that they do not have to be able to see outside to know how roughly high they are and what attitude the aircraft is in. Dickson:

'It's a massive big equation that's always in your mind. It's different to each individual and includes aircraft height, attitude – whether the plane's upside down, nose-down or whatever – speed, the terrain, weather and where the other aeroplanes are, and it goes around and around until the moment when you ask yourself "Do I feel happy?" If you come back with the answer "No," that's when the old butt starts puckering.

'There's nothing more brain-sapping than strapping a helmet to your head, a mask to your face and your body to a seat, in a confined space that has extra noise plus three different voice radio inputs and the cockpit intercom. The calls are coming in thick and fast, plus it's a fairly physical job. We say that you lose fifty per cent of brain power whenever you get your flying kit on; fifty per cent of the remaining amount on strapping in; and a further fifty per cent when you get airborne – all due to the extreme environment – half your brain in a bucket on the floor. I find it very tiring.'

Pilots say that once they are in the air they are totally absorbed in what they are doing. When they are part of a team of six or eight aircraft, they cannot afford to let the others down by flying at less than the best of their ability. Everybody concentrates very hard, starting with a lengthy briefing two and three hours before the flight and finishing after the de-brief. A one-hour flight can mean a 6 a.m. brief and a working day that finishes eight hours later at around 2 p.m. Flight Lieutenant Graham Stobart:

'You learn what to concentrate on at what time, what you should be listening out for, looking for. You have to develop an awareness of what's coming over the radio, of when you need to listen, and when you can talk to the other aircraft. Even just trying to listen is quite sapping.'

The most difficult thing about being a fighter pilot is maintaining the picture of where the enemy and your side are in space and time. Flight Lieutenant Mike Jones:

'It's discipline – listening to what the AWACS tells you, looking at your radar and the plan display. There's nothing chivalrous about air-to-air warfare. You want to pick on the guy who has split off from the others, has a single engine failure or some sort of problem – and kill him.'

Flying the aeroplane must be second nature if the pilot is to concentrate on the battle – and this is the standard he has reached once he arrives on the squadron. However, everybody has their own limit for the amount of information they can absorb. Jones:

'There's an awful lot of information in our displays and everybody has their maximum capacity. If somebody's working at full capacity and is told something extra that input can get filtered straight out – especially if it's not over the aircraft intercom – and he'll ignore it as he can't cope with it. You can reach that stage, and you've got to recognize it. If your nav. shouts "Break left" because you're about to collide with someone in mid-air and you don't hear it, there are obvious safety implications. People have to work really hard at it.'

The picture can be complicated on a mission. The pilot knows from the brief where his colleagues and four or five groups of the enemy are, where the jammers are, and where the AWACS is. But after the initial move it is chaos. Jones:

'You try to do each task as it comes along, looking for the guy you're going to target, then concentrating on killing him. I try to divide my attention so that I'm only doing one thing at a time, plus listening to the radio, but covering everything. It's a constant scanning technique – I decide what I'm going to look at and what I need to know from it. I look out of the aeroplane then briefly at the plan display, then at the RHWR to see if we're targeted, then I look out of the window again as that always helps. I might switch to the radar for a couple of seconds just to see what the nav. is doing with it, then back out of the cockpit again, back to the RHWR. You're not just sitting there Feeling the Force! but picking and choosing the sensor you're looking at next.

'Obviously if the RHWR shows that the enemy has locked on to you with his radar and is about to shoot that becomes your focus of interest. You're being targeted, so you've got to make some decisions. Go to the radar; is the guy that's spiking me the same guy that's on my radar? The spike's coming from over there. The guy on the radar is in a different direction so, no, it's not the same guy. So do I have any information from the plan display on where that spike's coming from? Is he spiking me from eighty miles away? No I haven't – OK, so best I go defensive 'cos I don't know the range this guy is at. And then you turn, run, set your scope up again, look back at the plan display. Has AWACS or any of my buddies managed to put in the guy that's now spiking me? No they haven't and I still don't know his range, so I'll run a bit further. OK, set the scope up, and we'll come back left. Set it up for 60 azimuth on the left, we then go naked – when the RHWR indicator tells us there's nobody looking at us any more – so we come back again.'

Science has turned combat flying into a very technological game: men reacting to information from mysterious black boxes. Is there now a black-box mentality – technicians flying an electric jet, rather than fighter pilots flying by the seat of their pants? Wing Commander Martin Routledge:

'We'd all like to go back to knife-fighting in phone boxes with Spitfires because that would be a lot of fun. But technology marches on, and you have to make the most of what you've got. We've got a very technical aeroplane. The pilot flies it, and the navigator is there to help – a work-sharer, or load-sharer. The way the aircraft is configured, the radar workload is passed down to the back. A lot of it is still down to the man looking out of the window, and working out what he's going to do next. The navigator is there to help, to make it as easy as possible for the pilots to get in there and kill. We do it together.'

CHAPTER SIX

On the Ramp

Without reliable, safe aeroplanes, the squadron, quite literally, is useless. No matter how good, brave or well-trained aircrew officers might be, unless they have complete and utter confidence in their ground crew and the aircraft, they will be unable, either physically or psychologically, to push their aeroplanes to the limit – and do the job. The aircrew take the fighting to enemy and this is reflected in the structure and attitudes of the squadron. The ground crew, however, who prepare the aircraft for war, are integral to the effort. Engineering determines how well the squadron performs. On detachments away from base like Maple Flag, the preparation is more important than what happens on the det. itself and as much of the work as possible is pre-empted.

As senior engineering officer (SENGO), Squadron Leader Chris Gould is responsible for the engineering on the squadron. He joined the RAF in 1982 after serving a civilian apprenticeship as a mechanical engineering trainee. He was trained and worked on Nimrods and Canberras – and was a junior engineering officer (JENGO) on 29 (F) Squadron when it changed over from Phantom F–4s to F3s in 1987 as the first operational Tornado squadron.

In those days the Tornado was a simpler aircraft at a much lower specification; there were very few spares and the ground crew were unfamiliar with it. A few had worked on GR1s – its air-to-ground variant – but preparing the first F3 for the first tactical evaluation exercise (TACEVAL) was a nightmare as it was so new to squadron life. There was also high-level military, political and media interest. Having an aircraft straight off the production line was new and exciting – and glamorous. The squadron went on lots of overseas deployments, including a world tour called 'Golden Eagle' which took in Singapore, Thailand, Malaysia, Australia, Hawaii and the USA before coming back to the United Kingdom.

Flight Lieutenant Dave Mudd is one of the squadron's two JENGOs. He is also its piano player, specializing in late night, alcoholically fuelled sing-songs and honky-tonks. After being a full-time musician he had worked in computing and marketing, mixing with highly motivated people in the city:

'Like the ones I work with now – but I got cheesed off with it – and saw an ad for the RAF.'

Dave Mudd's aspiration was to do exactly the job that he is doing now – JENGO on a fighter squadron, the job every young engineering officer wants.

Coming to the squadron with its very fast pace of life and the responsibilities demanded of him was a big change: each of the two JENGOs is responsible for shifts of ninety people and many things that are in the domain of the senior NCOs and chiefs, so beyond their personal control. Trust, self-discipline and communication are the watchwords:

'It's no good just being an officer and telling people what to do. I'm the inter-face between the day to day requirements of the aircrew and the realities of what can actually be done, taking into account the needs of my men.

'Sometimes flying rates are planned that mean nobody gets a break and the shift stands out in the freezing cold for twelve hours on end – which I then have to say isn't on. Equally, when that sort of work rate is necessary, I end up being the middleman, getting winged at from every direction … Ground crew do spend a lot of time waiting – after running around a lot!'

The ground crew does two weeks of days, then two weeks of nights, in shifts which run from 7 a.m. or earlier in summer, until 5 p.m.; the night shift comes on at 4 p.m. and works as long as necessary.

Much of Mudd's work is manpower control. There is much less formal discipline than in the past. The ground crew work very hard and some of them are young and need to burn off energy. Because they are an autonomous unit, physically separate from the rest of the air base, with their own crew rooms, bars, etc., the JENGOs are able to quell problems that, as Mudd puts it, 'elsewhere might turn into a riot'.

Officially disciplinary matters are dealt with according to the book but, less officially, people can be punished without running to a charge – by being given the unpopular jobs, for example. The rationale is that someone who is only a few years from leaving the squadron and is not interested in promotion may not be bothered if he is charged; all he will get is a few days' restrictions. However, if he is given an onerous task he will think twice.

The air forces of other nations tend to have a centralized engineering maintenance system instead of specific squadron ground crew; their actual squadrons comprise aircrew only. In British fighter squadrons, high morale and team spirit is greatly boosted by the squadron being a fully functional, integral unit. Mudd:

'It's a very strong identity, and the ground crew are very proud of the job they do – even though they will slag off the aircrew. They are much happier being here than working in a base workshop.'

As an officer deep in the heart of non-officer territory, Mudd has to think rather more carefully about his status, and how he relates with his men, than do the aircrew:

'There's a very clear-cut line between officers and other ranks. I try to keep a certain amount of distance, because at times I've got to discipline these guys and so I can't be their best friend. You've got to be consistent. Sometimes the ground crew take the piss out of me, and other times I take the piss out of them. Sometimes I'll go out with them and have a good drink, relax a bit and be informal. On Maple Flag, I've been out once with all of them, and we've had a good laugh – but now I'll leave them to it just to keep that distance.'

The ground crew themselves understand this, but see the divide as being between aircrew and themselves – rather than being purely rank based:

'There's not much socialization – they're officers and we don't mix that often. We have to make allowances – as they've always been like that! Some are a bit superior, others not. They certainly stick together though.'

Mudd: 'I don't think the aircrew have any idea how much the ground crew takes the piss out of them. Our guys have nicknames for all of them, and know about everything they do.'

The traditional god-like status of fast-jet aircrew is maintained for the benefit of outsiders (and the squadron's reputation), but inside the squadron reality rules. Anything flyers do and think they have got away with is invariably noticed – and word gets around like wildfire. However, the ground crew would not tell outside the squadron – and anyway, Mudd says, it is good for aircrew to realize that they are human like everybody else.

Mistakes are greatly enjoyed:

'There's nothing like an aircrew cockup to boost morale! For example, the story about a certain pilot leading a fly-past for the AOC who missed the target by a couple of miles. That one lasted quite a while, with comments like "How can he complain about the navigation system when he can't even find the base that he flies out of every day?" They all love it!'

There is a whole hidden language of private and not-so-private jokes which

Flight Lieutenant Dave Mudd, one of 29 (F) Squadron's two junior engineering officers (JENGOs); he was a full-time musician and worked in marketing and computing before joining the RAF.

keep the more potentially god-like of the aircrew firmly in their place. Mudd:

'When there's a pilot cockup and aircrew ask us for a technical explanation, the ground crew report "stick-to-seat interface failure" or something like that. The aircrew don't always twig immediately what it means.'

Like the squadron as a whole, the ground crew structure is designed to make transmission of information as easy as possible. It is all about communication upwards and downwards – so that not only does Squadron Leader Gould know what is going on, but so does the senior aircraftsman who has to go out and service the aircraft: it is important that he knows why he's doing his job.

Despite being so technical, the safety of the jets depends upon the ground crew as people. Gould:

'They work very hard, and you've got to give praise when due, as well as stamp on them when necessary – and you can't be soft. They'll always take advantage of a soft person. Sometimes it's almost kiddology – a little praise goes a long way ...'

Gould is very aware of the divide between ground crew and aircrew and concedes that there will never be a perfect relationship between the two because their jobs are so very different:

'What the aircrew do is difficult – no doubt about it. It's a particular skill and we couldn't do it. Equally what we do is difficult – and they couldn't do it either.

'The secret is to get everybody working together, particularly on detachments like Maple Flag. Most aircrew appreciate what we do, and equally most ground crew appreciate what the aircrew do. Some on each side have a different attitude, but overall, it's all right.

'You must have a good ground crew/aircrew relationship, for which a good squadron commander will work hard. I've been on squadrons where it hasn't been good – which makes life very difficult and uncomfortable.'

The ground crew themselves are very clear about their role on the squadron:

'It goes back to the old cliché – you can teach a monkey to ride a bike, but you can't teach him to fix it!'

Within the ground crew, there are equally vehemently defined divisions, based upon robust competition. Electricians are called 'Greenies' and 'Sparks' among other things, and appear to be universally 'disliked' by other trades (as seems to be the case in other industries too); avionics technicians are said to be 'fairies' who replace black boxes without really understanding what they do; engine techs are 'sooties' or grubby 'spanner-wankers'; and armourers are 'plumbers', so devoid of personality and intelligence as to go round in groups of at least four so that one can think, while the others respectively handle walking, talking and listening. The ground crew are certainly far more critical of each other than of aircrew or anybody else. But they do agree that they lack job satisfaction – possibly because modern aircraft engineering has gone very much into 'black-box' replacement repair, so that its diagnostic and craft aspect is starting to be lacking:

'What we do is a job – with no glory. The aircrew look after themselves, and we have to look after everything else.'

'They're the glory boys, who climb back in after we've fixed all the snags and carry on. We don't get any job satisfaction seeing them fly off the runway ...'

'Until it goes up!'

'If they said thank you now and again, it would help.'

'If they do well, they come down and say "We did really well". But if they were shot down all over the place, as in a recent exercise in Belgium, they moan about marks on canopies that make it hard for them to see the enemy – but they don't moan to us, but to the bosses, and make a big deal out of it.'

Gould would like his men to be more aware of what aircrew do with the aircraft – both tactically and in terms of the stresses and strains they put each airframe through. Exercise Maple Flag will not be particularly useful in this respect as the Cold Lake weapons range gives the ground crew no way of seeing what happens on missions. In the United Kingdom the air combat manoeuvring instrumentation facility (ACMI) allows them to see exactly what is happening in the air. He believes that it is very important that the aircrew make an effort to keep the ground crew informed:

'When we do "lock-in" exercises back at Coningsby, after three days sitting in a hardened aircraft shelter without somebody keeping them in the picture, they'll start mushrooming away. Some aircrew are very good at talking to people, while others are no good at it at all.

'The very good ones, who usually get on in the air force, do make the effort – and do get on with ground crew. They'll never make good squadrons commanders if they don't.'

Where serviceability of aircraft is concerned, the only acceptable standard is perfection – a state which is very precisely defined, and also limited, according to the ubiquitous book of rules. A less than utterly perfect aircraft may be permitted to fly within carefully proscribed limits, but as far as the diagnosis and treatment of its ailment is concerned everything must be totally correct and completely accurate. Perfection has to be fully and perfectly documented too. Gould:

'It's easy to criticize the rules and regulations. I find myself wondering why we have to do things in particular ways. The guys sometimes see an easier way of doing a job, but in aircraft maintenance there's no room for somebody doing the wrong thing. Even though there might appear not to be a problem, somebody in the past will have had one. You just cannot afford to take a chance.

'At management level we have to ensure that people understand the reason for the rules and regulations.'

The men on the line can see it too:

'It's not like a civilian airline, where time on the ground is wasted money. With us, the aircraft have got to be absolutely right first time – you don't get second chance. It's pure safety – which is expensive. The jets are probably over-serviced, but who are we to say that.'

'A civvie airliner has got to be fit for purpose – to get from A to B, then do it again. Ours have got to be completely serviceable every time – a subtle difference in terminology that costs the RAF millions.'

Trust and self-discipline are integral to safety. Squadron engineering has to be largely self-regulating, a chain of command in which the people at the top trust those further down to get things done properly. Gould:

'If things don't happen, then we've got a problem as we rely on people getting on with the job. It's not army discipline – telling people to get down immediately or they'll get shot.'

People are expected to think for themselves, and make decisions:

'If I tell them to change a line replaceable unit, say number 10 on the radar, because that's what I think is wrong, there's no point in them doing that if, in fact, it's LRU 11. Technical spares and aircraft components are very expensive, in short supply, and repairs take a long time. If we acted like that, we'd never get the job done.'

Spares are a finite resource, and with feedback from the ground floor the ground crew reaches a group consensus even though Gould or one of the JENGOs makes the overall decisions. On shift change-overs everyone involved will discuss what needs changing. However, they can be autocratic where safety is concerned. Mudd:

'Aircraft are very different from any other sort of machine, in that if something does go horribly wrong you can't just pull over to the side of the road or stop the ship. Through experience we know what we can afford to limit on the aircraft, and aircrew know what they can afford to do with it in the air.'

If the ground crew concentrates on just the aircraft that are unserviceable, it can end with those taking up all the spares leaving the others at risk of not being able to fly. Juggling is required, which is a team game: by shuffling spares around, everything can be kept flying. The secret is to follow a critical path that will keep the majority of aircraft going with limited resources.

Planning the engineering effort requires looking ahead. Back at RAF Coningsby, the JENGOs get the next week's flying programme on a Thursday, then determine the number of teams needed to handle aircraft that are to fly – and thus how many people are left over to carry on with servicing and repairs. Mudd:

'When dealing with other units, formations, even air forces, plus coping with the weather and so on, critical timings change and people can get run ragged. Everything changes day by day, which the crew don't always understand.'

Servicing and maintenance is an enormous task that has to be planned very carefully. This process is relentless and carefully documented, and can only be done in conjunction with the flying tasking. Although servicing limits can usually be extended by a few flying hours they can never be waived. Apart from scheduled servicing, there is also 'out-of-phase servicing' (OOP) on engines and other specific parts that get replaced at different times, so cannot be tied in with the scheduled servicing on the airframe. Some parts, like ejection seats which are not actually used very much, are checked using calendar time. Engines have their own lives, depending upon the number of hours run, and go totally out of phase with each airframe every time they are changed.

Maple Flag required that the aeroplanes be free of scheduled servicing for 105 hours, which meant doing a primary on each of them before leaving the United Kingdom. Plans also had to be made to ensure that no major out-of-phase servicing would need to be done during the exercise.

The hectic weeks before coming over to Canada had been made very much worse for the ground crew by a series of engineering difficulties. Across the RAF Tornado force, a number of reported engine problems required modifications to be made immediately. The first was to prevent build up of pressure in an area that would otherwise destroy the engine. With only days to go before leaving for Maple Flag, 29 (F) Squadron's ground crew were required to make a number of automatic limitation modifications, followed by stringent tests that led to failures of entire engines. Next a number of pins had to be replaced and the hydraulic systems adjusted; then a predicted engine fault required all engines to be examined boroscopically – a boroscope is a fibre-optic instrument that enables engineers to see inside the turbines. The stringency of these checks resulted in four aircraft being declared unserviceable until their engines had been changed.

As soon as a fault is found, even if an engine is running all right and will probably continue to do so for hours, it has to be stripped down and the faulty part replaced. With so little time, making the aircraft serviceable turned into a nightmare. Only one spare engine could be found at RAF Coningsby so engines had to be swapped with other Tornados, which required special permission – and doubled the work involved. The required boroscopic tests duly revealed that some of the replacement engines were also unserviceable. Mudd:

'We were "robbing" components from other aircraft not flying on Maple Flag, but if you do this with engines the tests you have to make invariably lead to more engine rejections, which in turn leave holes elsewhere in other aircraft, and even more broken engines. Robbing engines is not advisable – but we had no choice.'

On the Friday before flying out, four different fleet checks had to be made –some on engines, others on the airframe. At 8 p.m. that night it looked as though they were not going to make it.

The ground crew are philosophical:

'It's all right for him, he just sits there and does the paperwork! The boys go out – the fixing fairies like …'

'In the rob, you've got to identify if the subject engine is going to fit the bill. Is its servicing history suitable, what modifications has it had ? And there are several other documentary and physical checks. You get all your tools together and take the two aircraft into the hangar so it's relatively warm.

'You then get the new engine out and unload it. It doesn't come ready to fit, so you've got to swap a load of components from the old one onto the new one, then put it in. Just a drop, then slotting another one in takes three hours, but dressing the new engine adds a couple more hours on to the job. You've got left- and right-handed engines, for which you've got to swap various components round, plus lots of other little things that allow it to operate.'

The ground crew worked all weekend and ended up with nine out of ten aircraft passing the tests. They had wanted ten, so that they could choose the best eight to fly. But they only just made the eight, as they did not want to take Bravo Zulu – which cannot take fuel in its fin, and needed paint on various surfaces.

All this effort had been greatly complicated by the aircrews' need to train for the exercise. Even though the ground crew tried to take only two aircraft per day away from flying training, the aircrew's practice was seriously affected.

The wiring for the air combat manoeuvring instrumentation monitor pods had to be removed and the mountings for Sidewinder missiles installed. This took one working day per aircraft, with the added nuisance that the missile system test sets did not function properly. Finally, the aircraft had to be painted which, with only one paint shop on station plus all the primary servicing to be completed, was not easy.

By the time the aircraft set off for Goose Bay they were still carrying small snags: a problem with one of the head-up displays, an avionics control unit and inertial navigation units needed adjustment and there were some communications problems. However, the ground crew had run out of time, so Gould authorized the aircraft to carry these minor problems to Canada, to be repaired on the first weekend there. Mudd:

'It was a great relief going out with the advance party, then seeing the aircraft arrive at Goose Bay.'

One of the Tornados diverted to Winnipeg with a battery problem but it was otherwise an uneventful trail to Cold Lake. But when the ground crew arrived there their site had no toilets, electricity, heating, phones or communications.

Getting ready meant doing four seventeen-hour days which, with the change from United Kingdom time (eight hours behind), left them confused and tired. A fast-jet ground crew cannot just arrive and start fixing things. Mudd:

'We have to get set up properly, with everything where it should be. Tool control is vital – you can't just forget about a spanner, which gets left by an air intake on a jet, to be sucked into the engine, the jet crashes and somebody dies … so unpacking properly took a lot of time.'

In Canada the ground crew are on the usual at-home shifts, with a few people swapped over and some 'A' Shift people supplemented by some 'B' Shift people. They are on duty from midday one day to midday the next, going back to the hotel to sleep when the work is done. This back-to-back shift gives them a full twenty-four hours without any work, so they can enjoy their nights out knowing they can sleep in the next morning. During the on-duty twenty-four hours they get up at five o'clock, breakfast and leave for the base. On arrival, the line teams go out to the aircraft to start servicing, while the 'rect' men take the weatherproof covers off.

Before flight (BF) servicing checks gases and oils, plus a full check of the aircraft: its switch positions, the ejection seats, a search for any airframe cracks, and panel checks. A book lists exactly what is involved and squadron line training takes the crew through all this. It has to be done to the letter. Once a 'liney' has worked from the book for six months or so he knows what is in it. The servicing is a real two-man job.

All aircraft are potentially dangerous. A modern military jet is designed to be lethal, so must be treated with very great respect even when it is stationary on the pan.

The first thing to check when approaching an aeroplane is the pins which prevent the ejector seat from going off when someone is sitting in it. The only people allowed to fit or remove these are aircrew and armourers. When the aircrew are strapped in they remove their own seat pins. The only pins the ground crew remove are the miniature detonator cord (MDC) pins, which blow the canopy in half if it fails to jettison, just before the seat goes. 'Man B' removes them before flight, because the aircrew can't quite reach them.

It is important to watch out for movement of the tailerons (the primary control surface at the tail of the aircraft) which move very quickly:

'Unless you're wearing headphones and are in voice contact with the pilot, you don't know when he's going to move them. If one comes down on your head, it's goodnight.

'And the blast from the main engines is very windy. The Americans walk under their jet pipes – ducking down. You can actually walk directly underneath them.

'When the APU – assisted power unit – is running, its air intake is a little door on the side. Its jet eflux is worth avoiding as APUs have exploded, and the bits fly out sideways. There have been cases where the navigator's got into the pilot's seat, and started the APU to get his computer up and running while the pilot is doing his walk-round. The pilot has seen this panel door open and, because he never sees it open as he's usually in the front seat, he wonders what it's for and tries to look into it. Some even put their hand up inside!

"There's lots of little things, which because we've spent so much time with the aircraft are second nature to us. The lox – liquid oxygen – is nasty. Very cold! When you come to disconnect the supply hose, it occasionally dumps itself on to the tarmac.'

The lox supply is replenished from liquid oxygen bottles which are potentially extremely dangerous. It is very unstable – a liquid that very rapidly turns into a gas because of its low freezing point – and can explode if subjected to any form of percussive action, with the usual huge sheet of flame that characterizes any sort of oxygen fire. Refuelling the avtur, which is considerably less volatile than lox, requires equal care:

'You've got to bond and earth the aircraft and bowser, connecting them both together to stop sparks, and not apply any sort of power during refuelling. Any spark will explode fuel vapours.'

Squadron Leader Gould and his two JENGOs are surrounded by experts who know their jobs inside out. The three officers earn their salaries by taking responsibility for everything, and making key decisions that enable the aircraft to take off and do whatever they have been ordered to do. In war, the rules change – for example, much scheduled servicing is deferred. The engineering officers have to make decisions based upon their professional knowledge and judgement, in line with various complicated rule books. For most missions, Dave Mudd has to sign legal documents stating that aircraft are fit to fly with particular snags.

'If we can't do that, the aircraft is declared unserviceable. And if we haven't got enough aircraft for the next wave, we inform air ops to ask if they can re-plan the mission. If not, we look to see if we can juggle with the scheduled servicing of aircraft not allocated to fly – maybe by delaying due servicing for six hours, and other jiggery-pokery!'

Overleaf: Despite arctic weather, ground crew get up at 5 a.m. to prepare aircraft for Exercise Maple Flag missions.

In Operation Deny Flight in Bosnia, a lot of the war rules do not actually apply, but in a full war, the ground crew would go through a concentrated period of preparation called 'transition to war' in which as much servicing as possible is done and everything cleared out of the way so that the aircraft can be left alone to fly. Modifications like certain chaff- and flare-fitting modifications that are impossible to get done in peacetime are authorized, the money suddenly available as if by magic.

There is only one spare engine in Canada, so the ground crew hope there will not be any major problems. Mudd:

'Engine surge can be serious. When a fault leads to overpowering, it causes either a popping bang, a series of popping bangs or one enormous great bang. This leads to loads of people getting their hands dirty, boroscopic examinations, engine changes and a lot of work.

'Radar problems are more common and generally require box changes – and because the electronics are so complicated many of these boxes interrelate with each other. What looks like a fault on one box, is caused by a fault on another.

'The other trades get quite amused with the avionics guys who sit there with their magic bones and dice saying, "Definitely looks like a box six to me." "Oh no, no, it's definitely a five ..."

'There's all these jokes about how they decide which box to change. In reality, it's complicated by a shortage of spares. It gets to the point where it doesn't matter how they've made the decision as we have to say, "Well we've got one of those, so let's try that ..."'

The biggest drama on Maple Flag would be losing an aircraft. At Cold Lake, with several large lakes, melting snow and a large population of very large birds about to migrate flying into one of them is a distinct possibility. Even a small bird can cause serious damage and make an aircraft crash.

As in war, the ground crew will prepare for the worst eventuality. The pilot will try to recover himself and the aircraft in order to make a landing in one piece. If it is a minor strike air traffic control (ATC) declares an Emergency State Two before he attempts to land. If he is worried that part of the bird has entered his engine air intakes he might do a precautionary single-engine approach. For this, the ground crew would be ready in their vehicles at the end of the runway in case he crashes.

CHAPTER SEVEN

Cold Lake
Air Force Base

Cold Lake is over four hours drive from the international airport in Edmonton. The highway is broad and high, deep ditches either side filled with grubby, road-soiled snow. The prairie is flat and monotonous: snow-covered fields, small farms and the occasional grain tower and thousands of square miles of forest, stunted, lifeless and somehow afflicted. For the first hour the monotony is eased by a radio station, '95.4 CLASSIC ROCK!', to which the hire-car tuner leaps on its first pre-set – always a good recommendation.

Grand Centre, the nearest town, starts with a hamburger joint billboard, then the usual declarations of Welcome to Careful Drivers, height above sea level and population statistics. After a bend, the road straightens out into the town itself, a string of motels and fast food emporia each with a couple of acres for customer parking. At the centre of town a road branches left to the Cold Lake air base, past a residential area with its outdoors playground still covered with grey snow. Then the town is gone and nine metre (thirty foot) high birch trees close back on to the roadside, leafless and stunted as if they are dead after the eight-month freeze.

The approach to the base is littered with stripped-out military jets looking like Airfix models, six metres (twenty feet) in the air on concrete stands. One hundred and eighty-five metres (200 yards) from the main gate an F–5, with dummy pilot, looks particularly unconvincing as it points at the sky, a black pipe shoved into its rear engine exhaust extruding down into a concrete plinth.

A long line of Avis hire cars files slowly toward the wire perimeter fence. Despite large signs at the main gate declaring 'Cold Lake AFB Welcomes All Exercise Maple Flag Participants', air base security guards are checking vehicle passes and the traffic light beside the concrete bunker-style police post is showing red. Military police the world over are exactly the same – especially the civilian variety guarding military bases. No pass, no entry – even though this is the Sunday before the exercise starts and the compulsory first briefing session in the air base theatre is due to start at 10 a.m. prompt.

On entering the base past the golf course on the right (and one warmly dressed stalwart towing a bag of clubs), the cars pass the married quarters, then the military police post, gas station and the Canex (base supermarket) before turning right for the gymnasium and swimming pool, its pot-holed car park filled with yet more hire cars. Fast-food franchises adjoining 'the recreational facility' are closed – a lost opportunity to sell to hungry, jet-lagged and possibly hungover aircrew too rushed to eat breakfast.

Flight Lieutenant Dave Mutty has arrived early at the briefing room with the rest of his VC10 crew, joined by Squadron Leader Bob Wilkie and his AWACS flight control team – all working out of Edmonton International, the civil airport. Everyone is wearing flying suits, unit shoulder patches making identification very easy. The officers of 29 (F) Squadron arrive at 09.50, *en masse*, their slightly subdued air suggesting the possibility of a lateish night and the odd glass of Labatts. They are living in the Imperial Motor Hotel in nearby Grand Centre which advertises air conditioning, a whirlpool (complete with bar, from which swim-suit-clad waitresses serve cocktails), sauna, and 'Ladies Nights Wednesdays', sophisticated, politically correct events, the illuminated sign outside advertising 'Three free drinks per lady before 10 p.m.'. A leaflet on the reception desk offers wild boar hunting, 'using your choice of weapons (bow and arrow, black powder, or rifle)'. Wing Commander Martin Routledge was disappointed:

'The whirlpool bar may have been advertised, but all we got was a backwoods barman and the worst G and T in the world.'

Despite these distractions, they are in good time – five minutes before 'the five minutes before'. As is traditional amongst all branches of the British military, nobody is dressed the same. 29 (F) Squadron officers wear various versions of the basic flying suit uniform: some with peaked service dress hats, others the less formal-looking side caps. A few wear dark blue leather jackets (a sensible precaution against the bitingly cold wind), while most wear short-backed, dark green, cold-weather flying jackets.

They enter the empty theatre and sit *en bloc* near the front to the left of the aisle, while outside the car park fills with yet more hire vehicles as the German and United States contingents arrive. The base theatre, tired-looking like the

Cold Lake Air Force Base has a full range of recreational facilities; Flight Lieutenant Justin Reuter (foreground) queues with other aircrew in front of the barbecue tent.

winter-battered car park outside, comes to life. A skylarking US Navy contingent wears blue shirts and a mixture of blue jeans or bell-bottomed sailor trousers. Steely looking US Air Force pilots wear sharply styled, square-angled side caps and the Luftwaffe look more relaxed with blue-grey leather jackets over their flying suits. Canadian pilots wear distinctive dark green, almost black, flying suits or a colourful grey-blue variation. In this exclusively male environment, the few women present really stand out. Female ground crew with the USAF and US Navy contingents wear combat caps and camouflage fatigues. 29 (F) Squadron's Vania Pearson wears a flying suit but is making no attempt to be one of the boys; and Canadian Captain Kim Reid, a tall, willowy, brunette F–18 pilot, wears 410 Cougar badges and a Hornet op flash.

Inside the theatre, at exactly ten o'clock with every seat filled and late-comers lining the walls, there is sudden silence, then the thumping of flip-up seats as everybody stands to attention.

Cold Lake air base commander Colonel Clark Little stalks down the left-hand aisle and takes up his position below the blank screen. The lights dim and he orders everybody to 'Sit easy'.

The briefing lasts exactly one hour, starting with an official welcome from the base commander, then a very detailed welcome from the exercise controller Major Rick Boyd, an F–18 pilot in the Royal Canadian Air Force, in which he makes clear the ground rules for the forthcoming fortnight's exercise. Standards of personal behaviour are clearly established:

'We don't want anybody coming in carrying switch-blade knives, guns or anything like that.'

He pauses slightly, as if reading from a list:

'Impaired driving – zero tolerance.'

'Illegal drugs, zero tolerance.'

And in a diplomatic reference to the European contingents' tendency to drive too fast:

'Our speed limits may take some time for you to get used to.'

Major Boyd then gets quickly into the real meat of the briefing – flying and flight safety. A fighter airfield is potentially a very dangerous place. With some ninety aircraft taking off and landing in around one hour, co-ordinating movement, particularly of vehicles, is a nightmare:

'Last year we had instances of people driving across active runways – which we don't want this year. We're going to start running defensive driving courses, starting this afternoon, for everybody who needs to drive out there on the ramp. We will be policing this very carefully …

'Telecommunications play a big part in this exercise. Cold Lake telecom have a small supply of VHF FM hand-held radios which can be provided to units for use during the exercise. Please clear the freqencies with wing telecom.'

Major Boyd pauses at the next item projected on the theatre screen: Personnel Harassment.

'This one's pretty straightforward people. Please read it. Get the word around. The policy of the Canadian forces is zero tolerance. No member of the Canadian armed forces will subject any other member or anyone they work with to any type of personal harassment, including sexual harassment. All foreign personnel are expected to adhere to this rule while they are here in Cold Lake. It is the right of all personnel to be treated with dignity and respect by peers, subordinates and superiors.'

The set-piece quotation from the rule book over, Major Boyd runs through a few less serious items:

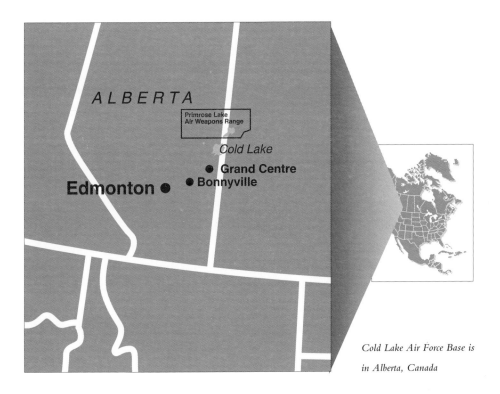

ALBERTA

Primrose Lake
Air Weapons Range

Cold Lake

● **Grand Centre**

Edmonton ● ● **Bonnyville**

Cold Lake Air Force Base is
in Alberta, Canada

'We have a kit and hot food shop running at Maple Flag ops (run by Mrs Boyd!), that takes all credit cards – with lots of Dr Peppers for the Americans. Feel free to come over at any time and see us. Constant coffee and cookies running as well.

'Plenty of recreational facilities here at the base – racquet ball, gym, weights, squash and swimming pool. Lots of good outdoor facilities – baseball diamonds, rugby for the Brits … Eighteen-hole golf course with special rates for Maple Flag – you won't find better rates anywhere. Hunting and fishing are big around here, especially when the ice starts melting off the lake. Lots of people will be going out fishing.'

As part of getting all nations socializing with each other the various contingents are encouraged to host parties in their own national styles – flying in their traditional foods and drinks. And Major Boyd is keen to get the 'Crud' tournament underway. This strange, very traditional – and inelegantly named – crew game has developed over the years. It is the air force equivalent of 'roller ball', played on a billiard or pool table by teams of suitably refreshed competitors who take turns to score billiard-type 'in-offs' with pool balls – but without the use of cues. 'Crud' can be very robust. Players must ensure that the balls do not stop moving, and play in order. Waiting players obstruct the person whose turn it is – with predictable results.

The microphone is handed over to Major Cash Poulson, the Cold Lake AFB flight safety officer. Short, bull-necked and taciturn, wearing a remarkably tight flying suit and black baseball cap, he comes straight to the point:

'Weather here can be severe, from clear to complete white-out. Birds are bad too – pelicans heavier than four pounds or so, mostly over Primrose Lake in the south of the range.

'There are no real towns to watch out for on the range, but the trees are a worse problem when you're flying at around 100 to 150 feet. When they step down from being trees to being scrub you can get fooled into flying too low. You'll see moose running past the windows – and they're real and heavy. So watch your altitude out there.

'There's also lots of helicopters and other slow movers out there, so please respect them. And watch your jet wash.

'If you bail out the biggest threat is what's on the ground, particularly once it thaws – swamp, mosquitoes and so on. Last year a helicopter went down and the crew decided to walk to the nearest transmission site. Thankfully we had our own helicopter out there and were able to rescue them from the swamp. There are serious mosquitoes and black fly … so if you eject get to high ground where there's some wind, and don't attempt to walk because it's very unfriendly out there. We'll get to you.

'We've got several flight safety videos of near misses we've had here, caused by lack of situational awareness, inattention, target fixation. They're pretty grim …'

A black-and-white cockpit view appears on the screen, cross-hatched with the lines and data of a head-up display. Suddenly a jet appears slightly to the right, swooping in towards the aircraft, swerving sharply, missing by feet, to vanish on the right-hand side. The room bubbles with sudden nervous laughter. Major Poulson starts a running commentary:

'A three-ship in close formation. Leader calls a right turn after they're spiked then, as you see here, for some reason turns left.'

As the three aircraft turn precisely and very sharply into each other at over 700 m.p.h. the cockpit view shows a miraculously close escape, eliciting cries of 'Shee-it' from the American squadrons.

'This next one shows how anybody can get fooled by the height of those trees I was telling you about. We had to dig the camera out of the wreckage – but the pilot survived.'

The screen shows a very low-level view as an aircraft skims conifers at high speed. The picture suddenly vibrates and the view drops so that some of the trees are whipping by above eye level, then goes blank. The pilot must have ejected very quickly indeed.

'So keep your heads up out there and have a good exercise. If you have one of your aircraft go down, come and see me. We have a great flight rescue and crash system. Otherwise, the only time you'll see me is when I come round trying to scrounge a ride.'

The theatre comes to attention as Colonel Little, Major Boyd and the briefing team walk out. Then there is a hubbub of conversation as contingents crowd into the aisles and file out into the crisp, cold air.

Two fighter squadrons – 410 Cougar Squadron, and 441 Squadron (the Silver Foxes) – are based at Royal Canadian Air Force Base Cold Lake. Both fly the CF–18 Hornet fighter-bomber and both have illustrious histories formed during the Second World War, in 1941 and 1942 respectively.

410 Cougar started as a night-fighter squadron, the same role as 29 (Fighter) Squadron, but flying single-engined Defiants. It was very soon re-equipped with radar Beaufighters then, in October 1942, the Mosquito night fighter – very much mirroring 29 (F) Squadron's war experience. In addition to normal night defence duties it also made offensive forays into enemy territory by day and night attacking trains, vehicles, canal shipping, airfields and aircraft. When the war ended, sixty-two officers and men had died, and the squadron had won forty-one awards including nineteen Distinguished Flying Crosses. Its badge, a cougar's head superimposed on a crescent moon, was approved by George VI in May 1945 with their motto *Noctivaga* (wandering by night) a perfect sobriquet for a night fighter unit. The squadron was disbanded in June 1945.

When Canada formed its post-war regular force 410 became its first fighter squadron, flying Vampire day-interceptors in the Royal Canadian Air Force's air defence group. In 1951, 410 was the first RCAF squadron to receive the F–86 Sabre and moved to Europe where again it was disbanded (in October 1956), for just a few days, before re-forming back in Canada equipped with the CF-100 Canuck. Then in 1962 it converted to CF–101 Voodoos in the air defence role until 1964 when, yet again, it was disbanded.

However … four years later 410's name was reincarnated as the All Weather Operational Conversion Unit at Canadian Forces Base Bagotville, training aircrew for the other three interceptor squadrons of Canada's air defence group.

Then on 12 June 1976, having survived the axe so many times, 410 Cougar Squadron received its Queen's Colours after twenty-five years of active service.

Four years later, the RCAF received the CF–18 Hornet and the CF–101 Voodoo programme was curtailed. This time 410's disbandment was purely so that it could move to Cold Lake Air Force Base in Alberta, to build a CF–18 training programme under its present name: 410 Tactical Fighter Operational Training Squadron. CF–18 training started in January 1984 when a complete squadron was put through the course (to become 409 Tactical Fighter Squadron).

In addition to being the training squadron, 410 Cougar Squadron is also a fully operational fighter-bomber unit. On Exercise Maple Flag it flies two sorties each day as part of the Blue Air bombing package.

441 Silver Fox Tactical Fighter Squadron is a purely operational, front-line squadron, also equipped with CF–18 Hornets, with air defence as its primary role. Formed in April 1942 in response to Japan's entry into the war and Germany's expanded U-boat campaign around western Atlantic shores, it was first known as 125 (F) Squadron and was based at Sydney, Nova Scotia. Its role was coastal defence using one Harvard and six Hurricanes.

In December 1943 the squadron sailed for Europe. In February 1944 it received Supermarine Spitfire Mk Vbs, and was tasked with dive-bombing. During the D-Day invasion it protected the eastern assault area, then its aircraft became the first British ones to land in France since the withdrawal of the British Expeditionary force, refuelling and re-arming near Evreux. Once the invasion was complete it returned to England to escort the Lancaster and Halifax bombers of No. 6 RCAF Group during attacks on the synthetic oil plants on the Ruhr. After escorting twenty-five missions it moved to the Orkneys to provide patrols to Scapa Flow. It was here that it adopted the silver fox badge, and the motto 'Stalk and Kill'.

The squadron moved back to Canada in 1945 just before VE-Day and was disbanded. It had suffered fourteen deaths, three pilots had been taken prisoner, and four had returned after having been reported missing. Nine Distinguished Flying Crosses had been won.

In March 1951 the squadron was reactivated as air defence, equipped with Vampires. In July that year 441's checkerboard logo was approved and the Vampires were replaced by Sabres. It was posted back to England in February 1952 and in 1954 it moved to Germany, then to Marville in France – for the next eight years. In 1967, having moved to Lahr in Germany, the squadron was integrated into the Canadian armed forces (when the Canadian army, navy and air force were combined). In 1972 the squadron re-roled to become a tactical fighter squadron and in the following year it received its colours from HRH the Duke of Edinburgh. It was stood down in March 1984, then reactivated as air defenders on 26 June 1987 at Cold Lake flying the new CF–18s.

29 (F) Squadron's five portacabins lie on a patch of snow-covered grass between the Canadian 441 Squadron's hangar and the apron. Their eight Tornados are lined up some hundred feet or so away, with a row of solitary US Air Force F–16s in front. The ground crew occupy the two portacabins nearest the apron. A third contains aircrew flying gear and lockers and to the rear, with duckboards in between, the ops planning cabin has a briefing room and the bosses' office. The cabin next to that contains the video de-brief suite and a crew coffee and planning room.

The briefing room is full, as Wing Commander Martin Routledge takes to the floor. As the most senior RAF officer present, he also has to act as detachment commander and is responsible for the AWACS E3D aircraft and crew, and the VC10 tanker at Edmonton. Squadron Leader Ian Gale, OC A Flight, is therefore in charge of all 29 (F) Squadron operations and the flying programme. Routledge starts by offering a trip for six aircraft and aircrew to the Saskatoon Air Show – which he describes as an all-expenses paid weekend. There is considerable interest in this mission; an air show offers enormous potential for a variety of interesting social opportunities. (In the end it never happened!)

Next Ian Gale runs through a selection of admin. points, then draws the squadron's attention to the latest letter from Air Officer Commanding (AOC) RAF Strike Command to aircrew, concerning take-off procedures – which urges everybody to ensure they determine the various critical speeds (V1 and so on), who is to call them and other basic drills that everybody carries out as a matter of course. A number of people make wry comments about the apparent isolation of very senior officers from the realities of day-to-day squadron life – and the lack of street cred. revealed by such missives. Ian Gale finishes by offering changes of crew if anybody is unhappy with whoever they are programmed to fly with and, with dry wit, changes of tasking:

'In case you want to do something more meaningful … ? If there are any errors, or anybody can see better ways of doing things, please let me know.'

Flight Lieutenant Tim Taylor talks everyone through the basic rules for the

Overleaf: CF-18s of Canada's 441 Squadron in very tight formation immediately before landing at Cold Lake, the base that has been their home since 1987.

detachment. He stresses the need for punctuality; that trying to get into briefings after they have started will be considered very poor behaviour. He also urges them to think through each mission as soon as they get back, putting on the head-up display (HUD) video immediately they return to the flight line to evaluate their shots. There will be two missions each day and the pace of running them leaves little time for the vital process of de-briefing, and no time at all for arguing the toss. Particularly in an international environment, arguing with other players or exercise controllers is considered unprofessional (in itself a serious 'offence'), which rapidly degenerates into self-justification — which the squadron call 'blubbing'.

'You don't just have to do a good job flying on the range, but report everything that you do on the mission accurately — which is actually very much part of the job.'

Taylor again emphasizes the need for punctuality, and stresses that he will be 'unimpressed with anybody who is late or unprepared — to the point of being very unimpressed.'

Aircrew high spirits start immediately, with several amusing but very pointed attacks (through the medium of large felt-tip-pen posters in the ops room notice board) on the non-flying duty adminstrative officer who is unfairly blamed for problems over hotel room reservations. (Aircrew call non-flying personnel 'blunties'.) Things have not gone terribly well, and the invective being heaped upon the hapless admin. officer — as 'chief blunty' — is very funny, but gets a touch out of hand. Routledge finishes off the briefing with a few low-key words about this:

'Let's back off a bit now guys, otherwise we'll get nothing more from him ...'

The squadron 'pigs' board has already started, listing the various 'Beanos' ('There will be no ...') in the operations cabin. This unoffical offences board details a series of fines for designated 'crimes' such as 'sharking' — chatting up anybody too overtly. On the 'hot poop' board, the AOC's missive about take-off procedures enjoys pride of place at top centre.

In the adjoining portacabin, with the coffee table and a separate office for the 'secret' viewing of mission video tapes, a table has been reserved for the editorial committee of the squadron magazine — the impenetrably named MDMITI, standing for 'Metal Detectors Monthly Incorporating The Irrigator'. (RAF Coningsby's station magazine is called *The Interceptor*.) Place cards are taped to the desk: Editor, Flying Officer N.O. Mates; OC C Flight (which doesn't exist) — the 'appointment' designates the senior squadron 'shag' (its youngest member); and

Fashion Editor, Cindy Crawford. Several large sheets of paper are taped to the wall showing a well-drawn cartoon story about the nefarious adventures of 'chief blunty' – with an unrepeatable punchline that causes the officer commanding the Goose Bay support detachment (who incorrectly believes he is the 'blunty' in question) loudly to question the parentage of 29 (F) Squadron aircrew in general, and of the artist in particular.

Wing Commander Martin Routledge is thinking about his crews and the forthcoming exercise:

'Crewing people and keeping them in balance is difficult. Each flight consists of roughly half the squadron, and has to be balanced in both experience and qualification. Each must have a weapons instructor, and the other squadron leaders (apart from the flight commanders) are allocated to a particular flight.

'Historically, the aces in air wars were fifteen per cent of the flying population, achieving around eighty per cent of the kills. The rest were really just cannon fodder, which indicates to me that it's better to have a few good crews than a lot of mediocre ones. It would be easy to put pilots and navigators into a pecking order, then put the best with the worst and so on – however, we try to match strength with strength while not leaving any really weak crews. We're lucky at the moment. There are few *ab initio* pilots doing first operational tours, although some have been instructors or flown other aircraft and are on their first tours flying Tornado F3s.

'Personalities come into play too – some people wouldn't want to fly together, although we don't get many people coming up and saying I don't like flying with so-and-so. In an ideal world, once your crews have been squared away you need to start pairing your pairs together – as we tend to work in elements of two aircraft.

'Without getting silly about it and saying that people have to go on leave and courses together, and always fly together, you should be able to fly sixty or seventy per cent of the time with the same pilot or navigator, and in the same two-ship. You need to know how the leader will react, to recognize voices on the radio, to know what people mean when they say things. Back in the United Kingdom, other commitments upset the equation.'

Routledge's main concern is with the continued serviceability of his aircraft:

'I've got an incredibly good set of ground crew who work really hard and well together – the fact that we arrived here all right and are totally serviceable for tomorrow is indicative of that. I hope the aircraft will remain serviceable long enough to give us maximum training value from the exercise. Other problems we'll take in our stride.

'However, the weather could become a major player on the exercise – particularly cloud. It's early spring here and we were expecting better weather than this – gin-clear right the way up to the moon is what I'd like.'

Maple Flag exercise controller Major Rick Boyd is 1.7 metres (five foot ten), verging on the forty-year mark and around 77 kilograms (170 pounds). With blond hair and a cigar to hand, he rules the roost at Maple Flag dishing out brick-bats and sparing praise with even-handed diplomacy. Known universally by his radio callsign 'Relic', he flies most days he can manage with the Cougars or his old squadron 441. Players on the exercise need to both respect and like Relic if the exercise is to be effective – which his great experience and calm friendliness ensures. He comes from air force stock. His father was in the military police and his wife's father was a Battle of Britain pilot who was shot down in 1943 and spent two years in a prisoner of war camp before being rescued by the Russians.

Boyd joined the Canadian Air Force in 1974, went through pilot training and stayed on as an instructor before going to Chatham, New Brunswick in 1979 to fly the CF–101 Voodoo all-weather interceptor. In 1985 he went to Colorado Springs (the home of the USAF Academy) and Cheyenne Mountain and spent four years there with NORAD Plans, then went to the Canadian Staff College in Toronto for one year. He has been in Cold Lake since 1989 as the deputy commanding officer of 441 Squadron, and at Maple Flag since 1993. This is his second Maple Flag.

He still does a lot of flying as senior standards officer for the wing doing all the combat-ready check rides for the pilots and annual TACEVAL rides.

Rick Boyd works hard to promote Maple Flag. In purely commercial terms, between $5 million and $8 million is brought into the local economy (mainly in foreign exchange) over the period of the exercise, through hotels, hire cars and so on. And the international fighter pilot 'season' spawns new local facilities; Dairy Queen and McDonald's franchises have opened in both Bonnyville and Grand Centre, with lots of local and Canadian media interest.

There is also money in the flying. With the restrictions on low-level flying training in western Europe, the wide open spaces of essentially empty countries like Canada and parts of the United States are becoming increasingly important for the operational efficiency of NATO air forces. Boyd:

'There's just over seven thousand square kilometres of range – four thousand square miles – which is a great big training aid. We can look around the world to see what the real scenarios are, then tailor the exercises for those situations.'

Major Rick Boyd, the Maple Flag exercise controller; he wants aircrew to 'run around the range literally with their hair on fire ...'

There is one very good reason why the Primrose Lake area immediately to the north of Cold Lake is uninhabited and therefore available for low-level warfare training. Its extreme weather makes running the range a challenging task. No work can be done on it until the ground freezes over – in the dead of winter, around mid-January – because the muskeg and large amount of surface water prevent any off-road foot or vehicle movement. Once the permafrost comes up high enough, the Canadians can take heavy equipment out and visit all the target arrays. These are three-quarter scale plywood mock-ups but, as they have to be flown in by helicopter, it costs money to replace them. By March when the range starts to thaw out, everything is ready to go again.

Developing modern air-to-air and air-to-ground ranges is very expensive and the price tag for the Canadians is about $3 million per exercise. The players pay for their own gas, food, accommodation and so on, but there are no fees for using the range, targets, etc.

'We hope to start recovering some of the cost from participants – including the Canadians – in 1996. We turn about two hundred sorties per day, and maintain a thirty-five day supply of fuel.'

Maple Flag could develop into a profitable business – provided the Americans also start charging for the use of their facilities so that Cold Lake does not price itself out of the business.

The Cold Lake air weapons range is designed to offer the same threat picture as a modern battlefield, with everything happening except actual missiles coming up at flyers. It has single and double digit SAM systems – SA–6s, SA–8s, SA–10s, 11s, 15s, 17s and 18s – Roland and CROTAL, plus the mock-up targets in 111 target complexes all over the range. The agile threat emitter is the prototype of a very sophisticated piece of equipment. The wave form of any surface-to-air missile can be put into it – more than a thousand examples are already programmed in – and will appear exactly like the real thing to aircrew. The emitter is 'destroyed' every day, but regenerated for the next mission. People come to Canada particularly to experience modern threats and the agile threat emitter is a big pull. The Americans also bring a lot of targeting equipment, adding to the reality of the exercise for participants.

This year's Maple Flag is based on a Gulf War scenario. The next may be something to do with Bosnia-Herzegovina. The aim is to train everyone to a higher threat than can be expected in war, knowing that most wars are going to be fought these days by Western allies who will have air superiority against a medium threat. If people are used to working in a high threat environment, they will have no problem handling a war in a medium or low threat one. Boyd:

' "Train hard, fight easy" – we throw everything we've got at them. We want them to run around the range literally with their hair on fire, going fast, knowing that they may have some MiGs bounce them, or be emitted from the ground with some threats – or even fired on by their own people … There are so many aircraft out there.

'I should add that from the safety point of view, it is all de-conflicted.'

The one thing that cannot be 'de-conflicted' – have the complications sorted out – is bird migration. There is an apocryphal story about a Polish or Warsaw Pact air force testing the canopies of one of their jets by firing a chicken at it with a cannon to simulate bird strike. The canopy broke and a technician inside was killed – because they forgot to defrost the chicken. Bird strike is a big problem during Maple Flag, and can stop flying. Baker Island, in the middle of the ranges, has one of the world's largest colonies of snow geese and pelicans. Last year a German F–4 was hit and grounded for over four months. At this time of year, with the ice melting, the birds are poised to go – *en masse*.

Radar is used to evaluate the problem. At bird level 5 everyone is ordered to climb to 1000 feet until they are near their target when they can dive to low level. At level 6 everybody has to fly everywhere above 1000 feet, and at level 7 the exercise shuts down. (Levels 1 to 4 are gradations that require extra care to be taken.) Boyd:

'The birds migrate in the middle of May, so we are at levels 5 and 6 now. When the winds veer to the south the birds really want to get moving – so we worry. The south-east quadrant of the range is the worst. The birds are our biggest problem, and there's nothing we can do about it. Although last year we had a Mayday call from one ground target party who we had to rescue from bears.'

The more elaborate and integrated modern warfare becomes, the greater the danger of what the Americans call 'fratricide' – the accidental killing of friendly troops. At very high speeds, and with the long distances over which air combat takes place, there is no fool-proof method of telling friend from foe, a radar signal from a 'friendly' SAM system, or the same signal from an enemy SAM.

Air forces these days have much the same equipment and aircraft. With former enemies now become friends (and there is nothing to say that they cannot go back the other way), the same kind of aircraft could fly on both sides – possibly with the same calibre of pilots – with the same type of weapons. Boyd:

'Here on Maple Flag, we have a lot of F–16s working on both Blue Air and Red Air sides. Tornados will be doing the same later in the series. There's no "them and us" like it was in the old days of the Cold War. Nowadays, we just don't know who "them's" going to be any more.'

The harsh reality of air combat puts a whole extra layer of demand on aircrew that they do not experience in normal training. On Maple Flag, eighty to 100 aircraft fly all the roles of full-scale war, from air transport re-supply to close air support, ground attack, bombers with fighter escorts, air-to-air defenders, plus all the possible ground emitter threats. The only thing missing is shots being exchanged. Boyd:

'Although the exercise is tailored to the junior combat-ready person, the learning curve is very steep and we've had people bow out of the exercise because it gets too busy. We can't have people flying low level, very fast out there unless they know what they're doing.'

Fighter aircrew are very determined – and aggressive:

'Any pilot flying on these Maple Flag missions wants to win. They're out there flying as if it was real war. Having said that, this is the environment in which to make mistakes. If you're going to fire on some of your own guys, put bombs off target or have to trash one of your missiles because you took a bad shot, do it here. They're all big boys – looking to learn as many lessons as they can.'

CHAPTER EIGHT

Firing Line

Over the decade or so that it takes to develop a fighter aircraft technology can change radically, as well as the use for which the aircraft was originally intended. The Tornado GR1 – the air-to-ground variant, essentially a bomber – was designed to fly at low level, which it does very well. By the time the F3 came into service it was already competing against F–15s and F–16s – newer planes designed for particular roles. The air force sets the specification for an aircraft, and much of the time it gets what it asks for. If the RAF had wanted a single-seat fighter that can reach 50 000 feet and carry a certain amount of fuel, it might have bought the F–16.

The Tornado is still flying the same role – that of an air-to-air interceptor – today as when it was introduced in 1987, although in those days it was specifically designed to shoot down incoming Russian bombers. Over the years it has been greatly modified, with updated engines, radars, etc.

Like several other present members of 29 (F) Squadron, Squadron Leader Chris Gould has been closely involved with the Tornado since it first came into service; he remembers it arriving like a new car, brand-spanking from British Aerospace, its ancillaries still in their factory wrappings, and knows well the usual and particular things that can go wrong.

He concurs that it is easy to knock the plane but insists that it is necessary to look at what it was designed to do and how it fulfils its roles:

'I don't think it's a disaster, which is what often comes across. Aircrew always compare it with the F–15 and F–16 because that's what they fight against – single-seat jets. It's not a fair comparison.

'Leaking or malfunctioning hydraulic actuators can cause major flying control problems, and take time to diagnose … Touch wood we won't have any on this det. Radars can inexplicably fail and keep on failing, despite diagnosing and changing boxes … Touch wood again.'

Sergeant Tom Berry of the rectification team is an avionics expert:

'The Tornado isn't really an "electric jet". They didn't go the whole hog and make it completely "fly by wire". It has a manual back-up. If the computers fail, I'm not saying it's flyable but it is certainly landable – which the pilots practise using simulators.'

The F–3's flight surfaces are controlled by computer. If the angle of attack (the maximum angle at which air can flow over the wing and still achieve lift) is exceeded, the pilot loses control and the aircraft flops around the sky. There are recovery techniques, but it is very frightening. The pilot cannot just apply lots of power. The engines need large amounts of 'clean' air (undisturbed by turbulence) coming into their intakes or they will fail, the aircraft will stall and the pilot will lose control completely. RAF rules state that if this happens at under 10 000 feet aircrew must eject immediately.

The Tornado's flight control system is reliable with redundancy built-in. Every system has computers: two in the automatic flight control system, plus two in the command stability and augmentation system (CSAS) auto-stabilizer – one for pitch, the other for yaw. Everything feeds into the main computer which generates warnings about other system failures. Software changes derive from aircrew requests which are written, trialled and eventually issued to the squadrons. There are little snags to be ironed out and changes in use. The main computer memory is 256K, small by personal computer standards. The complexity of the systems gives avionics engineers a lot of work and it can be a nightmare when every aircraft comes in with snags, most of which can take hours to repair.

Out in Canada, the Tornados are using four radio systems. They have VHF and UHF radios for talking to each other and the ground agencies. The HF isn't used very often, and is kept only for long range transmissions. There is also the emergency radio plus the secure 'Havequick' radio that flicks about between different frequencies to frustrate (amongst others) radio spotters who eavesdrop on airfields with scanners.

Very little radio traffic is coded. In any case, everything in an air battle happens so fast that no enemy would have time to use secrets gleaned from fighter transmissions. Havequick is pre-programmed and software controlled, and jumps automatically between frequencies, chopping everything up so that no useful information can be picked up by scanners. UHF transmissions do not carry very far, so coding does not matter when aircraft are flying in close formation. In a dogfight, everyone is so busy that even the enemy would not try to monitor them. Pilots and navigators both have radios, and monitor two frequencies each – their own plus the emergency one.

The fighters are also using the new JTIDS data link, and Exercise Maple Flag is to be its proving ground. Standing for 'Joint Tactical Information Distribution System', JTIDS creates a framework from which all manner of aeroplanes, weapon systems and other resources can be operated. It is a huge step forward in technology for the aircrew, allowing them to run away from a situation and regroup while retaining a full picture of what is going on behind them. Previously they had to listen to a voice on the radio and try to assimilate that information while coping with the pressures of working with other aircraft in tight formation, flying safely to gain tactical advantage. A visual picture gives radically more information than voice and gives it more quickly. The accuracy, simplicity and scope of this picture is absolutely critical in modern war.

The British airborne warning and control system (AWACS) is part of Red Air – the enemy on Maple Flag – training with 29 (F) Squadron and learning to use JTIDS. Although the system is radical it is not new, having been under development for twelve years. At its inception the Tornado was actually designed to be used with JTIDS (the box attachment holes have been drilled into the aircraft since it was originally built), and the present system has been under trial for two years. However, Maple Flag is the first time an operational squadron has used it out of theatre. With so many aeroplanes in the air it is the ideal opportunity to try out its possibilities.

Basically, JTIDS communicates a common air picture to everybody on the data link. The system works by dividing each day into small time-slots, which are allocated to particular people and aircraft. Each slot lasts only milliseconds, and there are 128 slots per second. Everybody on the link has slots. For example, an E3 (the aircraft that carries AWACS and operates as the airborne sentry) can transmit radar displays and other pictures to the F3s (and any other aircraft with JTIDS). Previously, the passage of AWACS data could only be done by radio – usually by voice.

There are slots for sending radar tracks from one F3 to others. On the time-slot map for Maple Flag, all eight 29 (F) Squadron F3s can update their displays in one second. There is as much relay capacity as there is information, so everything can be relayed if required. The E3 has a lot more time-slots than the F3s as it is gathering information from a wide range of sensors, plus relaying and communicating with aircraft and ground stations over a very wide area.

The full cycle of all communication slots lasts twelve seconds, but in peacetime only eight seconds are used. Every third slot is spare, around 7.8 milliseconds of nothing every sixteen milliseconds, making the system expandable for future demands.

All transmissions occur in very tiny bursts in these pre-programmed slots; and the system cannot be scanned because it changes frequency tens of thousands of times a second. JTIDS has therefore to be very carefully time-synchronized. Some of the transmission slots are allocated to voice and shared by everybody. The first man to hit the transmit button gets the use of the slot – like a radio net. It is very clear, but sounds a bit 'digital'.

There is an enormous amount of information flying around within the JTIDS system, which is not relevant to most people. To prevent the aircrew going into overload, this must be filtered – which is done by the receiver's terminal.

The digital data processor (DDP)is attached to the transmit/receive terminal. If a target is received, the main computer feeds it to the interface unit, which translates between computer and JTIDS language. For each message it has to send, the interface unit selects a message type from the huge list programmed into it. It passes this on to the digital data processor which does all the message formation and holds it until a time slot appears, when it transmits.

All messages come into each JTIDS unit, but the DDP asks the relay unit (RU) if it wants to see this message. The RU is programmed to accept certain messages, which it converts to main computer language, on to a display unit in the aircraft. Each type of platform (aircraft, weapon site, ground headquarters or even a ship) has a different RU to allow this. Everything in JTIDS interfaces with the navigation programming of the aircraft, the various numbered map lines of the navigator's display, the bullseye reference point, no-fly lines, etc.

Anything that can be converted into noughts and ones – video, word messages, diagrams, pictures – can be sent over JTIDS. One particularly effective use is to send weather reports to airborne F3s, complete with tables showing airfields, runways, and even the weapon reloads available at various places.

In an operational theatre, the E3 re-transmits everything it receives. On Maple Flag it will de-clutter around 1000 tracks per second from its own radar, creating a picture that JTIDS can transmit to everybody. However, because it uses a UHF radio link, JTIDS can only transmit to receivers within line of sight and therefore

Overleaf: The rotating dome on the AWACS (airborne warning and control system) aircraft – a derivative of the civilian Boeing 707 – contains the radar; the crew are learning to use the new JTIDS (joint tactical information distribution system).

needs intermediate relay platforms to extend its range to more than a couple of hundred miles. The system does this automatically by dedicating slots in every terminal for receiving and transmitting information, as well as for receiving and presenting it.

The effectiveness of JTIDS affects tactics and the way people think – even strategy in the widest sense. Data linking in this form is one step away from Luke Skywalker, and the system is the beginning of an instantly all-informed net. It is also, at least as far as humans can perceive it, a real-time data link – which has never before been achieved in fighters. A very simple system was put into the Lightning in the 1960s, but JTIDS is the Rolls-Royce version: secure, extremely flexible and very robust with massive capacity – more than the RAF operating on its own actually needs. Updating into the future will not be a problem. Having JTIDS affects the way aircrew react, and will bring about as significant a jump in their thinking as radar did in the Second World War.

The transmission language used by JTIDS is called 'Link 16', and 'Mercury' (the winged messenger of the gods) is its unofficial code word when it is operating in the air. Incorporating the system into the Tornado is remarkably easy as it uses the standard F3 display, fitting in with their radar picture. Flight Lieutenant Steve Pittaway is a Tornado navigator who has been trialling the system. He admits that the first time he flew with it, he was quite frightened:

'Normally you can only see aircraft in front of you. With JTIDS, suddenly this aircraft pitched up behind – which was very weird.'

JTIDS includes a navigation function that makes the aircraft extremely accurate in navigational terms. After an hour or so in the air it is possible to fly back to where the computer says an airfield is, and be there within fractions of a mile.

Flight Lieutenant Justin Reuter believes that JTIDS and other modern equipment have made the title 'navigator' obsolete:

'Today navigators work as the weapons control specialists, analysing the operational situation and managing the combat power of their aircraft. The twin inertial navigational equipment on board the Tornados is very accurate, backed up by a computer, which means that we don't have to navigate – as navs do in other aircraft.

'You know you will always be backed up by other fighters, ground or E3 radar and a tanker. You don't plan to work alone – although the AWACS might get shot down. Rather than navigators *per se*, we are actually weapon system managers, tactical managers at times.'

For pilots, being linked to JTIDS and the AWACS gives them the ability to shoot enemies before they are in visual range because the system allows them to be identified as hostile very much earlier. And as few aircraft have a rear-facing radar, Link 16 allows the pilot to keep an accurate picture of what is going on behind him even while running away. Flight Lieutenant Mike Jones:

'You can sit on the ground with the targets actually on your screen, and watch the enemy forces marshalling. A picture tells a thousand words, which is so much better than some controller giving you positions. You can just look down at the tube and see it all.'

AWACS can still commit aircraft on to groups by voice, giving what is called 'broadcast control', but with JTIDS/Link 16 they paint the picture of what the bombers and escorts are doing with their sweeps and the aircrew concentrate on this. Captain Doug 'Dog' Carter is a Canadian pilot on exchange with 29 (F) Squadron:

'In the United States Air Force, they have a squadron with JTIDS who are head and shoulders above everybody, kicking everybody's arse – and I mean everybody's.

'Unfortunately Tornado's JTIDS only has a single-colour display, so you have to really watch what you're looking at. You can be overwhelmed and lose track of what's happening. You think you know what's going on, then all of a sudden you go from having what you think is a very high level of awareness to having none again. With a colour display, it's unbeatable – enemy one colour, your wingmen, leads and friendly formations another colour, unknowns another – all of it over a moving map. You just look down and it's like a video game.'

The RAF are due to get a colour display for the F3s, but sadly with only two colours. The joke goes that when fighter crew asked for a colour display, the procurement people thought they wanted to paint the box.

Despite JTIDS, the F3 is never going to be as efficient as newer aircraft. Jones:

'At the end of the day, if you want to make a difference you're going to have to get in there and kill people. We're firing a semi-active rocket so we're behind the drag curve. They were firing semi-active rockets operationally in Vietnam when I was born, and we're stuck with this rather quaint technology. Most aircraft now are firing AMRAAM, which has changed the whole set of rules for air warfare. You can shoot at a lot longer ranges, turn away, motor back at high speed, wait for the rocket to do its thing, see if it's killed the enemy, then turn your formation back again, sanitize the whole area, see how many are left, shoot these rockets again at long range, and turn the whole formation away again.

'If they're doing it for real, people don't want to be surprised, and aren't particularly interested in visually merging. As soon as you go eyes-out in a single-seat aircraft for a single target, he's going to have his mate, so you're going to be vulnerable to his wingman. You can't concentrate on everything around you. You want to keep them all at range, do it all off the radar, employing your high tech rockets to kill these guys at range.

'On Maple Flag we won't be flying in the ideal conditions in which we'd like to go to war. It's daylight, flying on a good day against F–15s – probably the best air superiority fighters in the world. I'd much prefer us to do it on a horrible stormy night in cloud – which is how we fight best. We'd bring the jets over with night vision goggles – which gives us an advantage they don't have – plus in cloud a single-seat guy has a much higher workload trying to fly on instruments while working his radar.'

Being a two-seater is a tremendous advantage. Captain 'Tarzan' Tantarn, a Luftwaffe pilot on exchange with 441 Squadron of the RCAF (part of Blue Air), has flown both single-seat F–18s and two-seat Phantoms and believes that having two men in the cockpit is the Phantom's biggest plus:

'You can divide up the workload, so that you look out while the back-seater works the radar. Normally it's not so important, but on this exercise we will be very busy. With sixty to eighty fighters running around it will be a big advantage having the extra guy in the cockpit.

'In general, our Phantom is almost the equal of the F–15 – although we have to work much harder, and need the second guy to be successful. It's easier to fool a single-seater pilot. When I've got to engage somebody in an air-to-air fight, it's very basic. I'm concentrating on the guys in front of me and don't have much time to look around. The back-seat guy takes care of that. If I look around too much, I might lose the battle in front of me. You work hard and try to do the most you can, but a second pair of eyes helps out so much.'

Mike Jones has mixed feelings on the subject:

'In a single seater, you can lock somebody up simply by moving the radar screen markers across, whereas in the F3 I've got to tell the rear-seater to do it. Conversely at night when flying on instruments – which is much harder than flying by day – you have a guy in the back dedicated to looking at the radar which is a real bonus.'

Fighters go round in fours – or ideally on Maple Flag in sixes – because their mutual firepower, plus the fact that this enables them to 'volume search' the sky using all the radars, gives them an enormous advantage. Jones:

'In World War Two days, he who got the first tally-ho could call the engagement. Nowadays they've taken all that away and replaced it with the E3 that can see everything, the radar that helps you paint the picture, plus the ability to kill people beyond visual range. It's more difficult to move a formation round the

The navigator's cockpit in a Tornado F3; the two screens at the top of the picture indicate the aircraft's various weapons and radar functions and are controlled by a series of switches on the joystick.

sky, but operating as groups of aircraft allows you to sanitize the airspace so that nobody surprises you, and concentrates the fire power of four to six aircraft to shoot into the enemy.'

On peacetime exercises aircraft are usually fitted only with chaff and flares, and only rarely with live missiles or cannon ammunition. An operational load of live ordnance makes aircraft fly more slowly with greater momentum, so that it is more difficult to manoeuvre them. Armed aircraft must also be handled very carefully on the ground:

'You can't walk in front of an armed aircraft, or behind it or around it … You have to kind of levitate over it!'

The squadron armourers are responsible for all aspects of loading up and arming the Tornados, something they don't get to do all that often.

For day-to-day exercise flying, they attach small air intercept missile (AIM) 9L acquisition missiles which simulate the Sidewinder to the jets' pylons. These allow the pilots to lock on to targets and do everything except fire and gives them multiple shots. They use a training-aid pod fitted beneath the fuselage to simulate the medium range Skyflash. Each aircraft is fitted with a 27mm Mauser cannon but no ammunition. Every two years the squadron goes to Cyprus for four weeks to fire the cannons with live ammunition – and qualify for live firing. They also go to RAF Valley in Wales every eighteen months to fire live missiles.

The armourers will not be doing very much on Maple Flag. All the aircraft arrived with long range fuel tanks and as these use explosives, so that they can be jettisoned, they had to be removed by armourers. Long range tanks are usually jettisoned just before entering a dogfight to make the aircraft more manoeuvrable. The armourers also fit and remove ejector seats.

Before live ammunition and weapons are fitted, the electricians make sure each aircraft is electrically safe, with no spurious signals that might set live ordnance off by accident. Once it has a clean bill of health, the armourers arm it up. This is done either as a 'peacetime load' or as an 'operational turnaround' in which everything from refuelling to engineering checks are done at the same time. First the missiles are checked over as they arrive on the trolleys to make sure there are no breakages, and the launchers are prepared.

The GR1s have multiple loads – the actual weaponry depends upon their mission and role – whereas the F3 has only the Skyflash, Sidewinder and 27mm gun. This is its standard load and is the same for every sortie. The Skyflash is the medium range missile, which has to be kept locked on to the target. Once fired, the aircrew have to keep illuminating the target to guide the missile. Sidewinder is a short range heat seeker – a 'fire and forget' weapon. Once it is locked on to a target and has gone from the aircraft's weapon rail, that's it. Chaff pods are a couple of feet longer than the Sidewinder and contain bundles of very fine aluminium-coated fibreglass strands which are pumped out to confuse and deflect enemy radar signals. There are various settings for the chaff pods, with enough chaff for many goes.

The Tornados can carry four Sidewinders, plus extra fuel tanks that go in the middle between the two Sidewinder rails. Four Skyflash are mounted underneath – two at the front and two at the back.

Every Sidewinder weighs 200 pounds, and although two or three men can load it – it just slots on – Health and Safety at Work rules require four men. The front of the Sidewinder is a glass dome containing mercury thalium. The skin is very thin and if it is dented the rocket motor will be affected and give an uneven burn. A Skyflash is simply too heavy to load manually so a weapons loader is used to raise it on to a yoke, and then a hanger, before plugging it into the aircraft's electric system. The missile has a porcelain front that covers the radar seeker, and this has to be handled carefully to avoid damage.

It is important to ensure that no electric power is being applied to the aircraft while arming up, and that there are no radios within ten to fifteen metres (thirty-two to fifty feet) as broadcasting could set the cartridges off. The system is pretty safe, although a GR1 lost a Sidewinder some time ago, which led to further tests and precautions. It can start on the 'houchin' – the generator that gets the jet started – once it is all armed up.

Once the jets have been loaded up the armourers do a 'growl check' using an infrared torch to ensure the missile can lock on. They then check the missile management systems (MMS) to ensure that the aircraft knows it is loaded: if it has four Skyflash, the display will say '4 Ms' – or 'S' for Sidewinders. The missiles stay on until they are fired or develop faults that require investigation. Once loaded, the aircraft have to be pointed in safe directions so that if a missile goes off, it will not do damage or cause injury. All the munitions are fitted with armament safety pins which are removed only at the last possible moment. The aircraft only becomes combat armed when the pilot removes the last few pins just before taxiing.

Once the pins are removed, the missiles should be safe – until the aircraft is flying. There are various safety switches, including a 'weight on wheels' one that disables the system until the jet has taken off . The aircrew have to make the various weapons selections on the missile management system, and there is also a 'late arm' switch as a last accident prevention measure.

If an aircraft on a mission has fired, but the missile failed to come off the rails, the pilot comes back and lands, then taxis to a safe area. The armourers wait for thirty minutes from the moment the trigger was pressed. The aircrew come out of the aircraft immediately and tell the armourers which switches they used during the flight and which ones were shut down after landing. The armourers download the software control system, and check out the missile or the gun, trying to deduce what went wrong. The fault could be electrical – the pulse may not have reached the missile. Equally, it could be a duff cartridge that has not fired. They pin it up as fast as possible.

The Mauser cannon fires high explosive incendiary (HEI) bullets, or combinations of bullets belted up as necessary, at either 600 or 1000 rounds per minute – enough for only a couple of squirts. The gun is a last resort weapon.

The cannon is on the starboard side just under the pilot, and the ammunition goes in the other side. Rounds are fed in from the ammunition tank which fires then rotates. It is loaded initially with a 'speedy·brace' (a socket on a brace) so one round is 'up the spout' ready for firing. There is a pneumatic recocking unit, with five little cartridges that will continue banging them out, that will reject dud rounds twice before declaring that it really does have a problem and stopping.

Fuel planning is a constant, very real and life-enhancing occupation for aircrew, and they base their calculations on the following. In addition to the amount needed to get them back to base, they will need enough (600 kilograms on Maple Flag) to allow an aircraft to land on another runway or taxi-way if someone crashes ahead of them. If the weather is bad they will need enough fuel to allow them to overshoot from an approach at their base and then divert somewhere else. And in a real war they would also need combat fuel, the amount needed to fight their way home. Jones:

'If you were doing this for real – as we were in Bosnia-Herzegovina – you would be carrying fuel tanks, so you would always be fat for gas. You take off with tanks full, then go straight to the tanker to top off fully with fuel, then go to the area to do your roving CAP, so you're down to a sensible fuel weight. After the initial attack, when you start shooting rockets, you ditch your tanks as you come off the commit and hope that you have enough fuel. The tanks alter your manoeuvrability quite considerably! They impose g limits and put too much drag on the aeroplane. From then on, you'd have a jet that's full of fuel – you hope. If you have to "no shit" fight somebody right at the end of your slot, you don't want to be going in there thinking, "Oh my word, I've got to conserve petrol". So at a sensible fuel weight you depart the area and refuel. You never want to be short of petrol if you've got something to do. You calculate some figure to get you home; I'd use around 1500 kilograms of combat fuel, which is a high load.'

At maximum power without using afterburners (max dry), the aircraft burns 40 kilograms per minute of fuel – 80 kilograms for both engines. At re-heat it burns and blows so much it cannot be measured. Jones:

'Re-heat basically throws a load of fuel into the jet pipe and sets fire to it – which burns gallons … loads and loads more – around 600 kilograms a minute at low level. We don't have a fuel gauge big enough. If you're going to thwack on the burner all the time you're only going to be up for a very short time.'

A ninety-minute flight burns around 4000 kilograms of fuel, plus the extra from the tankers.

Bravery and aggression are very carefully calculated commodities in fighter aircrew. Foolhardiness, however, plays no part in their mental profile. Fighting and running are equally important tactics, and are decided as much by technical considerations as by basic human reactions. The limitations of man and machine must be fully understood – as well as capabilities and advantages. Jones:

'The criteria by which a pilot decides to leave a fight are fuel and the load that he is carrying.'

CHAPTER NINE

Flight Line

Maple Flag Ops is located in a complex of yet more brand-new portacabins (destined for oil exploration camps up north) freshly erected beside 441 Squadron's hangar. It is a three-mile drive from 29 (F) Squadron's flight line, requiring everybody to leave air base security, then re-enter through a second guarded gate. To the left, in thick woods, is the 'ammunition compound', long rows of soil-banked bunkers housing the base's training and war stocks of small arms and aircraft weaponry, located (in case of explosion) well away from every-thing – except the police sentry box. A lake remains frozen, with only the odd reminders that spring is supposed to be on the way: moose were seen among these trees last night, and several deer are in there now – any one of which could damage, if not write off, a car.

Beside the portacabins a larger prefab building, low and square with steps and featureless windows on one side, houses the nerve centre of Exercise Maple Flag: Maple Flag Ops. Another similar building houses the operations and planning cells of the various United States squadrons (including the Aggressors), and is the co-ordination centre for both Red and Blue Air – the two sides in the forthcoming air war. In between the two buildings is a barbecue area, picnic tables standing on concrete paving slabs, with two large, green military tents to one side, one for the hot dog and hamburger stand, the other selling Exercise Maple Flag souvenirs – the obligatory T-shirt, flying suit flashes, baseball caps, coffee mugs and pewter tankards – everything a fast-jet jock could ever need. This is a family business; while Major Rick Boyd (the exercise controller) keeps the war running on schedule, his wife and pretty daughter sell the merchandise.

Briefings for the aircrews start at 6 a.m. each morning. To speed things up, the leaders on the morning missions get the relevant information the previous afternoon and start their planning then. On the cold, icy morning of 1 May 1995 29 (F) Squadron aircrew arrive fifteen minutes early, filing up the wooden steps and into the warmth, past coffee urn and cookies. The twenty rows of chairs in the briefing room are empty, so with the usual rectitude of an experienced audience they start filling the large, square room from the back row forward. The front of the room has a lectern inscribed with Maple Flag's motto 'Send Us Your Very Best', marker-pen boards and a large television projection screen fed by a bank of computers on tables to the right-hand side of the room.

Two Canadian Air Force officers are feeding information into the personal computers, while the screen shows CNN Headline News – repeated on smaller television screens to either side halfway down the room. The walls to the rear are covered with maps of the range. The Germans arrive, then a surge of people fills the corridor filing into the room through its two doors. On the screen and monitors, CNN is replaced by a large digital clock; the seconds tick away relentlessly. A Canadian Air Force officer stands behind the lectern and announces:

'Five minutes.'

Exercise staff gather at the front and greet base commander Colonel Little as he arrives and sits in the front row. The officer at the lectern announces 'One minute'. The crush of people has stopped and only a few latecomers push into the room, to stand around the walls as all the seats are taken. 'Twenty seconds.' Then, 'Ten seconds' and the clock counts down to zero – 'Close the doors'.

Briefings for this first mission, and all that are to come, follow exactly the same format each time and although the aircrew complain that they contain very little useful information, with so many aircraft and nationalities repetition of what might seem obvious to some is better than any risk of dangerous confusion. After a roll call of call signs, both Red and Blue Air receive a general brief on the range, weather, and safety – starting with a meteorology briefing from the base weather man:

'Upper level winds from one all the way up to five thousand feet are south-westerly, five to ten knots. Light rime icing in cloud above the freezing level – at around five thousand feet, moderate mix associated with the convective cloud, with moderate turbulence …'

It is detailed, comprehensive and important, staccato information delivered fast over a hand-held radio microphone. The weather determines what type of a war the mission will be; whether it is split, restricted full or low, depends upon cloud. With so many aeroplanes flying it can only be a 'full' war on a nice day with clear blue sky. With eight-eighths cloud it is difficult for aircraft to penetrate this solid layer safely as there is no way that they can know whether there is another jet underneath that they may crash into.

In an emergency, the aircrew might have to divert to another airfield. They need to know about weather conditions over a wide area:

'For Saskatoon, again a similar situation there – some local stratus. Visibility as low as a half mile 'til 17 Zulu, cumulus developing. Snow showers also.'

'Expected take-off weather for 14 Zulu, scattered mid-level cloud based around seven thousand high, scattered to broken conditions above, good visibility. Two degree temperature.'

Aircraft altimeters measure air pressure, and so have to be calibrated to indicate height above the ground rather than above sea level. The met officer gives both the height of Cold Lake above sea level, and the air pressure at that height – that is, at ground level. With impending spring, migrating geese and other birds (many quite large) flying at low level do not mix very well with military jets – particularly as birds do not adhere to air traffic routing or air combat safety conventions. Today the bird count at 0615 local time is level one throughout the range, meaning there is no threat. Major Rick Boyd takes the radio mike:

'OK, birds are light and are expected to stay light – between zero and level three. The big number to watch out for, is if they go to level four.'

If they do the information will be transmitted over the AWACS and Guard emergency radio nets and aircraft will be restricted to 1000 feet and have to climb.

Boyd indicates various locations on the range map:

'There's a spawning camp here until fourteenth May at the north end of Primrose Lake. It's important to fish and wildlife, so it's "No Drop" – there's people out here until the fourteenth inclusive.

'This is AMOCO oil – a no drop zone; and this is the Esso Resources area – it's no drop too. At the end of this road there's an accommodation complex so no supersonic over here. Other than that, we have the usual weapons-free zones. Don't go into those or we'll be looking for you with AWACS.

'With weather, the only thing you've got to watch is this part of the range where there's reduced visibility down to four miles in some rain showers. We've got some targets there today. The whole range is pretty well based, clouds at 3.5 [thousand feet] topped at 11 to 17, clearer to the west than it is to the east – and it's moving off to the east. So keep an eye on the weather.'

Overleaf: An F–16 of the United States Agressors; the squadron acts as the enemy during Maple Flag and uses Soviet-style tactics.

Cloud cover has forced exercise staff to divide the air war into two distinct height zones: low level for the bombers, and air-to-air only above 7000 feet.

The late spring means that the usually reliable good flying weather has not yet arrived. Flight Lieutenant Mark Gorringe:

'We were on Exercise Red Flag last year, in Las Vegas where the weather is blue from the ground up to the heavens. In the desert, there was no problem going low to kill the bombers. However, with the weather here, if we can't see the ground there's an absolute bottom level for us of four thousand feet – the safety altitude – the height of the highest bit of land plus a safety allowance to stop us driving into a mountain while dogfighting.

'Splitting the war lets the bombers scoot through under the cloud, while we are stuck above, unable to get our radars angled low enough to kill guys on the deck – a purely exercise problem ...'

Captain Pete 'Pistol' Smith gives the air traffic control brief. Talking fast with the radio mike touching his lips, like the air traffic controller he clearly is, he is very jargonized and partly incomprehensible, prompting the comment from one navigator: 'Talk fast and everybody thinks you're sharp.'

Smith bangs through his slides and ends up asking for any questions in under one minute.

The intelligence briefing is just as brisk. Red Air's country (to the west of the range) has invaded Blue Air's territory (to the east). To the north and south are neutral countries. This scenario is developed as the 'war' progresses, but it is already clear that apart from the various map lines it generates – particularly the forward edge of the battle area (FEBA) – nobody pays too much attention to it. In a real war, by contrast, political developments and all snippets of intelligence would be pored over in great detail.

The microphone changes hands again, to Captain Jeff Hough, the package leader of Red Air, from the American Aggressor Squadron. This unit flies strangely painted F–16s and acts as an authentic 'enemy' using Soviet-style tactics. Hough details the 'blocks' – the altitudes in which the two sides must fly: Blue Air up to 4000 feet, and Red Air from 5000 feet to 9000 feet. For dogfight safety, the fighters keep out of the 'bubbles' of inviolable airspace allocated to other aircraft: 3000 feet from AWACS, the tanker VC10s and other heavy transport planes, 2000 feet from helicopters and 1000 feet from everybody else. All the low altitude rules will apply at anything below 7500 feet. Hough reminds everybody of the safety conventions for dogfighting. If aircraft attack each other from the front, making head-on passes, the convention is that everybody keeps to the right to avoid collision. In general, during the last seconds of an approach at speeds greater than 1200 m.p.h. people keep going in the same direction. Somebody with his aircraft's nose up is going to go high. The maximum number of jets permitted in one dogfight is eight, so Hough advises that:

'If you're having to start counting guys, just watch that fight and stay out of it, pick the guys as they come off.

'If you do get killed out, or you've got a merge with another guy and you think you may have been killed out, then make sure you go beyond visual range from that fight. Best thing to do is just flow on to another fight.'

He tells them to 'terminate' for any training rules violation. Wing rock – waggling the aircraft's wings – is the quickest way to get a termination as everybody is not on the same radio frequency.

'And watch your fuel as it's the first day and there's going to be a lot of people trying to get back in at the same time. Make sure everybody's got cloud clearances, and we'll set a hard deck if required.

'As far as defensive manoeuvres are concerned: basically a level to climb, and 180 degree turn, is the max of what you can do.

'Keep your visors down – remember those birds.

'Make sure you break off your attack by nine thousand feet so you can keep outside of those bubbles.'

Hough addresses the air-to-ground players: the Blue Air bombers:

'I know it doesn't apply today, but when you are doing level deliveries it's hard for Red Air to tell when you are going in to bomb. If you don't want us attacking you, then just rock your wings and we'll come off. If we don't, then get your whole flight to wing rock and Red Air will come off. If we still don't come off then ignore us and we'll de-brief it afterwards. Watch successive attacks on other guys – and watch your min airspeed down to low altitudes. No successive attacks, or big, rolling, vertical-type manoeuvres. If you see one of the Red Air guys come off in a big vertical move we're trying to tell you to look down front, 'cos maybe you're in danger of hitting the ground or something. Next slide.

'If you get a "knock it off" call get back to your blocks – where you started from, and contact Maple Flag Ops.

'Any questions for Red or Blue Air? OK, Red and Blue Air clear to off.'

The aircrew split off into Blue Air (the good guys) and Red Air (the bad ones). On this exercise, as on all exercises, the good guys have got to win.

They then split into their separate briefs, which for Red Air is eight Aggressor

F–16s, the Canadian Air Force's four CF–18s and 29 (F) Squadron's eight Tornado F3s plus support from two Canadian T–33 jammers and a Challenger spoofer (a chaff-layer and communications jammer). About twenty-five minutes of collective briefing takes them to 0715 then 29 (F) Squadron drives back to its quarters for a thirty-minute brief for its section.

Flight Lieutenant Tim Taylor, its qualified weapons instructor, starts the pre-flight brief. He starts with emergencies, which are particularly important for the first mission on a strange base. Wingmen and element leaders look after each other, with the AWACS acting as overall look-out to keep everybody flying safely. On the radio, 'Squawk' is the basic emergency signal with the usual 'Maydays'; and 'Pan' for less serious emergencies. Combat rules are standard and were covered at the morning briefing. Supersonic flying is allowed almost everywhere, and collision avoidance procedures are the same as the squadron's. The safety signal for 'cease combat' is also standard; for emergencies, 'knock it off' will be transmitted three times, followed by the nature of the emergency.

Taylor also reiterates the dogfighting rules. He tells aircrew to 'keep their noses out' when eight or more aircraft are involved, and only go into a radar fight if they have good situational awareness. Any missile launched at an aircraft means it is 'killed', and must get out of the combat area.

29 (F) Squadron are air-to-air fighters trying to stop the 'mud-movers' (bombers) from getting to their targets. Locations are described over the radio in relation to a known point called the 'bullseye' – which players have marked on their radar screens. The defending fighters wait around a combat air patrol (CAP) point, orbiting while they wait for the enemy to arrive. Tim Taylor runs through the 'airspace' part of his brief – who is where, doing what. The idea is to have a CAP as far back as possible in order to keep the enemy at arm's length while giving the fighters the maximum distance over which to accelerate on the 'commit' (the initial attack). This gives them the longest possible time for finding and locating the enemy. The squadron operate within their fighter area of responsibility (FAOR), within which they can engage targets freely. The 'reset gate' is a rendezvous for fighters returning to the CAP to regroup after an engagement.

Taylor's package is organized into two 'four-ships' – autonomous units working to his overall plan. He gives the navigators the CAP point and navigation point locations to feed into their computers. However, because of the way the software works, the only way the navigators can draw circles on their display is by feeding in this information as if it were a missile engagement zone (MEZ).

Both four-ships have a second CAP point entered as 'MEZ Two' with a radius of ten miles … with various lines to keep the two separated laterally from each other. CAF CF–18s will be resetting through 29 (F) Squadron's area, so the second CAP point will be vital to keep everybody safely away from them.

The CF–18s are working as part of the Red Air fighter package, so the plan keeps both them and the US Air Force Aggressor Squadron in separate blocks from the F3s. However, the CF–18s with their long range AMRAAM missiles are out in front taking the initial long shots, and will need to run back through the Tornados' blocks. There are also Red Air airborne jamming aircraft. Taylor:

'Here on jammers' CAP is the Challenger and two ET133s, so a wise man wouldn't push it past the edge of the box more than about a hundred miles.'

Timings are critical, as the fighters must go into a fight with the maximum fuel and spend as little time as possible orbiting the CAP point.

'1540 Zulu is the time to be on CAP up the top here between fifteen thousand and ten thousand feet, with my element operating in the low half.'

Air warfare is in three dimensions, with as much difference between the altitudes of aircraft as their linear distances from each other. Fighters at exactly the same map grid location can be up to 40 000 feet away from each other – eight miles in the vertical plane – invisible, and far from easy to spot, even on radar. Within their boxes, fighters often 'stack' across the range of height blocks they are covering.

'If the weather's clear, the F–18s – call sign Flogger 31 – will be stacked up in the next block. Expect the odd sweep of the radar as they look for you, or even look over your shoulder and see them there.'

Getting into the plan, Taylor details the circumstances under which the Tornados will attack. They will be too far away from the incoming enemy bomber stream actually to see them, so the decision to commit has to be taken according to what they can see by radar. GCI is the ground control intercept system, radar-using ground-based fighter intercept controllers, which for Red Air today is replaced by the E3 AWACS sentry aircraft. The AWACS can see some 300 miles and, staffed by fighter controllers, is the most reliable source of information, using Link 16, the top-secret data transfer link that constantly circulates and up-dates the fighters, AWACS and other RAF radars with real-time information from all the radars in the JTIDS network.

Taylor decides the Tornados will attack anything that passes west of bullseye, and that committing off E3 information is marginally more reliable than JTIDS, and JTIDS more reliable than their own aircraft radars – even though all three should always be working off the same information. He needs to make this very clear to his crews so that they know exactly how the critical commit decision is to be made in case (for example) of data link failure. Taylor will call the commit: '31 commit'. If he is unable to get airborne Squadron Leader Ian Gale, the leader of the second four-ship, will call '35 commit'.

In the overall plan the F–18s are to appear from behind the F3s, taking shots at a very much longer range than the enemy package will be expecting. In all the tension and decision of the commit, Taylor is not convinced that the Canadian planes will manage to get out in front, and thinks that one of his Tornado four-ships may end up in front of them. On the commit the orbiting aircraft have got to get into line to attack in formation – which means that those rotating away from the enemy have got to turn and accelerate very rapidly to catch up with the rest. The gap between the lead aircraft in the two four-ships will be ten to fifteen miles so the Tornados at the back will have to move quickly to catch up and close the gap. He reminds aircrew that they are all going to go at the same time:

'When you hear the word "commit", it's time to get your fingers out of your bums and go to work.'

The plan is then to stay in the 15 000 to 19 000 foot block and attack down the extended centre line of the target package. The F–18s will use their excess power to stroke on up in both speed and height, to get out in front between the two F3 elements. The rules of engagement are that each pilot must have situational awareness, or E3 or JTIDS picture, and must decide which one of them is giving the best information. If a target doesn't produce a mode one squawk (indicating that it is a civilian aircraft), and is not in the F3 block of airspace, the pilot can fire provided he has situational awareness:

'We will always commit the CAP, even if it only appears to be a singleton coming in – 'cos we don't know that it's only one. In any case, GCI, and even E3 will only call a group.'

It is vital that both groups of fighters hit the enemy at exactly the same time and Taylor stresses the importance of trying to keep their ranges the same:

'What I don't want to see is a gap appearing as some guys take sixty degrees of turn while others take ten degrees. We want to do a co-ordinated manoeuvre and move out ...'

In his attacking manoeuvre Taylor has the two four-ships flying one behind the other, spread laterally across the sky. The first four-ship then splits right and left in pairs, leaving the second four-ship hammering in behind to go between them. The second four-ship keeps together but widens the spacing between aircraft – so that on the enemy radar screens two fast-moving blips suddenly and confusingly turn into a wide line of eight aircraft. The next task is for each aircraft to sort out its targets from the oncoming bomber and fighter package, ensuring that no aircraft is either targeted twice or omitted. The drill is to sort and shoot, with an engagement range equal to the overall coverage for the JTIDS, then go 'on to the beam' to shake off enemy radars, followed immediately by a drag back to the west to reset.

Going 'on to the beam' means turning to present a sideways aspect to the enemy, which throws the radars of other aircraft: it puts the plane's trace into a zone of maximum clutter, while messing up the Doppler shift by which its speed is being determined, and drastically reduces the likelihood of the enemy achieving a good firing solution for a missile launch. Fighter crew describe quitting dogfights as 'running away bravely', an essential part of their tactics, which Taylor insists must be done as rigorously as everything else:

'When we do the resets and aborts, you've got to be very aggressive, and stay as pairs. So even call signs, get your act together and be there!'

Odd-numbered call signs are the pairs leaders, so the even numbers have to follow them, in some circumstances following their every move in close formation. Staying in pairs is vital for survival. Two aircraft can search the skies far more comprehensively than one, drastically reducing the chances of enemy fighters creeping up without being detected and engaged. Every action must be co-ordinated with other friendly aircraft in the area, a task which the AWACS with its all-seeing radar overview of the whole area is best able to do. When aborting or resetting, the crews watch their radar screens very carefully, to get back to the right place safely. Without the E3 or JTIDS, they still have to get back to the right height block, in the right place, on time and facing in the correct direction as briefed. Once there, they start taking height splits covering the different height blocks with their radars.

'Hard walls' are absolute boundaries between predetermined airspace zones, which cannot be crossed. Controlling the chaos of air combat requires simple rules limiting friendly aircraft flow. Any aircraft not adhering to the rules and crossing hard walls is assumed to be hostile – and shot down simply because of its position and direction, a vital assumption which saves time, effort and the high risk of getting close enough for visual identification. Taylor now directs how the dogfighting – the engaging and killing of enemy lead elements – will be done. Each aircraft's radar forms part of a co-ordinated pattern, taking different heights and directions and so extending overall coverage, which is laid down as a standard operating procedure (SOP).

Flight Lieutenant Tim Taylor briefs aircrew before their first mission; he is the squadron's qualified weapons instructor but was at first reluctant to fly fast jets.

The element leader and wingman of each four-ship will take the enemy lead aircraft, and numbers three and four his subordinates. Everything is co-ordinated in pairs, according to the SOPs – one looking high, the other looking low, on radar and visually. Taylor advises that if people are together with another F3, but not sure who, 'a wise man would search the whole sky. If there's any doubt, you have to cover the whole lot. Don't let anybody get through.'

After resetting, the order is to commit on any enemy aircraft that is further than fifty miles from the bullseye reference point. At this point, everything will be very confused, a close range battle which all survivors will get stuck into. Any element lead can call the commit.

Sorting out who is going to shoot at which enemy aircraft is also standard operating procedure and depends on the F3s' formation and the formation of the target group. It is pre-planned so that everyone knows which target to take without discussion. At this stage, only aircraft not themselves being targeted can press home an attack. There is no point in getting shot down for nothing. Taylor says that if there is nothing on the aircraft's radar homing warning receiver (RHWR), which produces a telephone-like ringing sound indicating hostile radar, at twenty-five miles they can press on in to take a short range shot at ten miles.

Getting in close is important for the Tornados with their short range missile. However, they can only risk this if they are untargeted by the enemy fighter escort. It is very risky, and has to be finely judged. If they have detected an enemy radar searching, but not actually locking on – known as a 'search spot' – they go on to the beam and try what is called 'ropey-dope', a tactic to try and drag the enemy off to one side and entice him to chase them so that the wingman can shoot him. Getting in close enough to do this is even more risky than playing victim. This is the endgame, the time when the risks are highest. Everybody must get involved. Taylor:

'You're now the thin red line, and there's nowhere left to run. You've got to start trading shots. With the enemy fighter and bomber flow engaged and the single guys getting spiked it's now starting to break down.'

Unless people know from JTIDS exactly who is who, nobody can risk crossing the hard walls from one side to the other.

'So if we're all up and running, no problem, you can flit in there – just wander through the line to get a shot if you see someone trying to get through. But if there is doubt, you stay on your side of the line, and we let people get past us. Don't get too tricky, we don't want any blue-on-blue. It becomes soft-walled when we're all happier, and you can do a bit of bending through it to get a shot, but you've got to flow out if there are any problems with JTIDS or radar.'

When targets cannot actually be seen the decision to open fire in the confusion of a mixed dogfight depends upon how much situational awareness the pilot has.

'If you're happy from GCI, JTIDS and your own radar that a target is not friendly, lock him and shoot him – without any worries. But as your SA degrades, your willingness to hose off missiles also has to degrade accordingly.'

The F3s' game plan is dangerous, and assumes that some of their own aircraft are going to be shot down. The 'what if' plan if they are down to two radars, or two aircraft pair elements, is to press on and to start shuffling aircraft so that they have workable equipment. They pretend to be eight aeroplanes until there are only four, then they reduce to a reset CAP, in the south.

Next Taylor covers communications, which must be economical and to the point. The HF frequency is only for emergencies:

'If you haven't got radar or JTIDS and you really are Captain Cluedo, use it, and have a listen to what's going on … There will be twelve aircraft on the main frequency, including the F–18s, so listening is more important than transmitting. Be concise, be precise, those are the kind of calls I want to hear. Any questions before I draw up the big initial game plan?'

He goes to a large plastic marker board at the front of the room.

'OK. Two elements on two CAPs, with the F–18s stacked high. On the commit, with us in blue …'

Taylor tries to use a blue marker pen, which turns out to be red.

' … so we change colour, red in fact …'

Pen fails.

'Oh dear, pen failure.'

He takes new marker pen.

'And now, us being black, we commit off the F–18s, going high, and they go off to do whatever they want to do. We come down the back as the second stage, as F3s with a ten miles trail, all the way down for anything committing across the bullseye. Action ranges are standard.'

Taylor goes through the tactics. The aircraft are in a ten-mile-long line (trail), then hit the action range and go on the beam. They hold this to drag enemy missiles and radars on to them then, having evaded them, flow back round to rejoin the fight. It is important to hold the beam position long enough to confuse the enemies' radar. The F3s' second element are still coming through down the back and within the allocated height block there is not much room to run and hide.

At the same time as going on the beam (called 'pumping'), they must also change height radically, right down to the bottom of the height block – and run back. Resetting must be aggressive and fast using afterburners to get back. Anybody who is untargeted ('naked'), and has sorted the enemy bomber group as it drones on towards them, can take a shot at optimum range. But movement is restricted to no more than a mile or two because it is getting close to the F–18s' fighter area of responsibility.

'They'll kill anything that isn't an F–18. They've never seen an F3 in their life … to be honest. And don't lock up the guys coming back down the other side. Track-cross scan if you wish, but remember, that's just annoying someone else's JTIDS picture.'

Taylor does some more drawing on the board.

'Red team are now resetting their CAP down to the south. The back guys have hit their action range, and it's exactly the same. Flow if you've got no shots, and then back to your CAP point.

'Obviously both teams of four have crossed to the wrong side, and you have different distances to go. That's why you get paid so much, so use the aircraft's performance. It's a one shot, two shot thing, to get back over here. The ranges, around thirty miles, give you time to beam, holding for twenty, then do a 150 turn rather than ninety, to get yourselves back on your side of the line as quick as you can.

"These tactics are different from what we do in the UK – it's structured, forced, academic numbers, so therefore you might think there's no brain power required to do it. Wrong! You have to have your wits about you to do things at the right time, at the right speeds, and gauge things from the right place. Otherwise you'll end with eight F3s in this bit, some in the wrong half, some without JTIDS, and it will turn into a rolling goat.

'Right, anybody got any questions … Sir!'

OC A Flight Ian Gale waves a hand. He wants to know what to do if the Phantoms turn and run while his second element is coming in without having sorted, with the first element still out in front. Taylor:

'Go back to your reset … We'll press as far as we can, but then we're going to be resetting as well. Trying to co-ordinate the F–18s with us is just too difficult on Day One – unfortunately … Anything else?'

Tim Taylor's navigator, Flight Lieutenant Paul 'Vicars' Vicary, stands up with a few words for the navigators:

'We've got three minutes … When coming back to the reset CAPs, use your JTIDS and radars for CAP spacing. Be sensible about that. Be careful with your

BVR [beyond visual range]. Remember that people are going to be joining later than you might expect. Make sure you call that soft wall separating the two four-ships of F3s on the radio as you cross it – as a heads-up. Report kills on the main frequency so the E3 can co-ordinate.'

Taylor has a word about tanking, which on this exercise is not actually useful for the squadron as they are not carrying long range fuel tanks:

'We realize this is a bit of an academic exercise. The first guys will have less fuel when we've finished tanking than they would have had if they'd gone straight to the area. We'll see how the timing goes, and how people go through the baskets. We might take the first four-ship back for a quick plug at the end – but don't hold your breath …'

Ian Gale: 'If we're late getting people airborne, are we just going to kiss the tanker off?'

Vicary: 'Sorry yeah … If you can't make the tanker don't worry. If you can make 0940 on task, be there. Problems on the ground with computer reloads and that kind of thing are very possible within the time scale.'

Final word from Taylor:

'Remember the JTIDS, remember the flow, remember the radio transmissions. And above all else, remember we're in a strange base doing strange things, so watch out for the recoveries – getting back on to the ground. Shortage of fuel will bite, take it from me.'

The aircrew queue behind a desk at the rear of the briefing room to draw and sign for the latest navigation and JTIDS tapes. Mission data is fed into the aircraft by pre-prepared cassette, with coastlines and route lines, areas to avoid, and common reference point positions. One of the squadron navigators prepares this putting in latitudes and longitudes of air force bases, tanker tow lines, etc. On a long transit route lines and points can also be fed in. The 'init' (initial) data for JTIDS contains the specific communication time-slots allocated to each aircraft.

Taylor shouts above the general hubbub:

'OK then Flogger, let's listen-in for the "out-brief".'

The out-brief is known as the 'TCIC' (Thank Christ It's Covered), in case of an accident and Board of Inquiry and covers all the mandatory points: that everybody is qualified to fly the mission, that the aircraft to be flown are on the board, and that JTIDS is matched to the correct aircraft.

Taylor covers take-off speeds, diversion runways, speeds back to the airfield:

'We've all signed the orders. No warnings affecting the area. Note the one near our reset CAP which is six thousand feet only – below our air combat training.

'The current fuel and time rules are really going to bite you. You need to be properly dressed for cold weather, dry ops, so you want cold weather kit on.

'Authorized for two four-ships, and signed out by all of us now. Flight plan's gone in, birds have been briefed on, and we've got two hours.

'The range slot starts for us at 0940.

'They may have flares, they may have chaff, they will have jammers – so watch out for those. We're all current for the sortie. Any final points before we walk?'

They leave the portacabin and walk across the grass to the flying clothing portacabin where their helmets, g suits and flying equipment are stored in tall, green lockers. The g suits are like cowboy chaps, fastened on with a Heath Robinson mixture of zips and laces. They would look rather fetching in black lace (and are known as 'turning trousers' or 'speed jeans'). The crew then walk to the flight-line office to go through the documentation of the aircraft they are flying in the mission. They often request the same aircraft if they've had good sorties, so it can become a lucky talisman, although in general aircraft allocation is random.

The ground crew's A Shift is on duty under Flight Lieutenant Dave Mudd.

The line teams came in at 0700 and checked that each aircraft's servicing was complete and that all entries had been done. Complicated rules apply to rectifications, servicing that has become invalid and limitations that are imposed, so the corporal in charge has a very responsible job. Documentation also has to be checked to make sure the after-flight servicing was done correctly after the previous mission, and that reported faults have been properly dealt with. The teams work autonomously, without supervision, doing checks which can become monotonous. But people's lives depend on these checks …

Before flight (BF) servicing takes around thirty minutes. Mudd:

'Something missing is the real nightmare, as you get what's called a "loose article hazard". Say, for instance, a switch has broken off. It then falls down somewhere and jams, short-circuiting something, or gives the pilot a control restriction so that he can't fly the aircraft.'

While the before flight checks are being carried out, the 'rampie', a corporal, drives around with the liquid oxygen pot (replenishing the oxygen from the pot is hazardous and takes time) and nitrogen trollies, moving repair teams around, dealing with problems. Mudd himself gets in at about 0730 and starts going through the aircraft logbooks, checking what has been done so that he can answer questions when he goes for briefing with the aircrew. There may just be time for the ground crew to have a cup of tea before they are told that the aircrew are walking, on their way to the Tornados. The line teams go to their aircraft to receive them, taking the logbooks.

The aircrew go to the ground crew office and examine the 'F700' book, the limitations log, 'to see what standard the aircraft isn't at'. Different limitations affect the handling and operation of each aircraft. There is also an acceptable deferred defects (ADD) logbook which lists acceptable defects on the aircraft. They check the flight servicing certificate, then check the work log to see what has been done since the last flight. The aircrew may be asked to make a report for the ground crew on the repair of some fault that they cannot reproduce on the ground; for example, the correct operational use of re-heat which can only be checked in the air.

The line team are already out on the ramp, having spent the last fifteen minutes setting the aircraft's switches, aligning the navigation system, cleaning and polishing the canopy. When the documentation checks are complete and the aircraft signed for, the aircrew walk to their jets where they are met by two men, 'Man A' and 'Man B' on each aircraft. Man A helps the navigator strap in, while the pilot checks the aircraft, that all the bungs, blanks and safety locks have been removed and stowed – that everything has been done. 'Man B' goes with him.

The ground crew have done their own run-ups of the aircraft's inertial navigation system. Once the navigator is inside the aircraft and ground power has been applied, he checks this and loads in the mission data – which takes an extra five minutes or so. The pilot gets into the aircraft and tests communications.

Man A has the headset on and can talk with both crew members. He monitors each step of the starting-up procedure. The pilot does cockpit checks. General maintenance panel lights indicate if there are faults. The ground crew can speak with both pilot and navigator, and either recycle a fault and clear the computer or stop the start-up process.

As the pilot starts each engine, the ground crew watch for fire. Then once the engines have been checked they check the controls via the headset, asking the pilot to put flaps into their various positions – mid, fully down, mid and then back up – and to test the air brakes, then tailerons, making sure that the controls do whatever the pilot wants them to. If there are any faults, the line team rectify them or call in the hit team to try to fix it. The hit team are very experienced, and can tell whether this can be done quickly, or whether it will be necessary to shut the aircraft down and get the crew out.

The decision as to whether to fly or not is up to the pilot as 'captain' of his aircraft. In war, when staying on the ground might put others at risk, he might decide to take off with otherwise unacceptable faults. It is his decision, which *in extremis* could earn him a bravery medal, or a court martial. If an aircraft cannot be made fit to fly, others are ready to go. In addition to those on the board to fly, every plane on the flight line is before-flight serviced, switches set, power ready and inertial navigation systems (INS) aligned, ready for combat in every way except for starting the engines. Each one should be able to take-off in five minutes.

On Exercise Maple Flag, the aircrew are very keen to fly – both to achieve the exercise's aim and to maximize their personal experience. On routine training exercises in the United Kingdom, not getting airborne because of a fault is not as much of a problem as it is in Canada.

The aircraft finally taxi off on their first Maple Flag mission and return ninety minutes later. Sorties vary from around forty minutes to three hours or so – depending upon how much after-burner is used and whether the planes refuel in the air.

When the returning aircraft are ten minutes away from landing, the ground crew get a warning call through air ops, who give a code: 'X Ray' means there are no snags; 'Yankee plus a number' means that there is a snag and the number describes what it is; and 'Zulu plus a number' means the ground crew have a serious problem on their hands. The coding allows them to get the right people together, then check the aircraft's records and so on.

The aircraft taxi back to the shelter area and are waved into their specific flight-line slots, locked and chocked. The aircrew get out and a line team starts the turn-around servicing; or the more thorough after-flight servicing if no more flying is intended that day.

The aircrew come to the ground crew's line control area and deal with the '700' logbooks. If anyone had a snag they call over the relevant tradesman and report the fault. Back home at Coningsby this is done on the computer. The rectification controller joins Mudd and the line controller and they work out how they are going to fulfil the next mission – whether each aircraft can go out again as it is or, if not, whether it can be fixed in time. If the ground crew have spotted a leak or other damage they must decide whether or not they can live with it.

There was one problem on this first mission of Exercise Maple Flag – with the aircraft that the boss, Wing Commander Martin Routledge, was navigating. While inserting the Tornado's probe into the tanker's basket during air-to-air refuelling they poked the basket's outer ring, which consists of several metal

Overleaf: Tornados take off on their first mission; it was basically a familiarization flight and lasted ninety minutes.

vanes that can shear off and cause terrible damage to engines. The ground crew had to check the F3's engines in case some of the drogue bag had been sucked into them – which luckily had not happened.

The aircrew de-brief is very much part of the mission. While the ground crew are sorting out the aircraft, the aircrew analyse their own performance with equal care. They try to reconstruct exactly what happened – when they took shots, when they think they were shot – and play back the mission on the video de-briefing facility which gives heights, speeds, positions and headings of any event or shots. The de-brief is chronological and because of strict Maple Flag exercise timings is limited to forty-five minutes, rather than the hour or more that is really needed. The squadron then collates all the information before going to the mass de-briefing at Maple Flag Ops.

As de-briefing is the aircrew's only means of learning from the mission, cutting it short (the mass de-brief lasts about thirty minutes) seems rather a waste of the effort and expense of the mission itself. Maple Flag Ops de-briefs are no-nonsense, brisk events in which quick decisions are made as to how everybody did. Anyone who does not have exact data to hand will end up feeling hard done by. Argument is curtailed. International diplomacy is at the fore, disputes between nations quickly extinguished by Maple Flag Ops staff – if only to prevent these sessions running over. The de-briefs run exactly to time. The afternoon wave will be taking off hot on the heels of the morning wave – and, having got up at 5 a.m., nobody wants to stay on base any longer than necessary.

Today's de-brief starts with a summary by the air-to-ground Blue Air package commander, highlighting problems and lessons that have been learnt. Then each of the Blue section leaders says how they dropped their bombs on target on time: 'We were great.' Or, occasionally, 'We couldn't drop our bombs on time because we were bounced by the air defenders, but we dropped our bombs – which was a mission success anyway ...'

The day finishes at about 2 p.m. After all this effort, this first mission can be summed up in two sentences. Mark Gorringe:

'The first day was basically a familiarization flight, and we ended up fighting with the F–4s. However, the Canadian F–18s tied them up, so not a lot of trade came our way.'

CHAPTER TEN

Team Games

The AWACS (airborne warning and control system) mission crew are ready to go to war with the tools of their trade: laptop computers and briefcases. For normal civilian air movement the Boeing 707 E3 Sentry aircraft is call sign 'Ascot 9022', but on operations (and this exercise) it uses the AWACS call sign 'Magic 41'. It has been a very cold night, and de-icing has taken longer than expected. By 0720 the job is still not finished – cutting things a little fine for the planned 0800 take-off. Squadron Leader Dave Buchanan, captain of the AWACS aircraft, leads the pre-flight briefing:

'We're taking off with 80 000 pounds of fuel, with a great weather forecast – stratus in the northern area, up to six nautical miles visibility by landing time. With the lakes frozen up, we won't be ditching – just crash landing!

'0800 take-off, on station by 0845, ready for first trade at 0845.'

Flight Lieutenant John Coffey is the tactical director:

'The threat today is running from east to west. The range is set up as normal. Weapons brief: it's vital to keep out of the south part of Primrose Lake. No supersonic flights are permitted in there.'

For this mission the the American Aggressor Squadron are planning to do figure of eight manoeuvres while 29 (F) Squadron F3s will play more of their normal game plan. Different types of aircraft require to be given navigation details in various formats. Coffey reminds his intercept controllers of the specific compass bearings the Tornados (call sign 'Flogger') and F–18s (call sign 'Viper') require: degrees true for the Tornados, and degrees magnetic for the F–18s.

John Coffey has spent hundreds of hours airborne monitoring the no-fly zone over Bosnia-Herzegovina, directing NATO fighter aircraft on this real-world United Nations mission. Actual air operations involve far more aeroplanes than the usual training exercises, often from various countries with very different operating procedures, aircraft and experience. Co-ordination is vital, and is provided by AWACS.

Sponsored by the United Nations, NATO aircraft are tasked to support the UN protection forces (UNPROFOR) on the ground in Bosnia. Nine or ten NATO nations are taking part, with the full gamut of military aircraft: bombers, fighters, reconnaissance aircraft and AWACS, often flying twenty-four hours per day making sure that no other aircraft fly in the Bosnia no-fly zone. In the three and a half years up to March 1995 the AWACS put in over 60 000 hours.

Two AWACS are airborne during daylight; and one stays up around the clock. They are very much the lynch pin of NATO and UN operations, to the extent that without the system in location many operations simply don't go ahead. Fighter and bomber crews rely on the 'eye-in-the sky' to give them the warm feeling that someone is not only speaking to them, but is also looking out for their interests. Although RAF AWACS are not involved, American AWACS are keeping constant watch over northern Iraq and southern Arabia. The AWACS is very much an aircraft in demand; its political masters want to use it for just about every type of situation. Whenever anything happens one of the first aircraft to go in these days is an AWACS – to show presence, and get information back so that commanders can make an accurate assessment of the situation. Coffey:

'On Operation Deny Flight in Bosnia, operating from Italy, we often take off during bad weather deliberately light on fuel, and tank once we're airborne. We're also re-tasked to different areas, and take on fuel as we depart. Tanking gives us great flexibility – and in fact is the key to air power – and to us being able to do our job.'

Coffey believes that there is very little difference between an exercise and the real thing:

'Bosnia for example is very tense, and although "not war" could turn into "war war" any time you go flying. You therefore have to be guarded in everything you say. Over Bosnia you have to put a safety catch on your brain. Calling an "engage" would have serious political consequences. I've worked for many, many hundreds of hours over Bosnia, from July 1992 onwards, more or less continually. Most of us have done more than a thousand hours over Bosnia.

'Here in Canada we are teaching fighter crews to operate as part of large formations – which is very tricky to organize, and they have to sort themselves out. It's a very dynamic situation and they have to think on their feet. At the end of the two weeks, they will be flying very hard missions, at the edge of the capabilities of many fighter pilots – in a large piece of sky which enables them to train to their absolute maximum.'

Air force people refer to the AWACS aircraft by its role as the 'Sentry', or by its aircraft type – the E3. An RAF E3 crew comprises seventeen people: a flight deck crew of four (captain, co-pilot, navigator and flight engineer), and a mission crew of thirteen led by the tactical director. Nine people sit at the aircraft's radar and communications consoles: the surveillance team and weapons team, all fighter controllers. Extra people can be added for longer missions, although the size of the lavatory can limit the amount of time that can be spent aloft: for reasons unknown the Americans have two lavatories and can (apparently) stay up longer. The E3 can do ten-hour missions without refuelling.

Each console operator has access to four radios and three secure intercom nets. Net One is used for rear-to-front end co-ordination within the E3, particularly between the tactical director and the captain on the flight deck. Net Two is used by the weapons team, who are the intercept or fighter controllers. Net Three is used by the surveillance team.

One problem with the E3 is data overload; all the operators have to cut their minds into seven or eight quadrants in order to listen to all the radios and nets at the same time. With Link 16 and other new systems and improved packages, there is too much information for one person to cope with, which is why the crew is split into surveillance and weapon teams.

The weapons team is led by the fighter allocator and speaks only to fighters (and to tankers if refuelling). It allocates fighters to enemy aircraft, guiding them into combat intercepts, sorting out complications and confusions, keeping them as safe as possible. The surveillance team collates the information and radar pictures that are received, then assesses the radar tracks, identifying them by type: civilian airliners, hostiles, or friendlies that might be working for several different agencies and are not under the E3's control. It is important to make sure that only the enemy are intercepted. The processed and collated information is then disseminated appropriately. There is also a communications specialist, and three technicians – for communications, computers, and display and radar. The communications team ensures the eight UHF, three HF and two VHF radios plus satellite communications are working. There are also five data-link systems and a data-management computer.

The AWACS, or E3D to use its full title, is a derivative of the civilian Boeing 707 which has been modified for military use with a 1.8 metre- (six foot-) deep frisbee containing the radar on the roof. It is slower than the civilian 707 as the frisbee's struts cause handling problems over .8 Mach (just under the speed of sound). At .84 Mach the shock wave from the rotor dome impinges on the rear stabilizer. The aircraft's speed is therefore restricted to a maximum of .78 Mach, and it normally flies at around .72 – whereas the civilian aircraft cruises at between .82 and .84 mach. The E3 always flies with its nose a little up, the original angle designed for optimum civilian passenger comfort.

If the E3 is under threat its main defensive tactic is to run away. Its safety is a team effort and the crew use both their passive and active systems (radar and listening devices) to detect threats at a very long range. As the aircraft cruises at eight miles a minute, a fighter cruising at twelve miles a minute has no problem overtaking it. However, the fighter does not have as much fuel, so the E3 should be able to outrun him provided it starts running early enough. Although E3s can be given a fighter escort, using a fighter two- or four-ship to protect just one air-craft is too expensive. E3s do practise 'high value asset' attack manoeuvres (HVAs) in case they are targeted (as a high value asset). On Maple Flag, however, they are restricted by airspace and HVAs will not be practised by them.

The E3 is entered through the one rear door, on the port side underneath the huge tail fin. A cooking and tea-making station is possibly the most important piece of equipment on board, apart from the rear lavatory and three rows of fold-up bunk beds strapped to the side bulkhead. Four rows of airline seats face aft (in regulation, RAF style), then after a space for stowing cargo there is the console cockpit where the work is done.

The first console – that of the weapons team – faces aft with tactical director John Coffey in the middle, the electronic warfare controller to his left, and the fighter intercept controller to his right. With barely three feet between the backs of their swivelling airline seats, the six consoles of the surveillance team and data links manager face each other. Forward of them, the weapons controllers sit at their own consoles, with the communications team consoles further forward, just behind the flight deck. There is plenty of space, which is vital for the long operational flights the aircraft has to make. Team boss Squadron Leader Bob Wilkie:

'A battle commander could run his war from up here. With access to satellite data, the scope could be enormous – but there is a danger of over-saturating the guys with information.'

Four groups of fighter aircraft are flying on this morning's sortie: on the Red Air side, call sign 'Flogger' are 29 (F) Squadron Tornado F3s; 'MiG' are F–16Cs – the Aggressors; 'Viper' are standard F–16 fighters, also controlled by the AWACS. In addition, also on the Red Air side, are 'Yogi' – T–33 jamming aircraft which mimic and spoof Blue Air radar and radio frequencies. They simulate somebody else's picture and pass on wrong information to degrade that arriving in the Blue Air fighter escorts and bombers' cockpits. 'Ivan' are CAF CF–18s, very capable aircraft, controlled by ground radar.

Each group of Red Air fighters is given an area to protect, and Blue Air have been given targets to bomb. The Blue Air fighter escorts are trying to harass and engage Red fighters before they get near the bombers, which are trying to press on with a cunning plan to get to their targets and drop bombs on target on time. The Yogis run in front of a bombing package and spoof, then run away when they get too close to being shot down. The Blue escort fighters then go in and harass the Red fighter packages.

Red Air are organized into four-ships, within their different call signs. Each group of four aircraft in its allocated piece of sky tries to stop the Blue Air fighter escorts – and most importantly the bombers – getting through. Shooting down a fighter does not achieve very much, except that it cannot live to fight another day. Stopping a bomber getting to its target defeats the enemy's strategic goal, and requires him to send more bombers to try again. War is a process of attrition – wearing the enemy down so that he can no longer achieve his air task.

Flight safety is just as important in war as it is in peacetime. Wilkie:

'Modern aeroplanes are so expensive that we can't afford to shoot down our own. Fighters do not leave their allocated boxes of airspace, so you know that any unidentified aircraft entering is hostile. The fighters know that anyone coming through their wall of sky will be a bad guy.'

The fighters circulate at a combat air patrol (CAP), in a holding pattern in the sky waiting for the enemy to arrive. Being already airborne saves the time involved in taking off, checking equipment, getting to height, and into position, and means that fighters are instantly available. Ground force commanders want them there, fully serviceable, ready to pounce at a moment's notice, ensuring that anyone who tries to get through is attacked as early as possible.

The planning of an air defence battle requires tremendous co-ordination. The defence is constructed in layers, with different weapons systems attacking the intruders as they attempt to penetrate. It is in depth, with fighters out in front, then surface-to-air missiles, with ground-to-air artillery protecting specific

Overleaf: 441 Squadron's Captain Kim Reid, Captain 'Tarzan' Tantarn, on exchange from the Luftwaffe, and Major Rick Boyd (right) discuss a mission; they are part of Blue Air, the enemy, and 29 (F) Squadron and other Red Air aircraft, controlled by AWACS, will attempt to wreck their plans.

ground locations, each element trying to cause maximum attrition at all times so that in the end no enemy aircraft can get through to the target areas.

In the Gulf War fighters accompanied the bombing packages, with CAPs of fighters behind them in case the Iraqi aircraft decided to make their own attack. Any Iraqis that got through then had to penetrate the Allied surface-to-air missile belts, through which our fighters would not go. Specific targets like Ryadh were protected by missiles or by triple A – the highly effective, old-fashioned wall of lead – in case any bombers got through the SAM belts.

The surveillance team on the E3 consists of Flight Sergeant Mick Collins as controller, with Squadron Leader Geoff Cooper monitoring the enemy close in while Flight Lieutenant Dave Clarke monitors them far out. Analysing enemy intentions is a vital part of these two desks and they work very closely together, confirming and then identifying traces, trying to work out the enemy's game plan. Coffey faces forward with Flight Lieutenant Steve Larry to his left, and Flight Sergeant John Belcher to his right. Facing aft, on the port side, Flight Sergeant 'Woody' Woodford runs the electronic warfare desk, countering enemy jamming and clearing up the JTIDS picture for transmission to the fighters. At the middle desk is the weapons fighter controller Flight Lieutenant Tim Leffler and intercept controller Flight Sergeant 'Grog' Shaw.

The crew straps in for take-off and the aircraft climbs rapidly to operating height and starts orbiting in a wide figure of eight pattern. The radar screens are glowing, full-colour displays on which the various tactical battle and navigation lines have already been drawn. Bullseye, the range area and the southern tip of Primrose Lake (to be avoided because of the bird threat) are marked on everybody's displays, whereas the fighter boxes and hard walls appear only on the weapons team displays.

The AWACS system can detect fighter-size aircraft out to about 200 miles over both land and sea, even when flying at low level. Today the E3 is orbiting at around 30 000 feet and is, quite literally, an eye-in-the-sky looking down at a huge amount of airspace, with a god's-eye view of six miles of vertical airspace: a cylinder 400 miles across containing around 10 000 cubic miles of air (some 1300 square miles on the ground). If it was forced higher this single aircraft would look into even more airspace. Even if fighters' radars are merged as a four-ship or larger, they cannot cover more than a very limited amount of airspace and in any case their radars face forwards and only to a limited extent sideways – but not back-wards. Furthermore, the big problem with airborne radars is that they present information about a three-dimensional airspace on a flat surface.

The AWACS, however, by calculating the height of all aircraft using IFF sources (friendly forces' 'squawk' data), secondary radar returns (from JTIDS) or their own primary radar (the latter a less accurate method as it is still essentially a look-down radar), produces a three-dimensional picture. This information is then coded and passed digitally through Link 16, or by voice, using the 'bullseye' format. This is an agreed reference point on the ground that the E3 and fighters use to determine the position of aggressor aircraft. AWACS provides anything from a god's eye view of everything in its full 300-mile range to the tighter and more localized pictures needed to control individual intercepts.

The nine men in the 'the pit' – as the console area is called – are strapped in and working. The fighter allocator and his two controllers are preparing to run the intercepts with the air defence forces allocated to them by ground agencies. Once the threat to Red Air is identified, they will determine the tactics the fighters employ (within the plans already briefed), and the number of missiles and munitions left in each group of aircraft. Everybody will receive this data on their JTIDS – circulated over Link 16.

The surveillance controller works with the radar technician to keep the primary sensors – the radar and IFF – working to optimum efficiency. He also has the data link manager, an electronic surveillance monitor (ESM) operator, working the passive radar detector to pick up sea-, air- or ground-based radars to enhance the air picture. He also has two trackers who manipulate both the active and passive systems to produce the air and surface picture.

Today's mission is not proceeding as it should. Cold Lake air traffic control have become worried about cloud cover, which is closing in – and whether they will be clear enough by the end of the mission to get all the aircraft back in again. The met report indicates that this afternoon will be fine, so Maple Flag Ops take the decision to abort the morning launch. On board the AWACS there is disappointment, as they are not scheduled to fly for the afternoon war. After consultation, Dave Buchanan decides to stay airborne and play Sentry for the afternoon wave – which will mean tanking in order to have enough fuel. He explains the logistics of the day's mission:

'We started up with eighty thousand pounds of fuel, enough for the morning's session plus a couple of hours additional flying. When the morning session was cancelled, we had fuel until 1330. To fly this afternoon, we require a further two and a half hours' fuel. As we burn around eleven to twelve thousand pounds of fuel per hour, I decided to take on thirty thousand pounds of gas.'

It is very easy for an AWACS to rendezvous with its tanker, as the intercept between the two aircraft is directed by a weapons controller until the pilot takes it on visually at around three miles. Dave Buchanan is one of the RAF's most experienced multi-engine pilots. He instructs multi-engine pilots how to tank:

'Each aeroplane has its own optimum tanking speed. I prefer to tank this one at 260 knots indicated speed. On the join you need a certain amount of overtake, so you first establish the tanking speed, then close with the tanker at 280 knots, a thousand feet below. At about half a mile I'll leave the power, and just raise the nose, converting my excess twenty knots into height. In an ideal world you just cruise up there and click in beside him, on the right-hand side. The reason for going echelon right is to prevent collision. Until we are visual with the contact – the tanker – we are not allowed to leave this thousand-foot level below him. Years ago there was an accident when a Buccaneer crashed into the tail of a Victor, with a lot of casualties. He was joining from astern, with too much overtake. The rules were changed, and now we always join on the right, get stabilized, get the picture sorted out, and then move in … a little bit of power off, into the astern position, and go for the contact.'

Most of the work is done by the pilot. The co-pilot normally operates the radios and monitors everything, particularly the aircraft's attitude and the bank angle. The pilot watches only the tanker, latching on to him, in close formation, and using him as his artificial horizon. There can also be other aircraft in very close proximity, but the pilot keeps concentrating on the tanker alone. Buchanan:

'So I'm not looking outside other than dead ahead and scanning this tanker. Everybody else should be watching the peripherals. The co-pilot should also comment on closure speeds, although that's fairly obvious when you get close. The further you are away, the more difficult it is to judge. The navigator monitors our position – although as formation leader the tanker has the final say. The engineer puts the fuel into the correct tanks to keep the centre of gravity correct, and monitors the engine settings. It's very easy to put too much power on and over-boost the engines, particularly if you get into a tail chase.'

The Boeing 707 was not designed with close formation flying in mind. All the tankers – the Tristar, VC10 and 135 – have significant wing-tip vortices. The VC10 has three hoses and baskets, and because of its vortex the E3 is only allowed on the middle one. On a wing hose, the vortex would bash it from one side to the other. To compound the problem, the 707's engines are located away from the fuselage, out on the wings, and unless engine response is even (which it seldom is), the fact that they are so far off the aircraft's centre line creates left and right movement – yaw – which has also to be compensated for. All this makes staying connected a very complicated and continually altering process that requires very precise mental calculations. Pilots adjust their own position in relation to the 'picture' they have of the tankers' rear:

'We teach the trainees to hold that picture – peg it. Don't change it. It's just practice …'

A 707 is very heavy with a lot of inertia, and its pilot has to manoeuvre while the tanker stays steady at 260 knots. To speed up, the AWACS pilot has to open the throttles, then wait for the power to increase his speed. He also has to anticipate power reduction. Coping with this inertia and momentum, and anticipating the controls' time lag, all have to be learned.

Another problem is that multi-engine pilots like Buchanan do very little formation flying during their training – anyone who is good at this is usually put into fast jets. On average, it takes around nine one-hour sessions to learn to tank. Tanking is very fatiguing as big aeroplanes were not designed to fly very close together. Buchanan:

'It's very difficult initially to hold both a line and a pitch … but after about five or six sessions it all settles down and it's nice and relaxed. It's like riding a bike, it takes a while, but once you've learned it, you've got it for ever!

'Tanking pilots have to learn to detach themselves from reality in order to concentrate on that big chunk of metal in front of them – so much so that at first they can't do anything else. With time and effort, you find that little bit extra mental capacity. You can never totally detach yourself from the crew and aircraft, because they are always your responsibility.'

As they make their rendezvous with the tanker, Buchanan tells its captain (Squadron Leader Dave Mutty) how much fuel he would like to take. The mission crew guide him to the intercept on their screens until, at three miles or so, Buchanan sees the tanker and takes over the intercept:

'As we close, I'll tell the tanker captain I'm on the right, and ready to go astern. He'll clear me, then I move astern, until I'm seven to eight feet behind the tanker, in the pre-contact position. At that stage I'm trimming the aeroplane, getting it really stable – which is the most important thing.'

Buchanan then checks that he is being shown the correct hoodoo indicator lights – initially red and then amber.

'Once I'm absolutely stable, trimmed out on the rudder and ailerons, I can go for contact. All I do is put half a knob of power on, hold the picture and go for the contact, to put the probe into the basket.'

Because the VC10 engines are located high in the aircraft's tail, its backwash impinges on the AWACS' rotor dome and rudder, heating them up. At higher altitudes, the turbulence gets worse. Buchanan has his own rule: that after about twenty minutes tanking he disengages to allow the rotor dome to cool down a bit. When the AWACS refuels from a Tristar its pilot throttles back the middle (tail) engine so there is not the same problem.

The AWACS can tank at up to a speed of 290 knots, which is necessary if the VC10 is very heavy with fuel and unable to slow down without risking stalling. It can also tank at up to 29 000 feet, although as the air at that altitude is very thin it makes the aeroplane unstable – particularly as tanking is always done with autopilot off. A VC10, however, cannot make it to 29 000 feet when it is heavily laden and tanking is best at done at around 20 000 feet where it gets more control response. Buchanan:

'We have problems if we come in too hard. The aim is to join with around three to five knots overtake speed, to make a nice firm contact. If it's too hard, we send a ripple up the hose, which is only a problem when the ripple comes back down – which it does very fast, so you haven't got time to resolve it. It'll take your probe tip off. Equally, if you get a soft contact and it's not enough, it waffles around, putting a brake on the tanker's equipment on board, stalls the whole thing so we've got to start again …

'When you are in contact, there is a zone of safety – a cone up-down-left and right – on the probe. If you go too far either side the probe tip can shear off and send safety bolts flying everywhere. If this happens, the tanker has to shut off the fuel very quickly indeed. Occasionally the valves don't open and you can't take fuel. The other real nasty is called a "spokes contact", when the probe pokes through the spoke rather than settling in the centre – which tends to happen if you take a dive at it! The inclination is to take the power off and withdraw the probe rapidly, which actually is the worst thing you can do. You've got to keep the power on and hold the contact, and try for a nice, gradual withdrawal.'

AWACS operate with other air forces and have to be able to take fuel from a wide range of different aeroplanes, particularly USAF aircraft. The Americans have a different system of air-to-air refuelling, from their KC–10 and KC–135 tankers. They use their 'boom method' in which the boom plugs into a receiving nozzle behind a set of opening doors in the roof of the AWACS. Its linkages and machinery are more complicated with (as Buchanan sees it) more to go wrong.

As 'Magic 41' moves towards its intercept with the VC10 tanker, and Dave Buchanan talks with its captain Dave Mutty, the seat belt signs come on. As the E3 tucks in behind the VC10 the turbulence increases to coffee-spilling intensity. It is a rough ride to get into position, but eases – marginally – once Buchanan has got everything trimmed out and stable.

Up in the cockpit, Buchanan is slumped in the right-hand seat, concentrating fiercely, left hand on the throttle, right hand holding the controls. He is constantly moving his engines up and down their full power spectrum, anticipating the responses of his huge, ungainly bird. Two feet from the windscreen, the tanker basket wobbles up and down in the slipstream, and Buchanan flies his probe smoothly home. He flips the radio switch on the control column, muttering into his microphone.

He is flying this aircraft as close to another former passenger aircraft as might a fighter pilot in close formation with his wingman. He is sprawled rather than seated, head cocked slightly to the right as he watches the enormous back end of the VC10 less than thirty feet away. Behind its rear engines the blast of hot air swirls, distorting the picture he is so intent on watching. He gives the strong impression that even if he was set on fire he would continue flying with the same concentration. He is nevertheless very aware of what is going on in the cockpit, occasionally asking questions or muttering jokes to the rest of his flight deck.

Back in the rear of the aircraft, after a short period of increased turbulence, the seat belt signs go out as Buchanan disengages and departs the tanker. While Magic 41 returns to its orbiting position, everybody starts getting ready for the afternoon war. Today the E3 is flying a figure of eight course within its allocated box, but can also fly a circle or an oval depending upon the weather and its task.

Slowly the radar picture develops, as Blue Air take off from Cold Lake, and group to the north-east. As they flow west, the surveillance team start analysing the radar traces, identifying individual packages, working out the Blue Air game plan. They talk of the incoming bombing package as the 'gorilla' – a developing trace that spreads out over twenty-five to thirty miles, and consists of seventy or so aircraft in different packages. The mission crew's job is to prevent the gorilla reaching its targets. Reports start coming thick and fast from the consoles:

'First jamming aircraft airborne, and the bombers are getting up.'

'Our first pirate will be laying chaff.'

'Weather good with a cloud layer seven to twelve thousand feet so the war will be a full, all out.'

'A lot of aircraft taxiing to get up at their slot time. Red and Blue are getting out to predestined start positions, from which the war will start.'

Although both Red and Blue Air are taking off from the same airfield, the build-up of aircraft is realistic. In a war, the mission crew would first have to work out whether the picture they were seeing was for an attack, a threat or

Overleaf: Squadron Leader Dave Buchanan guides the E3's refuelling probe into the basket of the VC10 tanker.

probing mission, or some kind of diversionary operation shielding an attack elsewhere. Predicting when and where the enemy will breach friendly airspace has to be done in time to get fighters in position with enough fuel and munitions to counter the threat. The enemy's electronic counter measure (ECM) onslaught has also to be countered so that the actual threat can be evaluated. Wilkie:

'The little green symbology are the six F3s going into the area. JTIDS is working well. A chaff-layer T–33 is going north laying chaff – you can see him there under the letter A in the rectangular box.

'The gorilla is getting airborne now, out of Cold Lake.'

The tactical director is managing the whole stream. The surveillance controller is getting the optimum radar picture with the AWACS' active sensors, and the link manager is helping with tracking – making sure the correct symbology is actually against the right dots – and that JTIDS is working. Wilkie:

'We don't know what the fighters are receiving, that's up to them, but we do edit the picture to make sure it's accurate.'

Flight Sergeant Mick Collins: 'F–15s coming.'

Squadron Leader Geoff Cooper amends a radar trace: 'Put "F–15 comma", so we give ourselves an element of doubt – so we're not committing ourselves too badly. He's very slow, not going anywhere at the moment so it doesn't matter too much.'

Flight Lieutenant John Coffey is tagging up each radar dot as the main radar picks it up, putting symbology against each of the tracks to indicate whether friendly or otherwise:

'We don't have an automatic track initiation to do this – we have to do this manually.'

Now the Blue and Red forces are getting into position, the packages forming up. One of the MiGs has cancelled and there are around fifty aircraft in the air so far. The AWACS team are trying to build up their situational awareness of what is going on. The fighter crews will also be very busy trying to do this.

The Flogger F–16s are all airborne – a six-ship – and are forming on their combat air patrol. Pirate – a Challenger (Red Air) – has just checked in and laid his chaff to confuse the radar patterns of incoming aircraft. He is ready to start 'comm jamming' – listening out on the radio frequencies from the incoming packages, playing over the top of the F–15s' radios, making their picture as difficult as possible. He can record a tape of their controller giving them instructions, then play it back so that the controller appears to be giving spurious information. He also plays music to drown out their transmissions, or background noise in order to make it difficult for the pilots to hear what their control agency is telling them.

Only the Americans have the capability to stand off, out of the air battle, and jam. They use the EF1–11's powerful jammer and target acquisition radars; plus a specially modified Hercules to control and monitor the jamming operation, working out who to jam and where; and the Wild Weasels, which attack the surface-to-air missile sites when they turn on their radars. Coffey:

'It's all a game of cat and mouse, trying to get one over on the other guy.'

Jammers try to affect communications and radar; and each radar is affected by different types of chaff and electronic counter measures (ECM) depending on whether they are pulse or Doppler radars, and the frequency they are operating at. So what might affect a fighter will not necessarily affect the AWACS. There are several ways of dealing with jamming: by changing to a predetermined frequency on a given code word if it gets too bad; by employing anti-jam radios (which are in service on the E3); or by achieving ECM resistant communications by using Link 16, which works despite jamming.

The situation is now building up so that the mission crew can start identifying different tracks as hostile. 29 (F) Squadron F3s are still on the ground waiting to take off. Pilots and navigators will have the E3's radar picture on their display screens as Link 16 broadcasts the picture down from Magic 41. Even though they are still on the ground, this allows them to build up their situational awareness while thinking about how they are going to set their formation up, and what they are going to do. It is a very busy time as everybody jockeys for position at the pre-planned start positions.

At this time in a battle there is lot of co-ordination between the AWACS crew to make sure they don't miss anything and achieve the best possible information flow to ground agencies and aircraft. Leffler:

'In a war, with this number of aircraft in the sky, we would be up against a very large air force indeed. There's a lot of information to absorb, and the software needs to decode what sort of airframes they are, to identify the type of package – fighters escorting bombers, bombers, or both together.

'Looks like everybody is building up to the east, before starting their battle plan. It's a huge jigsaw puzzle which we have to put together before passing the information back.'

Leffler's controller sits to his left, furiously spinning the cursor wheel under his screen, punching display control unit buttons, trying to work out what is going on. The aggression and sheer mental effort going into this work is obvious. To Leffler's right, activity at the top-secret ESM desk is more considered; because

In the E3 Sentry aircraft Squadron Leader Geoff Cooper of the AWACS surveillance team monitors the enemy leaving Cold Lake Air Force Base.

Blue Air are not deploying a full-scale ECM threat there is much less on that screen.

Although it looks like an arcade video game, each dot on the screen is a lethal aluminium tube flying at over 600 knots across Canada. Blue F–15s to the north are sweeping a path for the main bombing package coming through, which is now being intercepted by some F–16s and F–18s. The main bomber package is now out further to the east, and the F3s will shortly be joining the fray.

The enemy are clearly identified with distinctive little red hats over their traces. Leffler is allocating fighters to the threat as he sees where the Blue Air enemy fighters are, and where the threat is coming from:

'Can we try and get that group if possible? I think there might be Blue Air F–4F's somewhere in there. It's a very confused situation, with a mixed–up picture, so it's hard to identify friendlies from enemy. With the Link-16-equipped aircraft, we have a great advantage as they self-identify on the screen.'

Meanwhile, outside the AWACS, the F3s on CAP are waiting for the order to commit. 29 (F) Squadron's Flight Lieutenant Mike Jones:

'From the push, we get set up in racetracks. The initial picture from AWACS shows where the enemy groups are coming from. The guys running the battle in the AWACS will determine where the heavy groups are coming from, and will decide when to send our various groupings in against them – perhaps leaving some guys hanging slack as goal-keepers. The CAP lead or element lead calls the commit. Or if AWACS can see it, he might commit you off even though there's nothing on your radar, knowing that when you arrive you'll fit into the picture. We commit on a particular group, leaving our pre-planned race track to go and prosecute an attack.'

Back in the AWACS, Leffler watches the traces of some fifty aeroplanes wheeling and streaming round the sky:

'It's very difficult to fight the war from this stage onwards. It's very much a question of picking out as much information as possible for the fighters, and passing it on. They're on their own, as we have very little idea of who is who. It's very generically based. All we can say is that there are bandits in certain positions, but we don't know if there are friendlies in there too, so the fighters can only approach with caution and shoot on a visual sighting. Beyond-visual shooting at this stage in the war is just not a play – there'd be too much blue on blue.

'We're communicating with the fighters down the link, not by voice. Sending them a picture cuts down the chatter on the radio, and also saves them losing so much brain power through having to listen. We use the best combination of link and voice, keeping it to the minimum, highlighting things they might have missed, trying to give them the best picture we can. There's a lot of flight safety at stake and the guys have got to keep themselves as safe as possible.

'They can only see so many tracks on their screens. Their system is track limited, and only sees their bit of the war – which makes it harder for them. However, now, with Link 16 working, they've never before flown with so much information available to them, so there is also the danger of data overload.'

Intercept controller, calling for attention from his console:

'I've been tracking with One and Two for ages, and I'm not sure they're engaged with anyone.'

Wilkie: 'It might be confusing him a bit.'

'I think that's a bad track.'

The intercept controller hits a button:

'Yeah, that just got rid of it.'

'He's probably been going round in circles trying to shake it off.'

The false radar trace would have appeared behind the F3s:

'He thinks there's one in his six.'

'Just check it's extrapolated ...'

'It is.'

'Just extrapolate it to check ... No, you've got the CAP.'

'All flow east of Mercury is still here.'

The fighter allocator allocates fighters and targets to his controllers, ensuring they have the right radio frequencies over which to work. The AWACS controllers give the fighters basic guidance from which they use their own on-board radars to pick up and confirm the target, then go after it and make a kill. If the fighters' radars are not working, the controllers provide enough information for them to get in close enough to achieve some form of visual identification, then go in for their own visual kill.

Fighter controllers are trained at RAF Boulmer in the north-east of England, where they go through a very vigorous training process – which has a very high failure rate. They then work on ground radar units, training with fighter squadrons doing intercepts. So when they come to AWACS they are very experienced, which is vital as they are required to work with any air force, anywhere in the world.

Fighter controllers have the basic problem of looking at a two-dimensional television screen and interpreting it in three dimensions. The volume of airspace is huge, and a controller is working with very fast-moving objects, using his voice to transmit his thoughts about how to get an aircraft into a position to intercept a plane approaching at closing speeds of over 1000 miles per hour. To experienced controllers, the problem becomes what they call 'transparent' .

They learn how to assess the heights and speeds of several aircraft, interpret the information and then put in a fighter to make the kill. The radar in a standard fighter can see only forty or sixty degrees on either side of the nose. Apart from that, the pilot has to rely on his own eagle eyes, which are very restricted in range. The controller becomes an extra crewman in the fighter's cockpit, with a 360 degree view over a wide area. A controller can see over 200 miles, and usually well over 100 miles from the fighter's position. He can provide its crew with the sense of well-being that comes from an accurate verbal picture or, with Link 16, he can send a picture to its cockpit screen showing where the war is developing, backed up by an interpreted mental picture related to the radar screen. Controllers also show how the enemy is reacting to what the fighters are doing. It is a very dynamic and continually changing situation for both controllers and fighters. Leffler:

'The controllers are talking on several different radios to different aircraft, their brains taking in multiple audio inputs as well as the visual. Sorting that information out is a really draining process.

'A long mission taking on a lot of fighters is physically tiring. You can sit in a seat for five or six hours, and although you haven't actually moved more than a few fingers on the keyboards, or feet to control the transmitters, you come away feeling physically tired. The mental processes are hard; assimilating screen information, converting it into the real airspace picture, then achieving with your fighters exactly what you want them to do.

'Less experienced controllers move their heads, trying to think "Are they moving left or right, do I need to go faster or slower to intercept?". As a controller gets more experienced, it becomes a more transparent process, and your brain is working overtime. Out in Bosnia, for example, you are responsible for over thirty aircraft – for the lives of each individual person involved. In training, you are also responsible for making sure each aircraft is flying within the safety requirements, as well as achieving their tasking. Concentration is running at a very, very high rate – like being in a hard exam all the time.

'Controllers are each different in how they do what is a very cerebral job. You have to be able to visualize how it is for the crew, particularly when things aren't going so well for the pilot, for example when they can't see the enemy aircraft – which in a whole lot of sky, is very small indeed. When trying to visually acquire, they often need help. We interpret what we see on the screens, and translate it into what they need, telling them what they should be looking for. When controlling several aircraft, you have to flick between three or four different cockpits within a split second telling them to look left, right, up or down – doing it from their point of view. Your mind has to continually flick between the different needs of your various aircraft. You might have some aircraft holding back on a CAP, assessing the situation, waiting for targets to come into their area, while others are engaged in a fight. You have multiple inputs, plus multiple thought processes in which you mentally discuss each aircraft – knowing which they are on the screen, and what they need.

'It's also very exciting – particularly when you are busy. Adrenalin levels run very high, even on an exercise, because you are so involved. You lose all track of time, sitting inside the cockpit of every aircraft you are controlling. You can easily lose two or three hours.

'It's a self-induced virtual reality, but with real people and aeroplanes – so you have to be one hundred per cent right all the time. In a busy fight, you have to make sure those guys stay safe. There's no putting a coin in the slot and starting again. There's a dislocation in that we can't actually do anything …'

As the fighter allocator, Leffler listens to what the controllers are doing and gives them everything they need. If the weather is changing he ensures that they advise the aircraft of this. AWACS also passes information on to ground units like anti-aircraft positions and headquarters. In Bosnia they also talk to a wide range of other agencies, for example, ships in the Adriatic. The information goes out to all the battle managers who need it.

Today's mission has now come to its final stage, the recovery back to Cold Lake – and is now in the hands of Cold Lake air traffic control. Leffler:

'In the fight, some people will have mismanaged their fuel so I hope there won't be too many emergencies. It's a real problem. We've just got rid of all our fighter assets and are heading for home. Unfortunately, because we tanked halfway through the day we had to guesstimate the fuel requirement, so we've got too much fuel on board. We need to burn some off so we can land at a weight that won't damage the aircraft. The flight deck are just calculating that now, then it's de-brief time, and home for tea and medals …'

At the AWACS de-briefing the question of hard walls and blue on blue came up yet again. Leffler:

'It was an absolute classic case, of the F3s wanting to cross the hard wall to chase some bandits. We refused, and they kept coming back asking. In the end the people they were targeting turned out to be a MiG formation – so it would have been blue on blue.'

Hard walls are vital for what is called 'zone co-ordination' to reduce fratricide – known as 'blue on blue' because the positions of friendly troops are marked in blue on a map. In this incident someone who was well out of the fight, and who had swept to the east when everything else was to the west, picked up a contact on his radar and wanted to attack it. Realizing he was close to the hard wall, he asked the AWACS for permission to cross. This was refused despite his asking several times. Leffler:

'If he had gone across and shot, he would have been even more embarrassed and probably several crates of beer poorer. You can't have hard walls with semi-soft centres. It's either hard or it isn't. Let's hope they take it to their de-brief and learn from it.'

Final word from the back of the room:

'Well I thought the fighter controllers were excellent.'

Laughter and:

'Well that's another slapping he's going to get tonight!'

CHAPTER ELEVEN

Beavis and the Red Baron

It is Thursday, 4 May 1995, and the morning is grey with wind-driven snow – icy, unpleasant weather, too bad for low-level flying so the morning war is cancelled. Instead, 29 (F) Squadron decide to do battle with the Luftwaffe in an informal encounter in the clear air above the snow clouds with the Phantom F–4F's of Jagdgeschwader 71 – the famous 'Richthofen Wing'.

29 (F) Squadron and Jagdgeschwader 71 are old friends, with a former member of 29 (F) Squadron (Flight Lieutenant Adrian 'Aids' Rycroft) piloting one of the German Phantoms on a three-year exchange tour. The two squadrons have had much in common since the start of 29 (F) Squadron's history in the First World War, when their DH2s would have come up against the German Flying Corp's ace fighter pilot: the famous Red Baron, Manfred von Richthofen who, between 1916 and his death in 1918, shot down eighty British and allied aircraft. The two units both have the sort of élite pedigree that in the rarefied world of fighter aircrew engenders strong mutual respect – and friendship.

29 (F) Squadron has its own aces. Its first operation in the the First World War – the destruction of several Fokker E–111's – was initiated by the then Lieutenant H. O. D. Seagrove, who was to go on to hold both land and water speed records, and be knighted. Others are Royal Flying Corps ace the former Flight Sergeant J. T. B. McCudden (fifty-seven kills, the Croix de Guerre, Victoria Cross, Distinguished Service Order, Military Cross and Military Medal); then in 1940 Flight Lieutenant Guy Gibson (later to lead the 'dambuster' raid and win the VC) and Wing Commander Wight-Boycott (who shot down four enemy aircraft on his last mission as commanding officer).

After the disbandment of the Luftwaffe in 1945, Jagdgeschwader 71 reformed in 1958 with Second World War ace Major 'Bubi' Hartmann (352 kills) in command. As a day fighter wing, it flew F–86s as part of NATO's central region air defence. On 21 April 1961, the German president officially named the wing after Manfred Baron von Richthofen, 'in honour of his military achievements and chivalrous attitude, as well as his extraordinary talent as a fighter pilot and his overall human qualities in times of tension'.

It converted to the F–104 Starfighter in 1963, before taking over the Phantom F–4F. The squadron flies air-to-air fighters and their two-seater Phantoms – old aeroplanes fitted with very new radar and weapons, and AMRAAM – have more in common with the Tornados than with any other Maple Flag contingent. Captain 'Tarzan' Tantarn:

'It may be thirty years old, but I love the Phantom. You can't turn as tight as F–16s or F–18s – and you don't want to get close to those guys as they'll turn inside you. The airplane's simply too old, and you can't keep up with them. But it's made of steel with not too many computers, so I trust it very much. It's reliable and fairly powerful and fast – faster than a lot of other airplanes round here.'

All fast-jet aircrew share Captain Tantarn's feelings for the Phantom, to the extent that, in 29 (F) Squadron, harking back to the days when it flew them, is a 'beano' – forbidden on pain of immediate fine. Squadron Leader Ian Gale remembers that it was a difficult aircraft to fly well and, because it was so demanding, very satisfying when he got it right:

'It has vices – not very stable, especially at high angles of attack, when it can easily bite back and go into a spin, so there were many cautionary words of advice during OCU.

'I don't know anybody who did manage to spin a Phantom, but quite a few, me included, got very close to it.'

At the time it was one of the best fighters. The F–15 was in its infancy so, with Phantom, the RAF was the only air force in Europe with an all-weather, air-to-air capability. And because it was equipped with Sparrows and then Skyflash, a beyond visual range, radar-guided missile, it had the advantage over more manoeuvrable aircraft like the F–16, which only had Sidewinders.

Like all Phantom pilots Gale is a tremendous enthusiast:

'When the decision was made to put Rolls-Royce engines into the Phantom, they spoiled it. It had more power, but also more drag. The engines were slightly more efficient at low level, which is probably why they made the change, but in terms of performance and engine reliability, the (purely American) F–4J was far superior – quicker and more fuel efficient at height, and it actually flew better.'

Flight Lieutenant Tim Taylor is in charge of the morning's mission, and gives as its uncompromising aim that the six Tornados will 'beat up on the four Richtohofen Wing F–4s'. The advantage of JTIDS will have to be exploited to the full, as Jagdgeschwader 71's Phantoms, far from being an interestingly old aircraft, have been completely re-vamped with all the latest technology – not the least of which is the lethal, 'fire and forget', American-made AMRAAM missile.

Captain Martin Pinneman believes that the up-grade of the F–4 changed things radically:

'Before, we had a bad radar and weapons, and were only useful as a good-weather interceptor. Now we have become an all-weather interceptor; we can see more, shoot further out, and on this exercise we are performing well against third generation aircraft like F–15s and F–16s and doing well – in thirty-year-old aircraft. We have become equal – which is a big improvement!'

The specific model of AMRAAM being used on Maple Flag is called AIM (Air Intercept Missile) 120. Flight Lieutenant Paddy Dickson:

'The American AIM 120 is superior to our primary weapon, so we will have a hard time getting in to kill them. If you have a longer reach, you're a better boxer than someone with short arms. We have to get in close and give him a good punch in the kidneys …'

Flight Lieutenant Justin Reuter is impressed:

'That's a great analogy. I must give you a round of applause.' Claps.

'Thanks for that … after all, we are all god-like …'

'Or horse-meat.'

'Quite.'

A big problem for 29 (F) Squadron is that most of the people they are up against on Maple Flag have AMRAAM, which is superior to their Skyflash. They did a lot of training against the American F–15s from Lakenheath who have it, devising tactics and ways of using JTIDS to defeat it. AMRAAM is active, its on-board radar taking over some time after launch to guide it into the target. The launching aircraft can then go away or attack further targets, whereas the Tornados have to follow their missile in and continue to steer it with their radar. AMRAAM can also be fired over far longer distances, allowing the firer to escape before the Tornados get close enough to use Skyflash.

Overleaf: The Luftwaffe's Phantom F–4s line up at Cold Lake Air Force Base; although the Phantom is thirty years old, and difficult to fly well, it is much loved by pilots and navigators.

Against such odds, the Tornados' only hope is to disorientate their enemy, to mess up his situational awareness using confusion tactics. They have also devised evasion tactics to make it hard for AMRAAM shooters like the Luftwaffe Phantoms to lock on and achieve a good shot. Most fighter radars calculate velocity by utilizing the Doppler effect, making calculations based upon a head-on approach using closing velocities. A standard evasion manoeuvre is 'going on to the beam', suddenly turning 90 degrees to the oncoming enemy to confuse his radar, while making massive height changes to take away his SA. Flight Lieutenant Mark Gorringe:

'If that doesn't work and we're still being looked at and targeted, which we can tell from the instruments in our aircraft, we just put him "track 6" – behind us in our six o'clock – and run away at the speed of heat. We run as fast as possible, to go faster than he's chasing us, which gives us more range so that when we do turn back to try to kill him again, we've got more time. You can waste up to five miles depending upon speed, by coming around the corner to face up again. So if you're starting off with not many miles behind, you'll have even less time to turn and face up again ... There's usually six of us out there so as three groups of two we can give him a problem of rapidly changing height, azimuth and depth, and see how he sorts it out.'

Dickson: 'The plan is to use all our advantages – JTIDS and having two people on board. The only way to do it, in my book anyway, is to screw over the guy's brain. His radar will see you, and his missile will certainly kill you over longer ranges than we can kill him. Therefore you've got to screw his brain so he's looking into the wrong bit of airspace with his radar; or doesn't get the chance to get his weapon away in time ...'

Reuter: 'Or if he does, you do tactics such that you defeat his weapon before it gets to you.'

Dickson: 'So we do a set-piece manoeuvre as a formation to survive their initial onslaught of missiles, and then be in the right place to do our job – which is to kill them. It's bugger-all use all surviving and coming back without having shot anybody down. So we've got to live through the initial manoeuvre, then go on to screw up his SA to such an extent that we can get in there untargeted. Once we get somebody in, we're very good at hosing them down.'

Phantoms are well known to be less than environmentally friendly aircraft, which will be to 29 (F) Squadron's advantage in the forthcoming mission. Taylor:

'They're dirty smokers, so we shouldn't have problems seeing them. Our aim is to kill as many F–4s as possible, while avoiding AMRAAMs. As soon as you hear the commit, open your throttles and leave JTIDS running. They need to spike you to shoot. Remember, if they see you at fifteen miles, you're dead. Change your height when you re-commit – make them work hard with their radars. If you are low on energy, it's better to stay with the F–4 than to run and try to out-run his AMRAAM – 'cos you won't … Let's go!'

The aircrew walk, make their take-off time and punch up through the cloud into a beautiful, clear day. All six Tornados are OK, and JTIDS operates correctly – except in the case of Dickson who has its picture, but for some reason is not able to transmit his own picture or position data.

After take-off the F3s form into their tactical formation – a pair, followed by another with ten miles in between; then another pair, ten miles further back with height differences. Ten miles is nothing in the air defence world.

The enemy is already having to work hard on his radar. He can see defence in depth, and at different heights. Fighters can also see height on their radars, whereas surveillance radars like AWACS can only say high, low or medium, but are unable to give height.

On that initial presentation there is about sixty miles between the first pair and the targets coming in. The call 'commit' is made (as the executive command for the formation to go in and kill the bandits, and also to let everybody including the AWACS know what is happening). The formation then splits. The first pair turn 30 degrees in one direction and the second pair turns 30 degrees the other way, so that there is 60 degrees between them – flying as a 'Y' formation. The third pair stay down the middle transmitting their JTIDS picture to the others so that whenever they do their defensive manoeuvre they will retain situational awareness despite radical manoeuvring.

As they scream in towards the enemy formation, coming from long range into medium range, the Tornado crews are trying to build up their SA. Amid the mind-numbing distractions of electronic counter measures they must know exactly where the bandits are and they hunch over radar screens working down all the data to the point where they can decide exactly who they will kill. Realistically, in this scenario, the enemy will attempt to target the first two pairs but, in buttock-clenching seconds of fear and data overload, the third group will not be a factor. If they have the time, they will just watch them – while the third F3 pair watches back.

As they burn down towards the twenty-mile mark – into short range – the Tornados will be trying to survive against the AMRAAM. To do this they make a big height change, and go on the beam – turning away. This is always done pre-emptively, regardless of whether or not a missile has been launched. The closer the F3s get to the Phantoms' AMRAAMs, the less distance they have in which to run away once the missiles are fired. Reuter:

'Because of the speed at which their missile travels it will get here before anything we fire at them. If you push on inside what we call the bubble – which is the distance we like to keep clear defensively – without having done anything to confuse them, you're effectively dead as soon as they see you. And there's nothing you can do about it. We call it the "no-escape shot".'

The size of the bubble depends upon the type of missile, the heights and altitudes of the opposing aircraft, their speeds and the aspect. Dickson:

'If you're head to head, his missile's got a longer reach; or if he's higher than you, chasing you down, it's going to overtake you; whereas if you are running away it's got a shorter range. We keep the size of the bubble in our heads at all times – as we both die if we screw it up …'

As the F–4s approach detailed assessment is difficult. Ian Gale is spotted and spiked and executes a very big, fast turn to the left. The jamming continues. Gale descends fast to between 6000 and 7000 feet, runs away and 'beams' – does a full 150 degree turn away, then another 90 degree turn, to stop the closure function of the enemy's Doppler radar. All defensive manoeuvres include drastic height changes of more than 15 000 feet. It is more usual to beam first, then pump – run away, but Gale decided that his initial left turn threw off the spike.

Squadron boss Wing Commander Martin Routledge detects a hostile emission on his RHWR and is spiked, so Flight Lieutenant Ian Laing, his pilot, turns hard left while Routledge starts narrowing down his radar scan to find whoever is targeting them. It becomes clear that there are a lot of enemy out in front so he opens his scan back up to wide again to ensure he isn't missing anything.

The enemy are in two groups, north and south. The southern group are at 30 000 feet, and are spiked at twenty miles by Taylor's four-ship which rides in down the track before turning. Their situational awareness is generally good, greatly helped by the quality of the JTIDS picture. Gale sees the contrails of the northern Phantoms – at two different height levels.

Taylor and Flight Lieutenant Paul Vicary, his navigator, are running back west (having turned away after the initial commit) with two enemy on their tail at between fifteen and twenty miles. Routledge and Laing are turning east to cover the withdrawal. Vicary calls for help as the bandits are too close to him. Gale and Dickson are running fast: 700 knots at around 7000 feet (the lowest they are allowed to fly today). The boss has no range information for anybody and he is running hard. He describes himself later as feeling like a sacrificial lamb:

'… and I was clearly the right person to be just that!'

Taylor and Vicary are now on the north-south 'beano' line. They pick up a spike, then a contact at eighteen miles. Taylor:

'So we were out of there rapidly – and possibly too late …'

They are in fact OK. Flight Lieutenant Boyes and Gorringe are also spiked and run north-west, initially on the beam. Gale is spiked intermittently, pitches left and right, then goes vertical. In the back seat, Dickson picks up a contact – the F–4s – and they decide to go for it.

At twenty miles Taylor's element goes defensive, hits the 7000 foot base-height and runs away. They re-commit a bit too early, turn back in without having gained enough separation – and get shot in the face.

Gale and Dickson are now targeted by a four-ship of F–4s that is ahead of them in two pairs. At twenty-two miles they go into their abort, and head due north at the same height: 23 000 feet. Flight Lieutenant Gary 'Gazza' Coleman, their wingman, does a really heavy dive at around 10 000 feet per minute to 8000 feet, then heads in the same direction aiming to distract the enemy's radar search pattern. The two aircraft are communicating by radio but, because both are expecting this manoeuvre, they do not actually need to talk. In Dickson's words:

'I still felt threatened, then we were spiked, so we turned away and put the enemy in our six o'clock and started a slow descent running north-west at supersonic, building up speed. We didn't want to descend too fast because that might drag his radar down to see our buddy. At about Mach 1.4 we're running away until we think we've got our separation.

'We can both see the bandits on JTIDS, and they start leaning north. We thought Gazza was targeted, and Gazza decides to come in behind them so he can't be targeted. We turned the other way, co-ordinated as a pair. He merged with them first and shot both, one with a radar missile at longer range, and the other with a Sidewinder. Once they started fighting, we did exactly the same: used two Fox Twos – Sidewinders. The best thing was that we got in completely unseen. They did not know we were joining that fight at all – and that's the best way to kill …'

Ian Gale shot two F–4s.

The morning mission has been a mixed success, with some of 29 (F) Squadron's anti-AMRAAM tactics appearing to work and predictable success on the part of the Germans, who combined suitable tactics with their superior weapon.

Gorringe and Boyes had had problems landing at the end of the sortie. At ground level the weather was appalling, visibility at Cold Lake verging on being too bad to even bother. The squadron's landing-slot times were scheduled for forty minutes after the fight was due to start. Gorringe:

'It was all-up combat, and you use a hell of a lot of fuel the minute you start cracking the burners in. The fight finished at quarter past nine, leaving us twenty-five minutes to stay airborne before our slot time to get back in here. We were not going to do it – our fuel was about ten minutes short. There were two of us, with the two others behind as singletons.'

Landing as a pair – side by side, as one aircraft – gets planes down quicker, in half the time. Air traffic control rules also require five minutes between the landing aircraft which necessitates even more time in the air. Gorringe and Boyes would get only one chance to land, then split and try for Edmonton where the weather was completely open.

Laing was leading. In the second aircraft, pilot Boyes was trying to fly in formation ('formate') with him, flying as close as possible – around 10 or 12 feet away. Gorringe:

'You fly as close as you dare. The thicker the cloud the closer you fly, to avoid losing sight of the other aircraft. If you do lose sight, then you both break outwards to prevent collision, and are on your own. It was fairly thick cloud, so we were pretty tight.

'Being wingman, Boysie is not looking out of the front at all, and can't see his head-up display. He's looking sideways, formating on the leader, trusting him completely to fly very smoothly, and not to fly us into the ground, or to do anything stupid.

'We had a PAR – precision approach radar – landing, so the air traffic control guy was saying "Left two degrees, right two degrees, a little bit more uppy-downy, etc." … and we're just flying, looking at Langers, trusting him to take us down. It's a very big trust thing. The weather was crap, and we knew it was crap, starting to verge on being a bit hairy.'

No one likes flying in cloud. When using an instrument landing system, pilots expect to come in down the centre of the runway – maybe shifting a little sideways because of wind. The system should take the aircraft right down to 200 feet, but with a mile to go they need actually to see the runway. When the cloud level is very low pilots know that if it is not visible when they start looking for it at that height they must over-shoot to get away from the ground. Gorringe:

'Visibility was down to about half a mile – pretty crap. So out of nothingness, as it were, Laingers saw the running rabbit lights, then the runway a few seconds later. I saw it as we were going over the threshold – which was pretty hairy.'

Back at 29 (F) Squadron Ops, the video de-brief confirms Ian Gale's two kills; and that he had got in unseen and not been killed himself. In the de-brief, Taylor summed up:

'Everyone was very aggressive, using the US-issue anti-AMRAAM tactics range information. From the video de-brief, I don't think anybody was killed.

'We can sharpen up on the bubbles. Some of us went cold too early. So as long as we've got SA from JTIDS, keep pressing on and work on the bubble.'

Vicary comments that, 'Aggressive height changes really do work.'

Taylor: 'Anybody get down to two thousand feet above ground level?'

Routledge: 'I wanted to!'

The boss suggests that they need to develop a standard operating procedure for singletons rejoining the formation so that radar coverage is co-ordinated.

Rank has no part in the discussion that follows. Gary Coleman – as the most junior present – suggests that the lowest call sign should take the lead. The boss wants to avoid radio transmissions and suggests they should work from the left-hand side inwards, one aircraft taking left, the other right. Vicary, however, does not like the boss's idea; he prefers the number method where the leader looks high, number two low, three looks high … and so on. The boss responds that they need to cover the whole sky as a group – rather than each aircraft covering most or all of it.

He does not mind that his idea was rejected:

'I felt that this was something we needed to think about, and still do. It's fine if they don't agree with me – the important thing is to have thought about it. Subsequently they came round to my way of thinking having tried and failed to make their idea work in a particularly busy environment.'

As far as the RAF is concerned, de-briefing is almost as important as the mission itself – and more important once the mission is over. How people approach de-briefing says a lot about how they think when flying. As package lead, Taylor chairs the de-briefs of his missions:

'Some people are better at recalling missions than others – and some can't remember at all. People remember the bits they need to remember. If you asked them exactly where they went, they might not be too sure, but they could tell you the order they did things in; that they went up, turned left, then ran away fast – but they couldn't draw it on a map, the places would probably be way out.

'What's gone, is gone. People don't dwell on the past, but think ahead, and the further they look ahead the less of a surprise it becomes. There are people who lurch from event to event and are always reactive, which you can see in the way they de-brief. Other people will look ahead, see what's coming, and try to use it to their advantage – or try to minimize its effect.

'The people with the best reputations are those who look ahead the furthest: "I saw a cloud ahead and made a small turn and went past it." Others say "Jesus, there I was in this huge cloud, and it was a nightmare …" Clouds just don't get you! Good pilots look ahead, in terms of both time and distance.'

29 (F) Squadron de-briefs are very straight up and down, with no reference to rank and can be brutal. Taylor:

'If I let someone off lightly, it won't stick in their mind, so they'll do it again. I can't afford for people to repeat mistakes. We fly so little, and have so little time to de-brief that it's better to deliver a short, sharp shock, and "Sort it out tomorrow – and this is what you will do …" Everybody expects it, will behave better for it, and will pass on their information that way.

'If you're all soft with each other, you turn into a soft outfit … it's a big soft world and we won't do anything nasty and hard to each other. There's only one result – that professionally, you all go down the tubes.'

However, on Maple Flag and Red Flag de-briefs everything seems to acquire a favourable gloss; everybody appears to have done well. Flight Lieutenant Mike Jones:

'The Americans are always saying "Good job", which from watching some of their game shows over the weekend, I've decided must be a national disease! I think it's to do with their culture – whereas we like to moan too much!

'We should be drawing all the points together from the floor – the guy up the front putting the hammer on it. We don't want to go out tomorrow and make the same mistakes. It's not necessary to jump up and down on people's cases, but we need to know why people went wrong. Was their SA low, radar not pointing in the right place, or did they just fuck up; do they say, "Yes, we had the relevant information, but made the wrong decision"? It's no good going out saying, "Good job, good job" but having your wingman shot down every day.'

Taylor is clearly intent on getting the maximum out of the morning's sortie. The bosses' job, however, is to keep a balance between personalities and to ensure that de-briefing remains constructive and positive. If a subject is not worth getting worked up about, then it's not worth doing – but the occasional touch of moderation does nobody any harm. Routledge:

'Timmy was haranguing people quite a bit in the de-brief, some of which was due to his personally having had a bad sortie. We had a chat with him about it afterwards ... calmed him down a little.'

This was a very valuable mission, planned, led and de-briefed almost entirely by Taylor. The squadron's relationship with the Germans is excellent, both on the ground and in the air so it was decided that a little very careful, cross-cultural, fighter information exchange should take place with regard to the AMRAAM missile. The Americans sell only an 'export' version, and refuse to release firing test data, so its performance cannot be evaluated – even by purchasers. However, in spite of not having this critical information, the RAF have been able to use general principles to develop useful anti-AMRAAM tactics – tactics that it is vitally important for friendly users of the missile to have, as they could otherwise become over-dependent upon the weapon system's supposed superiority. So 29 (F) Squadron would like to know more about AMRAAM; equally, Jagdgeschwader 71 would like to know more about the tactics others employ to defeat their weapon system.

Flight Lieutenant Adrian Rycroft is doing the interestingly named 'Phantom exchange' with the Luftwaffe and explains that the German air force is looked at very differently in Germany, to the way people regard the RAF in Britain:

'The guys go home at night, take off their uniforms and are civilians. At work they are the same as us. The big difference – and I was quite amazed at it – is the way they relate to the rest of German society.'

Unlike in the RAF, whose aircrew live as part of their squadron and move every three years, German units are not transferred; instead people stay for twenty or thirty years in the same place, in their own houses, often miles away from the air station, and are part of their village and the civilian community.

'The squadron has a much stronger sense of identity and spirit than an RAF squadron. These guys join the Richthofen Wing as young men, and they're there for ever. If they're posted to other jobs, they come back, and might eventually command it. They know their history, only – understandably – they don't talk about it.

'It is forbidden to sing any of the old Richthofen squadron songs in public, or mention the role it played in the Second World War. Officially its history starts when the squadron was re-formed as a NATO unit. There is a small museum at Wittmund, with a couple of Richthofen's bi-planes but, for example, we wear the NATO cross as our emblem, rather than the old 'R'. The history is there, but hidden away. Any mention of the squadron's war roles is forbidden. In our hall of fame the picture of Goering, who was our second commander of the wing, has been removed.'

Rycroft realizes that as far as 29 (F) Squadron are concerned, he is a marked man. He met his fate bravely at the British national night:

'When the Tornado came in, there was great rivalry between RAF Phantom and Tornado units. 29 Squadron realized that I'd gone from Tornados – with them – back to Phantoms with the Richthofen Squadron, which presents them with a great challenge. As soon as they knew that I would be coming out on this exercise, my card was marked, and at the first opportunity I was pinned to the floor and my moustache was shaved off. I'll get my own back eventually!'

He describes how, with the collapse of the Berlin Wall, the reunification of Germany and the change in German law that allows troop deployments outside NATO, the Richthofen Squadron has suddenly found its role changing from home defence with old aeroplanes to a world-wide role with a revamped Phantom and brand-new missile system:

'It's a quantum leap for them, and this exercise is the first occasion for them to practise with the new missiles and radar.

'The Germans do however have a very big problem – the age of the Phantom. Although it has had an upgrade there are things missing. The radar warning receiver has problems. Our SA isn't very good and we can't turn very well, so we need tactics to minimize the effect of all this – to kill people at a distance. In dog-fights it can't compete with the modern F–15s, F–16s and F–18s. AMRAAM is however a very long range missile, which helps equalize the problem. If you can kill before being seen, you stand a good chance. Also, although the Phantom's not a dogfighter, having two people on board, like the Tornado, you can keep your situational awareness a lot longer than a single-seat pilot can.'

When Rycroft first arrived, the Richthofen Squadron wanted as much help and advice from him as possible on how to use their new equipment.

'The exchange system is intended for such mutual passage of information. As the RAF have more experience in certain areas, you explain how it would go about things – politely and if they want it. There would be nothing worse than saying "No, try doing this" and them saying "Get back in your box Brit". In fact they were very keen to pick my brains and learn how the RAF do things – and equally the RAF are keen to know from me how the Luftwaffe are reacting to their new role. I'm not sure how the Germans will feel once they've been involved in a few "real war" operations – they cost an awful lot of money, and although it's easy to get into conflicts the hard bit is getting out again once you've done your bit. They're keen now to provide people and resources rather than standing in the background as in the past, forking out vast amounts of money – like they did in the Gulf War.'

Maple Flag is the Germans' first deployment using AMRAAM, their first chance to use the missile in a beyond visual range environment. Their job, along with the American F–15s, is to protect Blue Air bomber packages as they go *en route* to targets, fighting against the Tornados from 29 (F) Squadron, the US Aggressor F–16s and the Canandian CF–18s. Red Air is a very high-tech, high threat adversary, but the Germans have the F–15s on their side which tends to equal it out.

Because of the age of some of the Richthofen squadron's equipment, trying to work out who is friendly and who is not is always the big problem. Rycroft:

'With AMRAAM, we like to be out in front of everyone else. That way we know everybody in front of us is hostile, and we can fire at long range not allowing the enemy to get mixed in with the friendlies. Once they do get mixed in, we have to get in close to identify people visually, using heat-seeking missiles and guns to make kills. That's not actually very good, as the Phantom doesn't turn very well. The last thing that we want to do is merge and get into a dogfight.'

There are few aeroplanes a Phantom can actually beat in a dogfight – even an F3, particularly without wing tanks, can out-turn it. So after firing AMRAAM at maximum range, the F–4s move out left and right, still painting the targets with their radar so that the missile knows where they are. As soon as the missiles impact the targets the Phantoms drop down as low as they can and run away. They then listen to the ground controlled intercept (GCI) radar for other targets. When they decide they are far enough away, they turn back and take more long range missile shots.

When the Phantoms run out of long range missiles, it becomes very dangerous as they will have to end up merging with other aircraft. Their main aim, therefore, is to kill as many people as possible, from as far away as possible, then get to five to ten miles distance and run away to avoid a merge. They try to stay in the area for as long as possible to screen the bombers, but once the bombs have been dropped they leave them to get home by themselves. Without bombs, the bombers become very manoeuvrable, well able to protect themselves. Rycroft:

'As the Tornado is also a seventies aircraft, it's fun to dogfight with each other. You could put a hamburger in an F–18, and because the aircraft has so much more performance advantage, he'll win every time. Skill doesn't come into it. Phantoms versus Tornados is almost a fair fight – decided by skill.'

Flight Lieutenant Adrian Rycroft, RAF pilot, is on a 'Phantom exchange' with the Luftwaffe's Richthofen Wing; he believes that the Phantom's age is a big problem for the Germans.

The aim of the Maple Flag exercises is to determine which tactics work, and people need to argue and discuss things in detail. Rycroft:

'It's no good for somebody to come in and say, "We're wonderful and you're all dead". If it ends up that you get killed every time, you need to go away and work out why. If you can't validate your tactics through frank discussion with everybody else, then it's a waste of time coming all this way and spending all this money to do the exercise. For the Luftwaffe everything is completely new – post-Second World War they've never deployed anywhere, nor have they been allowed to be out in front firing long range missiles. They've always been the poor relations at the back of the fight, tagging along with the Americans. Actually being in charge is a great learning experience.'

One of the results of the reunification of Germany has been that the Luftwaffe have had to cope with the former East German air force. Some of its pilots have trained to fly F–4Fs. Others still fly MiG–29s, and some former West German pilots are also flying MiG–29s. Standardizing both tactics and equipment is a tough challenge. There is also the language barrier: East German pilots used to speak Russian in the air and now have the problem of learning English which is the common language of the flying business. Another problem is that because German squadrons have been based at home since the Second World War, the Luftwaffe is short of transport aircraft for overseas operations and exercises, and has to ask Britain or the United States for help, which in turn stretches these countries' capabilities.

The joint 29 (F) Squadron/Richthofen Squadron de-brief takes place at Royal Canadian Air Force 419 Squadron's ops building – a single-storey prefab beside Maple Flag Ops. The two groups of aircrew, the British in green flying jackets and the Germans in blue-drab leather jackets, are hunched forward because of a bitingly cold wind as they file into the warm corridor. The briefing room is large with a high ceiling and no windows, its walls lined with photographs and presentation plaques from past exercises all over the world. A low stage and podium stand in front of the inevitable white plastic board – a large supply of coloured marker pens ready for use. Both sides run quickly through the mission from their perspective, after which Tim Taylor outlines 29 (F) Squadron tactics, explaining the initial commit and the 'Y'-shaped manoeuvre, and their JTIDS advantage:

'We've got a data-link system working between aircraft, so we can pass radar contacts – you when you're hot, and guys who are cold. Also we can do the same kind of thing with the E3, plus we have E3 control.

'Our plan was to have a CAP somewhere round here – is that bullseye … yeah? Not bad for a pilot, eh? And when we saw you cross the western edge we were going to come all the way through … Your plan?'

The German package commander gets up and takes to the podium:

'Our plan was not that fancy actually. As a four-ship we just pretended to support a package behind us – as escort or something – to come in as a bandit formation very close together. And then upon "push", spread out by azimuth split and altitude split, which would have looked like this: one arm going here, the other arm going here, not giving you a chance to out-pincer us.

'That's the basic plan. Then, of course, trying to push you out beyond the target area, being more aggressive, rather than pumping out. Shoot, crank – turn away – then pushing forward into the area would have been our plan.'

Taylor goes through the mission blow by blow:

'At about thirty miles we start to get spiked, from what we believe is the southern group here. We've got two F3s that swept left – Boysie?'

'Sorry?'

'You swept left?'

'Only slightly – but badly.' Boysie admits that his defensive manoeuvre was not hard enough to have shaken off the spike.

'OK, we both get spiked. We assume you've launched AMRAAM but we don't know. So at about this point we both get on the beam and evade … Your southern group is pressing on at around the high twenties – around twenty-eight thousand feet, just under supersonic. The northern group have edged around … is that what you see?'

Taylor needs some feedback from the Luftwaffe:

'Out of interest, have you, er … shot yet? You see, we don't know that.'

He asks tentatively for a response to what he knows is a sensitive query:

'We know you've got a long range missile and we have to honour the threat.'

The German package leader responds:

'There was one missile, yes …'

Another Luftwaffe voice joins in:

'What range are you talking about now? Twenty … thirty miles?'

Taylor interjects:

'Stop, stop a second – we mustn't get too specific.'

Everybody relaxes. Taylor continues, drawing on the board using thick, coloured marker pens:

'I hope you don't use this information aggressively on Exercise Maple Flag!

Our aim is to kinematically defeat the missile, to drag your radars off and then pump through ... You've spiked out one or maybe two of us in the north, then a second guy – so that was good. We don't like it, but it was good! So it seems that you've done a pretty good job on us!'

Taylor smiles, and there is general laughter.

'These guys split up ... and these two are taking a bigger height split to try and get out of your way. The back guys are carrying on north-west, and this man has gone really low and is untargeted. Then he's definitely spiked, so you're aware of them. Oh dear. This isn't looking good. Any kills up to now or ... ?'

The German package commander prefers not to respond to specific questions:

'Maybe you just finish telling us your picture, then we come and show what we did?'

Taylor: 'OK ... so this guy comes round and takes a Fox One into one of them, which is a kill. This guy comes round and takes two Fox Twos, unseen entry – and we're claiming two kills. Times?'

Coleman: 'I've got the times here: between 0907 and 0908.'

Taylor: 'That's pretty much the end of our fight. The southern group were all dead, and the northern group were all alive, and we've killed two of you. That's how we see it.'

The German package leader stands up:

'Good ...'

Taylor: 'You should say that's a complete wank!'

General laughter.

'No, the picture's almost completely right.'

Gorringe: 'They gave us a good kicking, but they've got the big rocket so it wasn't very pretty. We fly quite a bit with the Germans, but I was surprised at how frank their de-brief was. It was really excellent and both sides benefited. The Americans won't tell you anything about AMRAAM or any of their equipment, whereas other nationalities will often give you a few top tips, even if they won't actually talk turkey and give you the ranges of their missiles. It's a bit sensitive, so I wouldn't like anybody to think that we've been told the ranges –'cos that would never happen.

'The Americans do sell AMRAAM – but the export version hasn't got quite the capability of the one they use themselves. They have equipment on their aircraft that we can only dream about, and they are very loath to tell us exactly what it can do. Although you do talk informally ... They're pretty good boys.'

CHAPTER TWELVE

On the Edge

There is a fine balance between placing yourself in jeopardy to shoot enemy aircraft down, and living to fight another day. Flight Lieutenant Richard 'Ritchie' Bedford:

'If it's a high risk mission – like shooting down an AWACS, which would seriously degrade the enemies' air picture and make it easier for our forces to get through, we might accept a calculated amount of risk, pitching back into a fight when we're not sure whether we're completely safe or not. Or we might run for the AWACS, deciding as a last resort to simply to go for it and see if we can shoot it down.

'Other things might not be quite so high risk – against maybe a fighter sweep, when the last thing we want to do is be shot down before we get at the mud-movers. Using a low risk assessment, we'd use as many defensive aids as possible to avoid them.'

Assessing risk and making judgements depends upon knowing what is happening. Just as aircrew have to battle to retain their situational awareness, they have also to monitor their own perceptions, which in the pressurized environment of the cockpit can alter disconcertingly. Flight Lieutenant Paddy Dickson:

'If you start getting really unhappy, then you've quite quickly got to demand from yourself and from your front-seater what's going on, because it can be very disorientating – even just flying and not even fighting.'

Flight Lieutenant Justin Reuter: 'There are so many illusions you can give yourself, of being in a different attitude, for example ...'

Dickson: 'With the little pendulums in your ear, when the aircraft accelerates heavily you get the feeling that you are going up – "pitch up effect". The natural inclination is to push the stick forward to go back down. But you're not actually going up – and would now be going down. If you do this just after take-off because you are in cloud with no other references and you don't believe your instruments, then you'll go straight back down, and have to cancel your life insurance policy.'

Reuter: 'And the late lunch you ordered.'

Lots of illusions at night are based upon autokinesis: if aircrew look at a light – a star or the light from an oil rig – for long enough, it starts to move. They become convinced that it is another aircraft and split from their formation and from their pair, to try to join on it. 'Break-off phenomenon' is when the flyer finds himself feeling as if he is sitting on the wing or tail of the aircraft, completely separate from the cockpit, looking into it from the outside. There have even been cases of people feeling that they are watching themselves inside, too tense to move the stick, feeling they are balanced on a knife-edge. Reuter:

'It's really horrible – more common with single-seat guys during long transits. If you're with someone you're talking most of the time, and you keep yourself occupied. On a long, boring transit we can have very little to do, so we talk.

'You would not believe just how extreme these illusions can be, and just how disorientated you can get.'

The 'leans' is another illusion: the pilot is convinced that he is in a turn when in fact the aircraft is flying straight and level. The seat of his pants is telling him that he is at an angle, so his natural reaction is to roll the aircraft. He really feels he has to roll it and the only answer is to keep telling himself: 'I am flying straight and level, I am flying straight and level'. Dickson:

'You have to believe your instruments – it's as simple as that. At least you've got to react to them as if they were true.'

Reuter: 'If you're the navigator in the back, busy doing something else when you enter a bank, your body doesn't realize what's happened when the pilot rolls slowly off it. You think you're still in the turn, but you look up and the instruments tell you you're not. You have to ask the pilot where you are. You have to keep on talking, convincing each other where you are.

'The bottom line is that you try to keep a mental picture of where you are and what your attitude is. Everyone has this alarm bell in their head which rings when it's all getting horribly frightening and you suddenly feel "Fucking hell! I am not happy where I am".

'The more you fly in a particular aircraft, the more you get to know which positions you can pull out of and exactly how far you can go before you can't – and that you will hit the ground before pulling out. You get a feel for it …'

Dickson: 'As a navigator, your arse is in the pilot's hands as it were. I trust him, particularly if he is a good pilot, between ninety-five to ninety-nine per cent of the time. If you trust him a hundred per cent you'll never check him, and everybody – but everybody in the world – makes mistakes. If you trust him a hundred per cent and he makes a mistake, you die too – the only consolation is that you die a millisecond later than him. You're not nagging at him, but you've got that five per cent pucker factor, so that if it is all going horribly wrong, and you think that he hasn't got control and you are imminently going to die, you will eject – just go – and he will come out as well.'

The command eject system on the Tornados means that if the pilot pulls the handle in the front, the navigator leaves first. Reuter:

'I think it's an eminently sensible idea. I've got no qualms about that. I'm very happy to leave about a quarter of a second early – excellent system.

'The back-seater's handle has a switch selection for "Both" or "Single", which most pilots ask to be set to Both, so he goes as well. The reason for this is that if it's got so horrible and scary that the back-seater feels he's got to eject, the pilot would probably like to come as well, because it's going to turn rather ugly. You can talk about it under the parachute, or in the bar.'

The ejection drill is simple – either the pilot or the navigator pulls the handle. Both should have both feet on the pedals, the pilot for his rudders, and the navigator because the transmit switches are there. Reuter:

'The handle is between your legs, so you reach down with your right hand, left hand on top covering, arms in, head back, neck back, eyes really tightly closed. You should have your visor down.'

The seat is a Martin Baker Mk 10, and has wide parameters for speed and altitude, limitations which in fact cover most eventualities. It is a very good seat and an awful lot of people have been saved by it at most heights and speeds, including aircraft stationary on the ground. As soon as the handle is pulled, all the locks and hinges disengage instantaneously and the canopy is blown away – powered by two rocket motors in the front. Then .3 of a second after that, which aircrew say equates to about sixty minutes of their lives when they are actually doing it, the navigator's seat goes, with a bang of explosives (that can damage his back) to get him clear of the aircraft, and a rocket pack to get him well clear. The pilot's seat goes .4 of a second later. If the aircraft is below 10 000 feet the seat deploys the small drogue parachute, then, as soon as it stabilizes the main chute is dragged out and the seat automatically disconnects leaving the flyer with a small personal survival pack, which was his seat cushion in the aircraft, strapped to him. This contains essentials like gloves, water and clothes – and a small dinghy that inflates automatically in water. Dickson:

'You can pull the handle and forget about everything, it all happens automatically. You've been in a nasty situation, and you don't really want to think about too much more – and most guys don't … It's a very good system. Guys have complete trust in it.'

The seat may even work in the improbable 'upside down one hundred feet above the ground' scenario although this would depend on the speed at which the aircraft was flying: at 600 knots it would probably get the aircrew out. It uses the airspeed to punch them out, not very far, but quickly deploys a drogue parachute that stabilizes them into a forward rather a downward motion which slows them down, then once the acceleration falls below 4 g it deploys the main parachute. It happens very quickly and the crew hit the ground fast. Reuter:

'The parachute isn't meant to get you on the ground in beautiful condition – you'll break things depending upon how you land. They say it's like jumping off the top deck of a double-decker bus.'

Unlike paratroopers, fighter crew fly in high surface wind speeds that can drag them sideways as they approach the ground and this increases the force of the landing.

Reuter: 'The only unfortunate thing is that quite recently there was an ejection involving a good friend of ours – who used to be on this squadron. There was a very serious emergency and they ejected. The pilot got out OK, but certain things happened and the navigator died. So although we have complete trust in the system, it really hit home; that in what should have been a very routine ejection, he still died.'

This accident is under investigation at time of writing. There is no suggestion that the Martin Baker seat was in any way at fault, or to blame. Although nothing can be said for certain until the RAF Board of Inquiry reports, aircrew are paying detailed attention to their postures, ensuring that they could get into correct ejection position. Reuter:

'You rely on the magic yellow and black striped handle – you just pull it and it's your "get out of jail free card". If you thought about the fact that you could die on each sortie, you'd probably never fly.'

The emergency siren starts trilling on the flight line outside, which usually signals an aircraft crash:

Overleaf: Canadian F–18s break formation as they prepare to land at Cold Lake Air Force Base after a mission; in addition to the stresses involved in air combat, aircrew can also suffer from disorientating illusions.

Dickson: 'Oh excellent, an emergency.'

Reuter: 'Bit of a crowd pleaser ...'

The siren stops – evidently a test.

War and the possibility of being hit by a missile is more remote than the day-to-day likelihood of ejecting. Dickson:

'If a missile hits the aircraft, it's a lottery whether you survive. If it goes off near the cockpit, you're going to die. We've had a fair amount of recent experience of this during the Gulf War. The best way to take out an aircraft is to kill the crew, so many types of missile carry fragmentation warheads designed to go off near the cockpit. Older, heat-seeking missiles go for the warmest part of an aircraft, which is its engines, so they have a good chance of detonating down its back.

'If you are hit, there's going to be a series of catastrophic failures, and you'll know you're going to have to leave very quickly. If not, it will happen so quickly, you'll be dead – so you're not going to worry about it.'

AMRAAM is virtually guaranteed to hit its target – a very real problem for fighter crew keen on staying alive. Reuter:

'You'll usually see missiles coming off – they make an awful lot of smoke, and you have all sorts of other indications that the enemy is on to you. It's difficult to say what you'd do. The pilot would be reacting so hard ... You'd do a last ditch manoeuvre to try and get it to miss you. You might succeed, or it might run out of energy. A manoeuvre might work, so there's no harm in trying. You wouldn't be thinking about ejecting, you'd be trying so hard to avoid the missile.'

The flight time of a missile fired at close range does not give aircrew much time to think, whereas AMRAAM fired at maximum range takes around one minute to hit its target. A Sidewinder is only fired when the target is visible, so although its speed is similar to that of AMRAAM the distances are a lot less, and it will hit much more quickly.

Ground crew are ambivalent about the dangers of their job:

'It's not very often we get missiles on the aircraft – and it's not as dangerous as you'd think. They're all pinned up when the aircraft is on the ground, with a lot of safety features, so walking in front of the plane shouldn't be dangerous. In any case, if you're that close to an aircraft when a missile went off it would take all the oxygen from the air around you and you'd die anyway.'

'I think chaff and flares are actually more dangerous than the guns or missiles themselves.'

A flight line is always dangerous, with or without live ordnance:

'Engine fires are usually exciting – but not too frequent. The jet pipe can catch fire, producing loads of flame out of the back. It's not really a problem as there's meant to be a fire there anyway – and an engine fire doesn't burn as hot as the engine itself. You can blow it out just by starting the engine.'

'Major fuel leaks are dangerous – with power on, the panels off and budoosh!! You turn the power off, then build sand castles in order to stop the fuel going everywhere.'

'When somebody has a problem on landing, they radio through and we send out the recovery team …'

'If there's a chance of the aircraft crashing, we all go outside and watch!'

'While the rest of us run for our cameras!'

'And take bets on whether the navigator beats the pilot in getting out first!'

If there is a state two emergency (the risk of a major failure), the aircraft might have to take the rotary hydraulic arrester gear (RHAG), the arrester cable which runs across the runway and which is always in position. A hook at the rear of the aircraft is dropped and catches on the cable which slows and stops it. The ground crew go out with a tractor and recover the aircraft.

'State one is pretty major – the plane has crashed!'

'We don't panic too much – the bosses do that.'

'Unless we've worked on the aircraft ! That's when you panic!'

Tuesday 9 May 1995

The Phantom is inside a heated hangar being examined by squadron engineers. Being an older aircraft, its front screen is made of flat sections of double-layered Plexiglass half an inch thick, strengthened and held in place by thin magnesium alloy columns. The bird had hit the right-hand, starboard side of the front screen, a glancing blow off one of the angled panels rather than a head-on blow to the flat, front-facing glass panel. The front layer is completely smashed and the second layer cracked with runs of dried blood in the space between. Inside the cockpit, fine, down feathers and small lumps of flesh have penetrated as far as the back seat area where the navigator sits. The bird may not have actually penetrated, but enough of its pulverized body has been hammered through the cracks in the inner screen to require a serious cockpit-cleaning exercise.

The engineering technicians are checking the air intakes and jet engine blades very carefully. Although, judging from the pilot's account of the incident, it is unlikely that any part of the bird has been sucked in, a full boroscope examination is nevertheless mandatory.

Major Roland Molter, navigator and commander of the Luftwaffe's Maple Flag detachment; he has vivid memories of a crash he was involved in five years earlier when he was on an instructor course in the United States.

First Lieutenant Heinrich Lendtvier is the Richthofen Squadron's engineering officer group commander:

'The screen is very strong indeed. You can hit it with a hammer and it will just bounce off, so the blow was very big indeed. We were lucky that it hit just a small panel.

'We'll have to order a new windscreen out of Germany, and fitting it will take time. We'll have to remove all the equipment from the cockpit, remove the windscreen, then fit the new windscreen to the right shape. The F–4 is a little tricky as things are not exactly the same size. We'll have to screw the windscreen in, then seal it – after which the sealant will have to dry. We then re-fit all the equipment and do some tests – and it will be all right. If we get the windscreen over from Germany by Thursday evening, working twelve hours a day, it will be ready on Monday.

Major Roland 'Moltex' Molter, a navigator, is the squadron commander of 1st Fighter Wing and also the detachment commander on Maple Flag. He describes the incident:

'I was number four of a sweep flight task. We re-committed out of our first push, then turned right back into the fight, then it happened.

'It was a bang – not as loud as I thought it might have been, then a lot of surrounding noise because we had a hole in the right-hand windshield and air flow was making this noise. We were at three hundred feet in a right-hand turn, at about 450 knots. After we slowed down to 300 knots, we climbed to four thousand feet and the surrounding noise lessened so we could communicate again pretty good.

'We asked for a chase aircraft to come with us, which arrived four to five minutes later. We had checked the windscreen to see if anything had entered the cabin, and felt that it would probably not collapse inwards – which would have been the worst thing that could have happened. (On further checking on the ground, I'm not so sure!)

'There had been a lot of birds around in the area. It's nothing like Germany or Europe, where you get small birds. They are very heavy around here! We knew immediately what had happened, as when it hit the cockpit filled with tiny feathers which flew around the cockpit – plus little meat balls and blood.

'Immediately the pilot told me that he had control and was OK. We declared a Mayday emergency to get the tower's attention, telling them that the aircraft was flying well so we didn't need any help. They had eighty to ninety aircraft in the sky, so if we had asked for maximum priority we could have got other aircraft into trouble with fuel problems. We were well to the north, a hundred and fifty miles, so as we flew slowly at 300 knots many of the other aircraft landed. We recovered pretty good – so nothing else went wrong!'

Moltex was involved in a crash five years ago when he was on an instructor course in America, learning basic fighter manoeuvres in F–4s. He was in a two-ship and both aircraft were running out of speed. When the F–4 gets too slow it stops reacting to the controls. The pilot of the other aircraft decided to set his lift vector, and pulled upwards right into Moltex's plane. He and his pilot were unable to react, to miss him left or right, so he hit them in their engine bay between the left and right engines with his canopy.

Moltex's aircraft was in a very high pitch at the moment of the crash, bent over as it turned. Its right engine broke out, taking the whole tail section with it. The right wing was also crushed so the aircraft went into a spiral dive.

'We had to eject straight away – there was no question of that. The problem was pulling the handle. The spiralling g was very strong, so getting a grip on the handle was very hard. I was bent over to the far left of the canopy trying to eject.

'I remember exactly what happened. The leg restraints pulled my legs back to the seat, the canopy unlocked, lifted a little bit – around one centimetre – before blowing away in the slipstream, then the ejection started. The doctors explained this phenomenon to me afterwards – that it's natural to be remembering everything from just one split second.

'We were at twelve thousand two hundred feet, and spent some six minutes hanging under the canopy. It's funny how you remember every detail. We had a lot of adrenaline, which makes your attention very high … and I can remember the seat separation, the 'chute deployment. The seat separation started immediately, and hurt more than the ejection itself – a real kick in the back. The 'chute opened, and what was really frightening was that our aircraft exploded in the air. The exploding metal parts were all free-falling in front of me like a bad dream. It was kind of interesting …

'The first thing I looked for was my pilot, who was half a kilometre away. Then we started looking for our two buddies. The only thing we saw was a drag 'chute falling down, but no other 'chutes so we knew what had happened. We screamed to each other, but saw nothing else.

'We then fell for some six minutes, to a very hard landing. The wind was around twelve to fifteen knots, but the ground was very hard and dry. Also, my 'chute had holes from the exploding debris so I was falling rather too quickly. I remembered the details of all my parachute training – stuff which day by day is of little interest, which now I look at with other eyes.

'For the next few days, I didn't really remember what had happened. The bad days started soon after that, and it took about two months before I could really say OK I've done with that. Normal flying was OK, but I was on the instructor course. I had to go on, and the next mission was basic fighter manoeuvres again – in which there are normally situations similar to what had happened. I had a lot of problems – particularly after three months. Today I think very differently. Before the accident, hearing about people who crashed and died, I always thought that it would never happen to me. Now I have crashed, and I see things with a very different perspective. I think it's a risk. If you take it OK, you have to live with it. If you can't take it, you just have to stay out of the aircraft.

'I try to teach my pilots to think about what they are doing, to evaluate the risk they are taking in everything they are doing. Especially low flying or slow flying manoeuvres. They have to talk about this within their crews, and think it through in preparation for whatever might happen.

'I do think about luck – sometimes you need to have a lot of it. Through your whole life you need luck. The same thing can happen on the autobahn when you're driving at 160 kilometres an hour and somebody's doing a wrong move. You have to rely on other people, and very often you can't control it a hundred per cent – you have to rely on others.'

'This bird strike today could have been a very serious accident, but it ended up pretty good. Right now I'm thinking about the young pilot I had in the front cockpit; he did very well and I'm very pleased about it. He did his procedure immediately. We had control at all times. Maybe tomorrow or this evening I'll feel a little differently – but right now I feel, hey, it's OK.'

The pilot was taken away immediately to rest and recover.

'If he has any problems like I did, I'll not let him fly in the exercise any more. I'll get him back into the air to get his flying confidence back, but not low level. After my first accident, when I started feeling bad, I used to ask myself if I had done anything wrong – maybe to cause the accident. It's a question you always ask yourself.'

As a way of coping, avoidance of bad and painful memories is a very common reaction to psychological trauma. After the crash, Moltex says, when he was in the air he thought about things that had nothing to do with flying.

'The problem is that you don't realize that you are having a breakdown. My mind changed when I was flying. I thought about something totally different – dinner the previous night and things like that. The problem with that is that you lose time – you don't realize that you have these breakdowns.

'After two months, when I recovered again, I realized that I should not have continued with the instructors course. I should have been pulled out of the course and sent home, then done normal flying in Germany to get my confidence back. The stress of the instructor course was high. But sometimes we need to go through these experiences, so we can tell other guys, "Hey, look out, this guy has problems and he don't even know it".

'If somebody with a problem can be shown that he has a problem, and reassured that it is perfectly normal, he is halfway towards getting back to normal. This is true. To get to talk about this thing that happened is very important.'

So how do fighter air crew manage to fly so close to the limits on a regular basis? It is a difficult and often dangerous standard that they must reach every day. Moltex believes their professional attitude helps them to cope:

'You like to do the job professionally, to do what you do as well as you can. We are taught to fly military jets from the age of nineteen. In my opinion, if you start at the age of twenty-five or twenty-six, you normally can't do it. You have to be young just to accept the training and go through with it. Younger people are responsible, but don't think so much about what might happen if things go wrong. Older people think too much about what might happen.

'The other part is that it's a kind of competition – who within the squadron is the best pilot? And the younger men are trying to improve their abilities. In the air, if they are thinking about doing their job, they are thinking about how to survive; how to make the intercept, make the shot correct – and not about the risks. After they land they might think about the risks if they had problems.

'Quite a few men have problems when they return to flying at about thirty, after doing a desk job. There's also a difference between being a bomber or a fighter pilot. Bombers try to stay away from other aircraft, whereas fighters have to seek them out and shoot them down – which is not natural.

'It's also similar when more senior men are flying. On the front-line squadrons, we have to put in more effort to get them professional again. Also, because older fighter pilots are very experienced, they tend not to go into the closing fight – they just stay out, which I guess is a pretty good habit pattern. Normally all our older pilots stick to this rule, and if they don't, we tell them to. We have good knowledge of their abilities, especially those of the staff officers.

'As pilots get older, their bodies start slowing down. I'm thirty-three and I've already noticed things happening with my body. It takes me a little longer to get used to new tactics. At the moment, I can average it out with my experience, but in a few more years some of the younger guys will be overtaking me.'

In Germany basic training finishes when pilots are about twenty-five years old. With a few years' experience in the squadron, they reach their peak, with the right combination of aggressiveness, reactions and professionalism, at the age of twenty-eight or twenty-nine.

'You can hold that for another five to six years, until your body just can't hold it any more. After that, you can hold it to eighty-five per cent of your ability until you are around forty years old. That's what the Germans have figured out, and after that it's better to leave the aircraft and take a desk job. People get sad when they reach that moment.'

The German system is different to that of the RAF. The Luftwaffe has a purely aircrew cadre who carry on flying until they are forty-one, then retire. And they do not have staff officers coming back to the squadrons they once flew in. Moltex:

'Getting married and having children starts people thinking about certain things they've done in the past! You analyse the situation and just don't do the kind of stuff you did – most probably. We have this training concept, which makes an older man responsible for a younger. With us, the younger men are controlled by older men until they get to about twenty-six or twenty-eight, when they have the experience that allows them to fly alone.'

F–18 pilot Captain Kim Reid is on another kind of edge as a woman in a very male-oriented world. Despite this, however, she qualified with no more publicity than her male colleagues. She joined the military at seventeen and after four years at a military college went to Moose Jaw, Saskatchewan, where she earned her wings. She moved on to the F–5, then the F–18 course at Cold Lake, and finally on to 441 Squadron.

In the Canadian armed forces, attitudes towards the role of women are positive, and sexual discrimination is very strongly discouraged. But even here, Kim Reid and two other female fighter pilots who were ahead of her in the training system were breaking new ground. And although the principle of equal opportunity is very much part of air force policy, there was a good deal of covert scepticism as to whether these trailblazers would be up to the job – the equal of men in very much a man's world. The other two women stopped flying F–18s after about eight months in the squadron. There was a lot of media attention on them, whereas Reid was treated the same as everybody else.

'It all happened fairly quickly for me. I always knew what I wanted to do – did it well enough and was allowed to go off and do it.

'Arriving on squadron was difficult because most guys were a little indifferent as they wanted to see how things panned out. It made it a little tough. But now after being on the squadron for close to three and a half years, it's perfectly comfortable – and all you do is learn from everybody around you. It's great.'

Inevitably people treated Kim Reid differently to other pilots. She was something new – almost a novelty – which, after proving herself on 441 Squadron, is no longer an issue, at least with her fellow pilots.

'There are still people who try to treat me differently, but all you can do is the best job you can. I'm confident that the senior officers on my squadron make no differentiation. If they did, I'd say something – or somebody else would.'

Being the trailblazer places additional pressure on that person which, added to the high pressure of flying training, requires him or her to be better than others – or at least to be able to cope with that pressure in order to survive. Fighter pilots are a radically more intelligent group of people than many other testosterone-oriented professions.

More importantly, they value performance above all other qualities; their lives depend upon the ability of the people they fly with. Trust must therefore be earned by every fledgling pilot. As in many other professions, acceptance for a woman comes more easily if she is one of the better pilots – an expectation that is tough when she is still learning.

'Perhaps there is that expectation but the further you go in your career, as you mature you realize that you have to make mistakes in order to learn. Everybody makes mistakes. I don't expect myself to be any better than the best lead on the squadron. I know what I'm capable of – I know my weaknesses and strengths. I don't expect to be better.

'The air force is cutting back with fighter pilots, and they wanted to send me back to Moose Jaw to be an instructor. At the age of twenty-seven I don't want to do that, so I'm leaving the military in a month, to go to medical school and become a doctor, maybe into aero-medicine. I'm going to keep on flying, but something like aerobatics – nothing standard. I'm really cherishing this last month on the squadron as I know I'm never going to be able to get into a jet like this ever again. It really tugs at my heart – but that's the way things go.'

Fighter pilots reach an incredible height of achievement, and just at its very apogee have to walk away. Many affect an indifference about this reality, insisting that they are relieved not to have to go on flying any more.

'Some people do try to avoid their feelings about this. You've reached a peak, done what you've dreamed of doing, and everything after that is a step backwards.

But unfortunately, you cannot keep doing this for the rest of your life – it just doesn't work that way. Flying tours are of a finite length of time. There's lots of other people who want to do it, so they cycle people through.'

People like Major Rick Boyd have jobs that allow them to keep on flying.

'You pay your dues to do that, though. Relic has done his ground tour, as a tutor and T-Bird tours – flying other jets. I had to ask myself a question: am I willing to spend three years as a tutor, three years on the ground, then maybe come back to the F–18. I also want to become a doctor – that's a real goal of mine – I really want to do that. So I decided, let's go do that!'

Reid has one disappointment: that more women aren't doing her job.

'Guys have two arguments: either that women shouldn't be doing it because we're absolutely different; or that I'm just very unusual – which I don't believe for a second. I've met enough women of my age and calibre, and greater intelligence. Thirteen- and fourteen-year-old young women talk to me with eyes as wide as saucers saying, "I want to do what you do". That gives me a lot of hope – but where are they? Why are they not coming through? What happens to their dreams between the age of fourteen and twenty?

'There are lots of reasons for women not coming to this job, but it is a real disappointment for me.'

Role modelling plays an important part. Until there are women doing the job, young women will not identify with them, or with those jobs. The Canadian air force had two other women flying fighters, and in 1995 the RAF had its first woman Tornado pilot.

'I can't relate to that because I've never really faltered in my goal, to being where I am. I haven't needed a role model. I just said let's go do it. I'm not sure why there aren't so many women just saying that.'

One of the obvious reasons for the lack of women pilots (from a male perspective) is biological. However, it is simply not possible to become a fighter pilot without a very well-developed sense of self-awareness, and women do know how their own bodies work. Female biology is a mystery to men rather than to women. Reid believes that to become a fighter pilot it is necessary to be a long-term planner.

'It takes several years. Similarly, if you want to integrate a family into all this, you also have to plan. You cannot be pregnant while you fly – it's just not compatible!'

Everything about being a fighter pilot is masculine; the aircraft are sleek, lethal, phallic, and astonishingly powerful. The squadron flashes, visually aggressive

Captain Kim Reid, CAF pilot; she has broken new ground as a woman flying F–18s and declares that her job is 'a rush … not a masculine preserve at all'.

symbols that indicate how each unit would like to see itself, show eagles and shafts of lightning, heraldic shields and private jokes (like 29 (F) Squadron's triple Xs); and they adorn these ultimate boys' toys, built solely for the purpose of screaming along at fence-post height doing 900 miles an hour, to drop bombs and destroy other aircraft. The whole 'top guns' ethos, far from being invented by the movie, was watered down by Hollywood into the usual story line of love, sex and derring-do. Captain Kim Reid, however, slim, athletic and very feminine, seems to disprove all this. She would not agree:

'I don't actually disprove any of what this job is all about, nor do I disprove what anybody else might think of it … because it's a lot of fun, a real rush. I really enjoy it, to the absolute maximum extent possible. I love the job.

'You might go in to the squadron before a mission or trip and maybe you're a little tired, or you've got something on your mind. But you come back with a big grin on your face. You're on cloud nine because of where you've been and how low you've gone, and how fast you've gone – it's just a rush. It's not a masculine preserve at all.'

CHAPTER THIRTEEN

Real World Problems

On every Maple Flag exercise mission, eighty-seven to eighty-nine aircraft take off from Cold Lake air base within forty-five minutes. At one every thirty seconds or so, it is a rate that no international airport would touch. They keep to one aeroplane in, one aeroplane out at any one time. Canadian squadrons that are not taking part in Maple Flag are also flying, and have to come in and out of the base. The air traffic controllers also have emergency medivac aeroplanes to bring down safely in the middle of exercise recoveries. The operation is run twenty-four hours a day, seven days a week, by sixty-four people.

Air traffic control plans and launches the Maple Flag exercise as in war, often silently, without radio transmissions, getting them in and out as fast as possible. Their big problem is getting aircraft across the inner runway to the outer one when there is a flow and both are in use. Pilots need to get organized and taxi at the right time, or they'll miss their take-off times. The controllers push them to keep to accurate timings, although if somebody has a problem they try to fit them into the flow.

Silent launches enable pilots to take off in radio silence so that the enemy has no warning of the launch. They do not talk to anyone; everything is done entirely by time. The package commander tells them what time to launch, and air traffic makes sure they can get across to the outer runway. If anyone has a snag and cannot get off on time, he waits until everybody has gone and is then fitted in.

Captain Pete 'Pistol' Smith is the Maple Flag air traffic controller. He started as an NCO in air traffic control, was commissioned lieutenant in 1992, and has spent twenty years in the military:

'If somebody has to stop on a runway, we have to get him out of the way so everybody else can continue. That's why on a silent launch everybody's got to monitor the normal radio frequencies so that we can prevent people driving into each other. The flyers normally all return at the same sort of time – sometimes strung out a bit. Visual flight rules are vital within the gaggle to keep separation. Our responsibility is to line them up for the inner or outer runways, and bring 'em home.'

Often people will land two together, side abreast to save time, a pair on each runway, or sometimes four together depending on the width of the runway. The ones at Cold Lake are sixty metres (200) feet wide. Regulations differ but here, as soon as an aircraft touches down and is 900 metres (3000 feet) down the runway, the next one can land.

The main rule for pilots is get to the tower side as soon as they are down and settled, so that if somebody behind has a problem and has to come in a little faster than normal, he still has half of the runway and can get by. Smith:

'Last year we had an F–15 with an aircraft ahead of him which hadn't pulled over tower side, so he had to apply more than the normal amount of brake. His wheel heated up, blowing the tyre, and he came off the runway.

'We can lose runways. An aircraft only has to take the departure-end cable, boom, we're down to one runway and have to use the other one. We play maximum flexibility – we have to! We do what we gotta do.'

Air traffic tries to put emergencies on runway 22 (its heading in magnetic degrees):

'We had an emergency yesterday, an F–18 which landed on the crossing runway – 22 – with his lead shepherding him. But his lead over-shot, which is why I come into all the briefings so much to stress the 2500 feet departure end of runway. We then had to over-shoot two aircraft on the outer runway, have them climb to circuit altitude and go round again. We landed them, and the lead went out and joined the pack waiting to land, and life just carried on.'

Smith also controls the emergency response and Cold Lake's crash facility response goes to level six. This means that it can take any aeroplane up to a KC–10, L1011 or 747.

Most of the fire trucks stay at the far end of the base with their own entrance on to the main ramp. During Maple Flag launch and recovery, one crash response vehicle is put on a taxi-way between the inner and outer runways to ensure a quick response anywhere on the airfield.

'If a pilot declares an emergency, or if we see something like a hot brake –

which gives a distinctive puff of smoke in his gear – we'll keep an eye on him if he doesn't react. Not all aircraft have indicators for everything, or maybe he's lost his radios and can't tell us. We'll activate the crash alarm just to be on the safe side – activated by the tower with a crash bell system. We hook up all the relevant systems into a crash conference line, ten different agencies on the one line, so we can tell all of them what's happening and get everyone activated.'

The response varies according to the type of aeroplane and the number of people on board – passenger aircraft also land at the base. Aircraft with dangerous cargoes or weapons can be put on to different holding areas all over the airfield. Emergencies involving armaments get put on to the outer runway.

'An aircraft with unexpended ordnance is landed on the outer runway, and held between the inner and outer until we can get an ordnance vehicle out to it. So long as it's not pointing at anybody we carry on using the runways. Pilots know exactly where to sit at arming and disarming points, the angles are calculated not to point at residential areas. They are expected to stay with their aircraft, but there was one occasion when the pilot took the first mule out of there and the aircraft was unattended. The tow crew had to bring it in alone! Pilots are people too you know! You're the pilot of the airplane, so it's fine if you don't want to hang around. We'll get your airplane, and put our mark on it – rights of salvage! It's ours!

'In a real war the airfield will get attacked, which requires a great deal more co-ordination. We've got an airfield engineer squadron here to repair runways. Silent launches will be the rule, 'cos anybody can tune into your frequencies and we don't want the world to know we're coming off. Our shift hours will get longer, and we do what we call "third manning" – so we end up working longer. It's like they say – war's hell!'

The other problem in war will be identifying friend from foe. Being such high-value targets, airfields have to be surrounded by anti-aircraft weapons and aircraft wishing to land will have to fly down specific safe approach routes to avoid being shot down.

'We practised a SHORAD – short range air defence – recovery yesterday, which gives the airfield's missile defence sites and radars a chance to practise identifying friends from foe. We rely on transponder codes that transmit signals automatically when they receive predetermined signals or the IFF codes that

Overleaf: A CF–18 of 441 Squadron, ready and waiting for the pilot to arrive; in war all aircraft take off in radio silence to ensure that the enemy has no indication of the launch.

identify friend or foe in normal air traffic control operations. Of course in war, the enemy will shut down his IFF so as not to be identified. We would go back to maximum flexibility again – to visual flight rules if we can, SHORAD procedures and silent launch. For a tower controller it's great, you just sit back and watch them go. They have to de-conflict themselves!'

There are two types of rules that aircraft must follow: visual flight rules (VFR) or instrument flight rules (IFR). For VFR to apply, minimum visibility must be at least 1000 feet vertical, aircraft must be three miles apart and there must be only a little cloud, which the aircraft must not go into as the ground must be visible at all times.

The aircrew, rather than air traffic control, are responsible for maintaining the three-mile distance between aircraft. Instrument flight rules are different in that the aircrew file a flight plan, making air traffic control responsible for their separation which is three miles, as with visual flight.

In silent launch and recovery, communication with the tower is with line-of-sight UHF radio. Short range VHF radios from a vehicle at the end of the runway are used to control emergencies. Flags are used to signal to the aircraft.

Thursday 11 May 1995; afternoon sortie, silent launch

An F–16 calls in with a hydrazine hazard problem – an emergency situation for which Cold Lake air traffic control scrambles the crash equipment. Captain Smith is out on the airfield monitoring the radio:

'ETA for the emergency aircraft is about seven minutes.'

'Copy, taxi left on to inner runway.'

They put up the arrester wires on the inner runway, and two F–18s waiting to take off are stopped by a red flag. However, with six minutes to spare before the F–16 arrives, the tower decides to get the F–18s airborne. The runway control team 'Oscar' signal them off, a nod of the leader's head, brakes are released and they accelerate down the track side by side, only feet separating their wing tips. The aircraft rotate, their noses lift together and their wheels leave the ground seconds later.

'Ground Oscar, you have control of the inner.'

'Oscar Ground, roger. I have control. Check the F–16 is going to exit off the runway and shut down, that he's waiting for a tow-crew.'

'Roger check that.'

Two F–16s come screaming in side by side, painted in the disrupted blues of one flight of the Aggressor Squadron. The jet with the engine problem lands while the other, who flew back with him to make sure he got home all right, flies along the side of the runway, parallel with his wingman, overshoots and accelerates over the end of the runway, climbing back up into the sky to rejoin the fight.

A bright yellow crash truck blasts past the Oscar control wagon, accelerating down the tower side of the runway as back-up to the two already on the scene, in case the F–16 develops a fire or some other problem. Smith:

'He's braking under his own power so it looks as though it's all right. It could have been almost anything – an engine fluctuation, fuel feed problems … the chances are he's secured the emergency by now, but we'll send the crash trucks anyway. The aircraft's turning off so it looks like it will be something for his ramp crew to sort out. About eighty per cent of emergencies declared in the air get down safely, they taxi back to the ramp and maintenance fixes it!'

The radio breaks in:

'Maple Flag Three, Ground. Can you check on that there van on the pan? He doesn't seem to know where he's going.'

'Ground, Maple Flag Three, did he request clearance?'

'That's negative.'

'Can I have clearance from present position 419?'

'Proceed, the van is blue and black when it appears.'

Captain Smith turns around and drives away from the runway toward the USAF ramp.

'He's probably lost – which is a real big problem round here in winter, particularly during snowstorms with snow obscuring all known points and beacons. It's not hard to get disoriented on an airfield anyway. In bad weather, the aircraft land on a beacon and we have only one that can be seen at night, on top of the tower. There's always somebody asking, "Where am I, can you see me?"

'I was on an airfield on the east coast. I went out with a technician to fix a TACAN in the middle of a snowstorm. It was only about a quarter of a mile from the hangar line, but took four hours to get back. The snow was blowing so hard that we needed a snowplough. He cut a path, but by the time he'd reached us it had blown back in.

'We couldn't see the tower, they couldn't see us. We inched our way forward, getting out to scrape snow – "Are we still on the pavement?". Finally, a guy came out with a skidoo and led us back in.'

In winter priorities are assigned to different parts of the airfield. Because it is a quick reaction base, the first priority is to clear a path from the air defence aircrafts' hangar to the runway. The ground crew then try to clear the snow 22 to 30 metres (75 to 100 feet) on either side of the centre line of one of the runways, then work on the other runway. It takes three or four days to clear this one as the ramps have to be swept clean of snow before the aircraft can come out of their hangars – a big job. Then they do the other runway.

The harsh conditions of a Canadian winter seldom affect flying, which takes place even at minus 40 degrees centigrade, although freezing rain, and ice fog when all the moisture in the air turns to ice crystals and it is impossible to see anything through it, can be important factors. There is not much wind at Cold Lake but when there is, at minus 40 degrees everything stops because with wind chill creating around 2250 watts per square metre of heat loss, it is too dangerous to go out of doors. On a normal day, at minus 35 degrees centigrade with light winds, the heat loss is about 1750 watts per square metre, which is bearable. The weather is gin-clear but very cold.

Summers are very hot and dry with temperatures in the low thirties most of the time, the skies are usually cloudless and visibility is superb. In the cockpit, the oxygen is dry and has a dehydrating effect. Aircrew get chest complaints, and sweat a lot and drink a lot, but they acclimatize.

Wildlife can be a serious problem. There are probably 50 000 gophers (Canadian ground squirrels) and their holes around the runways. They dig along the edges, the water goes into the holes, the ground gets soft and pieces of the runway start falling in. 'Oscar':

'And because they don't obey air traffic control they get run over a lot. They try to keep warm by nibbling on the lighting wires, and make excellent tunnels right under the runways. You fill one and they dig another one. We can't kill enough of them to stop the problem, and they carry a lot of disease. The authorities tried killing off all the grasshoppers, the gophers went nuts. Foxes and coyotes eat them – we get coyotes all over the airfield hunting them – but there's so many they just get fat. They'll try killing off the gophers, and the foxes and coyotes will go nuts. The trouble is we don't have anything large enough to go after them. I guess you need work out what's next in the food chain and import lots of them.'

Aeroplanes make very much less noise landing, than when taking off at full power. They coast in, shutting off power in the moment of touching down – with the exception of Tornados which add large amounts of reverse thrust in order to stop. A constant stream of military jets swoops in from the perimeter fence, to touch down about a hundred metres (330 feet) into the runway.

Three Phantoms approach in line, ten seconds between them. About 180 metres (200 yards) after touchdown, the parachute brake tugs out of the back to slow them down. Thirty years old, the Phantoms look rounder and more squat than the sleek, light-looking F–18s and F–16s. They land more heavily, make a lot of smoke and wobble like large geese splashing down on their home lake.

A crazy mix of aircraft comes in, F–16s with a big USAF F–15 in between. His back wheels touch down with a puff of black tyre smoke. The F–15's wide, wedge-like air brake comes up behind the pilot. The plane's nose is some thirty degrees in the air and the pilot and his front wheel remain well off the ground until he reaches the end of the runway and his speed drops right off. A Tornado touches down 100 metres (330 feet) in front of Oscar on the main runway, while a string of F–16s are landing on the outer runway. A singleton F–16 touches down in front, his port wheel first, then his starboard, making a lot of smoke, the airframe rocking violently from side to side. You wonder if the wing tips ever touch the ground.

The recovery is clearly organized, but appears haphazard; jet fighters of all types orbit the airfield in a long queue for one of the runways taking their landing as it comes, hitting the tarmac every thirty seconds or less. Many are short of fuel from using after-burners in air combat, and are anxious to get on to the ground before they have to declare an emergency and jump the queue.

The main body of the Richthofen Squadron are orbiting in line at around a thousand feet. Four F–16s fly close formation at 500 feet over the runway, indicating to the tower that they want to land. They break sharp right, to fall into echelon behind each other about 1600 feet apart, and orbit back to the approach heading. It is a short approach, so they have to lose height quickly while turning, then land one by one. An entire squadron of CAF CF–18s orbit round and come in to land, one by one. They don't need parachutes as they have very good brakes. More Tornados are landing on the far runway, after which the sky temporarily clears and a short peace descends on the airfield, bird song briefly discernible on this hot, clear afternoon. One lone Tornado comes straight down on to the main runway, its sudden roar jerking everyone back to reality. Then one of the ECM jammers – a twin-engined executive jet in drab olive green and black camouflage paint; then a Canadian T–33.

Things are different when training to fly in a war zone. The problem is how to train people with a very wide range of experience – from the very inexperienced (who lack confidence) to those who've done it before, so that they all achieve the same standard. Flight Lieutenant Tim Taylor remembers that preparing for Bosnia took three and a half months of hard work complicated by bad weather, people going off sick, unserviceable aircraft, and Christmas leave.

'It all ate in to the time, upsetting the grand plan, which started to crumble. As the time slips away, you ask, "What can we afford to teach them in theatre?".

The first squadron to go to Bosnia had just returned and the second one was already there. Because 29 (F) Squadron was only the third to go to the area they were guessing the priorities. They were operating in an unfamiliar configuration with unfamiliar equipment, using aircraft that performed poorly in heat. There were two radios on three nets (the United Nations command net plus the AWACS and, with so many people talking to the AWACS, also the squadron's own net), a modification to use night-vision goggles, permanent under-wing fuel tanks, weapons on board (which in training is unusual), defensive aids to counter radar missiles and radars, and infra-red decoys.

The radios were the least of the instructors' worries, as there were people on the squadron who had never even seen a real missile – and the Tornados carried six, plus special countermeasures. They had to teach people to fly in the dark with no lights using night-vision goggles, which are inherently difficult to use: seeing through them is described as being like looking down two toilet rolls, and they give no perception of depth. Taylor:

'It's only when you start looking at a flat world, that you realize how hard it is to take information from it, and how much you rely on depth. The goggles light the world like daylight, and headlights stand out like a huge, blinding beacon. A campfire will light up fifty or sixty miles of countryside. We'd watch artillery fights across the valleys, following the shells and tracer, with the night goggles. You could see the parabola, and sometimes we found ourselves underneath it – watching it go over the top of us.'

Trainees also had to learn to fly low-level day and night to find, chase and shoot down helicopters, shoot at ground positions … the range of what they had to do in a very short time was enormous, with the rest of the squadron life going on the same time. Taylor:

'It didn't work terribly well until we got to the panic stage – with some eighty training events to cover, and only eighty training periods in which to achieve them. We threw up our arms and demanded that our war training be made the priority. Normally you only train to do other training – like the work-up period to Maple Flag. In Bosnia trainees would be as good as they were ever to get when they arrived.'

Flight Lieutenant Mike Jones found Bosnia quite boring:

'We were on the 0100 to 0530 shift, tooling around at night at twenty-three thousand feet trying to chase the odd helicopter and watching the people on the ground beating the shit out of each other. Compared with training, there's not a lot going on – a low workload. You take off, go to the tanker, patrol the area for forty minutes or so, then back to the tanker. You do that for four and a half hours, until it's time to go home.

'We were doing five days on, two off, so just when you get into it, the week-end comes around. Others did ten days on, ten days off – which I didn't like, preferring to have the two days off!

'The area of Bosnia-Herzegovina is a lot larger than Wales. We were doing roving combat air patrols, and there wasn't much to see on the scopes – apart from the odd fire, tank shell or heavy machine gun fire. The night-vision goggles are literally a pain in the neck as they are quite heavy. Most of us used to take them off on leaving the area, stow them away, tank, then put them back on as we re-entered the area.

'There's very little decision making to be done – you have no powers until you're attacked. All the command and control came from the AWACS. It wasn't a question of being on edge all the time. Some people were fired upon using triple A, but I never saw any – apart from in the ground-to-ground role, both sides using triple A to fire across the valleys, burning villages and so on.

'Before every mission we had thirty minutes intelligence briefing on what was going on. When we were there, the Serbian 5th Corps were beating the hell out of various people in the Behac pocket. We avoided it as we reckoned it was the most dangerous place to be! There were a few occasions when we dropped flares to help out some of our army guys on the ground who were getting hassle.'

The squadron also chased Croatian helicopters which played a kind of game, landing in a big sports stadium that the Tornados checked regularly, having negotiated air traffic clearance over Croatian territory. The fighters would get to the stadium, count the helicopters, then return after tanking to find a few missing. They had been away for thirty minutes, so by drawing an arc of probability around the stadium they would know roughly how far away the helicopters were. They would then chase down valleys trying to find them – from 23 000 feet to stay above ground-to-air missile range. When they found them they issued the UN ultimatum to 'either land or we will engage you'. The helicopters knew

Overleaf: A Tornado on the ramp at Cold Lake Air Force Base wears an anti-frost canopy; the F3s will remain in Canada for the next British contingent to Maple Flag to use – this time as part of Blue Air.

they would not be attacked and would sometimes thank them and wish them a pleasant flight. All the fighters could do was report back to AWACS.

The squadron found these Bosnian sorties very restricting, especially the rules of engagement. Flight Lieutenant Justin Reuter:

'Working for the UN as a peace-keeper is very different to being at war. We've got our hands tied. It's frustrating, especially as the whole thing is guided by people who aren't actually out there. We know we could stop people flying totally but we can't do it because shooting people down could be turned against us, so it's very frustrating.

'The sorties are very long – more than four hours – and to be honest boring. You have to maintain a level of concentration that allows you to tool around at medium level not doing very much, but be able instantly to react to a missile being launched at you, or to aircraft taking off to bomb somebody else ... snapping into war mode. At the end of the day you go back to the hotel (it's only three star which is really bad for us), have a few drinks, a bowl of pasta and glass of wine, relax and chat – forgetting that the next day you could be captured and held as a hostage by somebody who says he's going to cut your bollocks off. It's very unreal.'

Identifying friend from foe is possibly the biggest real war problem. IFF has outlived its usefulness as a system to discriminate between the two as it can be jammed and spoofed. And although many aircraft still have it as their only method of identification, the RAF would not normally use only IFF for an airborne operation. Maritime forces use a system which deals in 'probables' and 'possibles' and although this was for many years the best method it has been overtaken by other types of discriminator. Track recognition based upon knowledge of the plan and the flow of aircraft works well, especially in set-piece scenarios, and is a common-sense way of avoiding firing on friendly troops.

The only really accurate system, however, is some form of non-co-operative target identification like cameras that show pictures of the target in the cockpit, or electronic identification from the radar picture, or visual identification.

Surface-to-air missile (SAM) sites present the same IFF problem in training when their positions are not known. In a real war, however, fighters would know where friendly SAM sites were. If they were chasing a target towards the site of a friendly missile they would haul off and let it do the work. The aim, after all, would be to kill the enemy and the SAM would have as much chance as the aircraft of doing this.

Wing Commander Martin Routledge remembers that before the collapse of the Soviet bloc and the reunification of Germany, the NATO war plan placed a belt of SAMs along the border zone, with the air defence fighters behind:

'The idea was that the SAMs took the first line of attrition, then fighters mopped up anything that got through. The likelihood was that the enemy would try to punch a hole through in one place, firing out all the SAMs, creating a place where all the attackers could pour through. The fighter force would be ready to block that hole, in the knowledge that there would be no leakers coming through at the side. This works in a land-based war with a clearly defined border. Today, we tend to set SAM clusters to protect particular sites. The fighters deploy forward covering the airspace.'

Some future war could create aircraft orders of battle that would make foe identification very difficult. With the break-up of the Soviet Union, the eastern bloc countries are now buying Soviet versions of MiGs and other Russian equipment rather than the less capable export versions, and any combination of allies could have Soviet MiG–29s on its side, against American F–16s and F–18s that have been sold to other nations. However, the high quality, American aircraft are still predominantly in the hands of friendly nations or in regions where Britain is unlikely to be involved. The Germans have inherited quite a few MiGs and Sukhois from the former East German air force – but do not fly them very often and would probably leave them on the ground in war.

Modern wars happen suddenly – rather than there being any convenient transition to war. Routledge:

'If we had to go to war now, we'd go direct from Maple Flag as the crews are all here and working. Back in UK, however, there would be a bit of bureaucratic juggling; some people wouldn't be able to go and a list of minimum qualifications might appear, which some aircrew wouldn't meet. I'd like to think that the squadron could simply up sticks and go.'

In the Gulf War aircrew had to have 'combat-ready plus' qualifications. This is also the case for Red Flag exercises. In war, two sets of crew are needed per aircraft, for round the clock operations. Like any RAF fighter squadron, 29 (F) Squadron is a training and administration unit which in war can absorb extra crews from other squadrons. In the Gulf War, the F3 force had 29 (F) Squadron and 43 Squadron as a mixed detachment. 29 (F) Squadron was the lead, but in reality it was a mixture of people and aircraft from both. A real war would be very different from Maple Flag. Routledge:

'You wouldn't be co-ordinating a set piece with the man in the next box. In a real war you'd find yourself with four aircraft to defend a sixty by thirty mile box. Anything moving in your box would die, which is a valid and viable way of doing business.'

Friday 12 May 1995

Exercise Maple Flag has gone well, with 29 (F) Squadron learning more than they had expected about certain things (AMRAAM in particular). It is, however, just another exercise. The next one starts in Spain in a matter of days and as soon as the last de-brief is over the hire cars are revving up for the boring four-hour drive to Edmonton, and a final night out in Canada. The Tristar that is taking the squadron back to the United Kingdom will leave early in the morning, so those who are determined to hit the town give themselves plenty of leeway to get back to the hotel. The air force makes a point of leaving exactly on time and takes a vicarious pleasure in the misfortunes of anybody who misses the coach to the airport.

The Tornados remain at Cold Lake for 111 Squadron to use for their two-week stint, as part of Blue Air this time. Nobody in the ground crew minds that another squadron will gain from all the hard work they have put in. They hope the aircraft will continue to perform well. As each one must be perfect for every mission, there is no difference between airframes, even if they have squadron markings on the tail.

As the squadron gather at Edmonton International airport, some of its members wear large cowboy hats – the obvious prairie souvenir, which will probably end up crushed by the end of the journey. It is clear that various people have had an enjoyable evening. The flight back to RAF Brize Norton is uneventful, the rows of passenger seats squeezed tight in a line beside the Tristar's enormous stainless steel freight compartments. The Tristar's cabin crew occupy rows of larger, first-class seats (intended for senior officers) behind a curtain near the front of the aircraft. This does not endear them to 29 (F) Squadron, who in any case regard them as inferior beings.

The aircraft lands in the early hours and after a fifteen-minute wait for luggage to be unloaded the squadron file through Customs (whose officials have not bothered to turn up) and on to coaches for the long drive from Oxfordshire across to Lincolnshire, and RAF Coningsby – their home base. Everybody is tired, looking forward to getting home and seeing their families again. It is a very familiar scene, to be repeated in a few weeks' time when they return from Spain.

Nobody is thinking about Maple Flag any more, and their next exercise is something they will think about after the weekend. Right now, everybody is looking forward to a kip on the coach, and tea at the other end … for the time being, the next phase can take care of itself.

Appendix

The Tornado F3

The Tornado is manufactured by Panavia and is a United Kingdom, Germany and Italy collaboration, made by British Aerospace, Deutsche Aerospace and Alenia. The RAF Tornado F Mark 3, the ADV (air defence variant) came into service in July 1986 and has been greatly updated since. Its top speed, flying level and clean (without pods, bombs or missiles), is 920 m.p.h., Mach 2.2 at altitude. It has one Mauser 27 mm IWKA cannon mounted in the fuselage, and carries a range of missiles on wing pods. Its endurance is quoted as two hours combat air patrol at 345 to 460 miles from base, including time for interception and ten minutes combat. Its intercept radius (the distance at which it can intercept another aircraft, which is determined by fuel) is more than 345 miles supersonic (1151 miles subsonic).

Flight Lieutenant Graham Stobart describes the cockpit from the perspective of the pilot:

'We climb in using a ladder, then check the seat and strap in. We put on the leg restraints, and one of the ground crew hands us the over-shoulder straps. We do a few brief checks of switches – that the cross-drive clutch is open so that we don't try and start both hydraulic systems and gearboxes together – then put the hydraulics into auto so that we can get some idling hydraulic power. Then we turn the radio on and start the assisted power unit – the APU – so that we can stop using the aircraft's battery. Nothing else really works until we've done that. We ask the ground crew, they give us clearance, and we flip the switch.

'We then run across the cockpit from left to right, checking in the correct sequence and order. The things you need are in front, duplicated in the head-up display. Once you've set the switches down the sides, they generally stay at those settings. There's an intercom and radio panel – cockpit voice recorder, UHF, VHF, HF and stand-by radio, intercom and missile volume, radar warning volume control, TACANAR for coding; then on the outside we've got the flying controls panel, and the command stability and augmentation system – the CSAS – which is the fly-by-wire system. It looks complex, but you put all the duplex lights on, get a green "Go", which you press, then you don't touch it again. If something goes wrong, a caption lights up on the central warning panel. You go to whatever it shows.

'The autopilot and flight direction system – AFDS – is on the left-hand side, and is not used for everyday sorties. For long trips across the pond you stick it on, and it saves you having to fly manually. You can select various different types of autopilot using the different buttons.

'The main computer controls everything. The inertial navigation system tells the pilot where he is and how to get where he wants to be. There's two of those in case one fails. The auto-stabilizer corrects for wind-buffeting, smoothing out the ride. The air data computer system gets information from the Pitot static head (which protrudes from the nose of the aircraft) and this combined with other information determines wind speed, airspeed, speed across the ground, ground track and ground heading – the pilot's heading and ground track are not necessarily the same as the wind may be blowing him off – and his speed in knots and Mach. This is very important, as various adjustments (to wing angles, for example) have to be made when you go supersonic.

'There are two throttles, one for each engine, in the "HP shut" position now – HP stands for high pressure. Pushing them up to "max dry" gives you maximum dry power with fairly economical fuel usage. Once you push it past the detent – what we call "Wopping it into burner" – you get up to "max re-heat" with very high fuel consumption and extra thrust, particularly at low level. The "combat" setting gives an extra bit of power on top of that. The wing sweep lever goes from 25 to 67 degrees of sweep. Rather than using every single degree of sweep, we narrow it down to four positions: fully forward, two somewhere in the middle and fully back. We use the wings fully forward for going slowly and turning as it gives you the best lift. You must pull the wings back as you speed up, or the aircraft is buffeted and won't go faster. Equally as you slow down, you must bring the wings forward otherwise you lose lift and become unstable.

'On the left-hand side, the air brake flaps indicator shows the position of the wings, air brakes, flaps and slats, leading edge manoeuvres slats, and trailing edge flaps. There's also the landing gear stick selective, and emergency jettison button, that allows us to get rid of any stores we may be carrying. There's an arrester hook that catches the runway safety wire for a rapid, emergency stop on landing. If we want to drop the hook, we press a button surrounded by yellow and black markings. The green light comes on and it's down. It's a one-shot hook which you can't raise again. You don't want to touch that button by accident.'

The aircraft is festooned with safety switches, to prevent missiles and other weapons being fired by accident:

'There's the master arms safety switch – MASS – at "safe" at the moment, then "stand by" as you start the jet, and "live" as you taxi out. If you were going to fire any missiles, you'd have it set at live. The "late arm" switch is another safety brake. Before going into combat you make sure that both MASS and late arm are set to live. The angle of attack indicator gives "alpha" units of air incidence against the wing – unitary limits that cannot be exceeded.

'On the left-hand side are the primary flying instruments. Attitude indicator, compass, and altimeter, repeated in the HUD which is focused at infinity, at a larger scale, and never goes out of focus – brilliant! When we try to fly without it, it's very difficult. The television screen behind the stick is purely a repeater of what the navigator has in the back. We can choose between his left and right TV by tabbing between them.

'The stick itself has a lot of knobs: the trimmer which sorts out the aeroplane in the position you want it to be in. Then the air-to-air over-ride button for the radar, which is used in close combat to take over the radar from the navigator. It has four modes. The missile select switch goes forward to select semi-active radar missiles, down for infra-red missiles, and pulls back for gun. The principle is that you sit with your left hand on the throttle, and right hand on the stick in the "HOTAS" position – that's hands on throttle and stick – doing everything else plus being able to look out .

'Engine instruments show revolutions per minute and temperature gauges for each engine, plus nozzle gauges that show how far the nozzles at the back of the jet have opened which indicates how much burner you're using. At dry power they don't move. It's only when you select after-burner that they start opening and closing automatically, narrowing down as you close the throttle and reduce power, and opening right up on after-burner, which gives you maximum thrust.

'The engine dials are marked with red lines to indicate limitations, which you only expect to see at the end of the runway as you take off as that's the only time the engines should reach their maximum. You don't expect to see them when you're airborne. The fuel flow indicator to the right shows fuel consumption in kilograms per minute, and only works in dry power.'

When using after-burner, fuel consumption increases so much that this indicator is useless.

'Below that is the fuel totalizer, which adds up all the fuel in the various tanks.

'On the right-hand side is the central warning panel, with seventy-two warning captions. You learn many of the emergency drills that follow these warnings by heart, and we have sessions in the simulator to keep up to speed on these. Some emergencies bring up several captions, and we test our knowledge by coming out with the immediate actions, some of which are quite complicated. The navigator has a set of cards in the back which he whips out to safety-check the pilot's reactions, then they continue the procedure. Some of the actions are several pages long and impossible to memorize, so pilots just learn the immediate actions to get things under control, then start working through the pages, setting switches, etc.

'Most of these actions are very specific. The engines drive the hydraulics, which power the flying controls so in a double-engine flame-out, for example, the aircraft won't fly unless you remember to put the ram air turbine out – but then it must go on to drive the hydraulics, off a supplementary system. It's not common sense or automatic – you have to memorize it.

'The missile management panel is under the head-up display, top left under the coaming – the raised frame around the cockpit – and shows the missiles on board, what state they're in, how many are left and which we have selected.

'Down the right-hand side are two rows of control panels – mainly navigation to start with: the instrument landing system and the tactical air navigation system. There's another control panel for the radar warning receiver which is displayed on the smaller television screen top right. It's very important and is quite excellent. It sounds like a telephone ringing in the headsets, and also gives a visual display of the direction from which the radar is coming. It's duplicated in the back, and it is generally the navigator's job to operate it.

'On the right-hand side of the radar warning receiver control panel is the engine control panel which you set up before you go flying, then leave for the computer to control. The ramps panel controls and reduces the air flow to the engine, which will not work efficiently at supersonic speeds. Front right is the refuelling panel, which looks complicated but is set up before you go flying, then left. If you go tanking, you have to make a few switch selections which the navigator reads off a card so you don't get it wrong. You put the switches back to normal afterwards. You can isolate certain tank groups, transfer fuel from one tank group to another – which is what you'd do in an emergency if you were hit.

'Behind is the radio. You dial up the frequency in the window, or you use the frequency pre-selected studs – which the Yanks call channels. It's UHF, and we rarely use the VHF in the back seat. The other UHF set is in the back seat.

'The environmental control panel adjusts temperature, pressurization in the cockpit, rain dispersal and windscreen heating. You don't need windscreen wipers, as at over 50 knots all water simply goes away. At slower speeds, the windscreen dispersion system blows it away and for foggy days there's a windscreen heater – gold film inside the Perspex. The windscreen is double thickness.

'In the back seat, the radar control looks like a flying control stick – but isn't. The navigator puts his right hand on the stick, and his left on to the radar control panel. He sets up a variety of different modes and sweeps the airspace using controls on the stick. The scanner at the front is pencil beamed, so won't cover all heights in one go. You can adjust the angle of the scanner and lock it in by pulling the trigger, and also initiate interrogations to identify friend or foe and other types of mode.'

The radar in the nose of the aircraft gets most use, plus the TACAN (tactical air navigation), which is used for things like rendezvous with tankers.

'The television on the right has the plan display – a God's-eye-view of where we are and where other people are – which is always north orientated and which can also show a map. You set up your own little box to work in, so you don't have to worry about where you are. JTIDS is in here too, controlled by the navigator, who can send out plan display information to everybody else on the same net. Before JTIDS, we had to transmit information by referring to the bullseye point. The plan display is excellent too – and unique.'

The navigator has two screens. One displays radar information, while the other can be set up with various data displays: general navigation of the area the aircraft is flying in. Tanker lines, ground-to-air missile sites and other information are all programmed in. The pilot can select various modes to see this information, and will change it round at different times. He usually elects to see nav. data until the aircraft gets to the fight, then switches to the radar.

'The rest of the back seat is a duplication of the flying controls, plus a Mode 1 Mode 3 IFF Interrogator on the right. If you "wear" a certain squawk the IFF system or ground air traffic control systems can tell that you're friendly. The more important captions are duplicated in the back-seat control panel and the navigator also has his own special captions that deal with computer failures. The squawk box is on the right-hand side.

'You load computer information – initialization data for JTIDS, plus navigation data – into the data entry box. With the double inertial navigation system the navigator punches in his position, and thereafter the system aligns to that so you always know where you are and how to get home. It drifts a bit, and after an hour it's usually about half a mile or so out which is pretty good. You can select the frequency radar channel you're transmitting on, so you don't have to co-channel interference with other radar. This is the missile management panel, with the radar homing warning receiver, a repeat of what there is in the front.

'And these silky cords are laced round leg-restraint garters on your g suit, pulling your legs in just before you leave aircraft on ejection'.

Index

References in italics refer to illustrations